D1601447

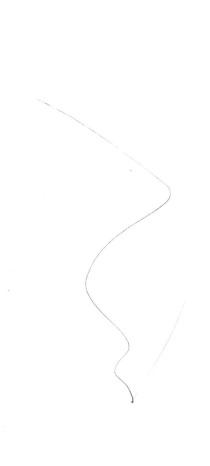

PROFIT SHARING

Does It Make A Difference?

The Productivity and Stability Effects
of Employee Profit-Sharing Plans

Douglas L. Kruse
Rutgers University

1993

W.E. UPJOHN INSTITUTE for Employment Research
Kalamazoo, Michigan

Library of Congress Cataloging-in-Publication Data

Kruse, Douglas.
  Profit sharing : does it make a difference? : the productivity and
stability effects of employee profit-sharing plans / Douglas L. Kruse
    p. cm.
  Includes bibliographical references and index.
  ISBN 0-88099-138-0. — ISBN 0-88099-137-2 (pbk.)
  1. Profit-sharing—United States. 2. Profit-sharing. 3. Labor
productivity—United States. 4. Labor Productivity. 5. Job
satisfaction—United States. 6. Job satisfaction. I. Title.
HD2984.K78   1993
331.2'164—dc20   93-23240
                                                                         CIP

The facts presented in this study and the observations and viewpoints expressed are the sole responsibility of the author. They do not necessarily represent positions of the W.E. Upjohn Institute for Employment Research.

Cover design by J.R. Underhill.
Index prepared by Shirley Kessel.
Printed in the United States of America.

Acknowledgments

I am indebted to a wide range of people for assistance and support in carrying out this study. My interest in profit sharing was initially encouraged by Richard Freeman, David Bloom, Martin Weitzman, and Lawrence Katz, and I am grateful for their continued support. Stephen Woodbury of the W. E. Upjohn Institute for Employment Research first encouraged me to apply to the Institute for funding this study. The Upjohn Institute staff has been remarkably helpful and understanding throughout the course of the research; I would particularly like to thank Kevin Hollenbeck for his comments, ideas, and oversight, and Judy Gentry for guiding this publication to press.

A number of colleagues have been generous with their time and comments. I especially appreciate the extensive comments by my friend and colleague Joseph Blasi of Rutgers University. Valuable comments on early drafts were received from Mark Killingsworth, Mark Huselid, Eric Schulz, and Mike Zigarelli. Other Rutgers colleagues who have provided various forms of support, ideas, and assistance are James Begin, John Burton, James Chelius, Angelo DeNisi, Steve Director, Adrienne Eaton, Charles Fay, Jeffrey Keefe, Avraham Kluger, and Barbara Lee. Valuable research assistance was provided by Hsiu-Yu Lin, Arup Varma, Paul Hempel, and John Maroon. Colleagues from other institutions who have given useful feedback, literature, or answers to specific questions include John Addison of the University of South Carolina, David Blanchflower of Dartmouth College, Tom Clifton and Ted Shepard of LeMoyne College, William Cooke of Wayne State University, Casey Ichniowski of Columbia University, Roger Kaufman of Smith College, Sanders Korenman of the University of Minnesota, David Levine and Jonathan Leonard of the University of California-Berkeley, Jeffrey Pliskin of Hamilton College, Martin Weitzman of Harvard University, and seminar participants at Cornell University and the Eastern Economics Association meetings (March 1993). David Wray of the Profit Sharing Council of America has similarly been very generous in answering questions and providing feedback. (Almost needless to say, I give everyone the typical immunity from responsibility for any mistakes.) My department chair, James Chelius, and the Institute of Management and Labor Relations (John Burton, Director) have been remarkably supportive in arranging the time and resources to make this study possible. I appreciate the computer systems help of Steven Wachtel, conscientious administrative support from Sherry Danko, Betty Lou Heffernan, Estelle Scaiano, Joanne Mangels, Betty Derco, and Hann Nee Kang, and valuable help in locating and obtaining literature from the Institute librarians Mamata Datta, Jeff Katz, George Kanzler, and Eugene McElroy.

I am clearly indebted to the executives at the 500 companies who responded to the confidential telephone and mail survey on which this study is based. The survey was carried out in a professional and conscientious manner by the Eagleton Institute of Politics at Rutgers University, and I am particularly indebted to Ken Dautrich, Janice Ballou, and Kim Downing for our highly productive working relationships.

This study would not have been completed without substantial support in many forms from family members and friends during a very tumultuous time. My deep gratitude and affection are given to Lowen and Ruth Kruse, Jorika and Betsy Wolf, Janet Schur, and Rita and Michelle Link. By far the most important person in helping me complete this study is the one I had the fortune to marry—Lisa Schur. Words cannot do justice to the value she has given this study through her ideas, energy, strength, and remarkable patience. My deepest hope is to provide such valuable help and insight in the completion of her Ph.D. dissertation.

Executive Summary

Profit sharing with employees is a longstanding practice that has recently received increased attention, both in the United States and internationally. Between one-sixth and one-fourth of U.S. firms and employees participate in profit sharing.

There are two major theories on the economic effects of profit sharing. First, profit sharing has long been advocated on the grounds that it can improve company performance by encouraging worker effort, cooperation, and sharing of ideas and information (the "productivity theory"). A second, more recent theory is that profit sharing can lead to fewer layoffs and greater employment and output stability, for firms and for the economy as a whole, by changing employer incentives to hire and retain employees (the "stability theory").

This study reports on a new database on profit sharing in U.S. companies with public stock. A telephone survey was conducted of 500 public companies—half with profit sharing for employees other than top management, and half without. To maximize comparability, an attempt was made to match profit-sharers with non-profit-sharers within the same industry. Data were collected on profit-sharing coverage, types, and formulas, as well as on company unionization and personnel policies that may compete or interact with profit sharing in affecting firm behavior (summarized in table 1.3). To provide evidence on the productivity and stability theories of profit sharing, the survey data were matched with publicly available data from public companies on financial characteristics and performance over the 1970-91 period.

What predicts the adoption of profit sharing? Eleven prior studies comparing profit-sharing and non-profit-sharing companies have not produced consistent findings on the relationship of profit sharing to factors such as unionization, firm size, employee composition, firm growth, capital intensity, and industry variability. Focusing on the adoption decision, this study found few variables that could help predict a company's adoption of profit sharing; among a wide range of variables examined, only unionization and increases in profit margins and stock prices were found to increase the probability of profit-sharing adoption in this period. This calls into question the studies that only use cross-sectional comparisons of performance, since profit sharing may in part be an effect, rather than a cause, of better company performance. Among firms that have adopted profit sharing, greater coverage of employees is predicted where the profit sharing is older and there is a higher proportion of nonunion and professional/administrative employees.

Does profit sharing affect productivity? A wide range of past evidence is surveyed in chapter 3, focusing on 26 statistical studies that attempted to estimate the effect of profit sharing after accounting for other influences on firm performance. A substantial amount of the prior evidence indicates that employee profit-sharing plans are associated with higher company performance, although the causality and mechanisms are unclear. Accounting for past performance and a variety of influences on productivity, this study found that profit-sharing adoption is associated with productivity increases of 3.5 to 5 percent, which are maintained with no subsequent positive or negative trend. The average productivity increases are found to be larger for small companies and for companies adopting cash plans, and are unaffected when accounting for personnel policies that may affect productivity. There is, however, substantial dispersion in the outcomes, and very little evidence on the mechanisms through which profit sharing may affect productivity, since it does not strongly interact with measures of information-sharing or other policies in affecting productivity.

Does profit sharing lead to greater employment stability? Fifteen prior studies are surveyed in chapter 4; most of the studies that directly measured stability found some association between profit sharing and greater stability, though the studies on how the profit share is treated in employment decisions had more mixed results. The stability theory requires that profit shares not simply be "gravy" on top of regular compensation for a given level of output; they should, instead, substitute at least in part for fixed pay. Such substitution was found to be unlikely for old profit-sharing firms, since average compensation levels were generally substantially above industry averages. For firms that adopted profit sharing within the sample period, the average small increase in total compensation was exceeded by the typical profit share, indicating that profit sharing is more likely to be substituting in part for regular compensation in these firms. After firms adopted profit sharing, the employment cutbacks accompanying decreases in product demand tended to be smaller than in the preadoption period, particularly where profit sharing appeared to partially substitute for regular compensation. For most of the estimates, however, sampling error could not be rejected as an explanation for the apparent differences in behavior. The relation of employment stability to profit-sharing plan types and formulas, and to profit-sharing participation by unionized employees and different occupational groups, gave several indications of mild support for the theory, but the evidence is not strong. The often favorable but not strong results may in part be explained by several difficult empirical issues in testing the theory, and by the broad definition of profit sharing used in this study, which includes a number of so-called profit-sharing plans that do not fit the requirements of the stability theory.

What are the implications for companies, unions, public policy, and future research? Chapter 5 relates the results to practitioner literature on group incentives and discusses union concerns, public policy options, and rationales. Given that the issues addressed by the profit-sharing theories—productivity, unemployment, and macroeconomic stability—are central to economic performance and security, further attention and research on profit sharing are strongly encouraged.

The Author

Douglas Kruse is an Assistant Professor at the Institute of Management and Labor Relations, Rutgers University, and a Faculty Research Fellow at the National Bureau of Economic Research. He received his B.A. and Ph.D. in Economics from Harvard University, and an M.A. in Economics from the University of Nebraska-Lincoln. He is co-author of the book, *The New Owners*, which explores employee ownership in public companies, and author of *Employee Ownership and Employee Attitudes*. In addition, he has published articles in journals such as *Industrial and Labor Relations Review, Economic Journal*, and *Industrial Relations* on the topics of employee ownership, profit sharing, pensions, worker displacement, and wage differentials.

Contents

List of Tables

PROFIT SHARING

*Does It Make
A Difference?*

1

Introduction, Trends, and Data Description

The idea of tying worker pay to company profits has existed almost since the emergence of capitalism. Albert Gallatin, U.S. Secretary of the Treasury under Thomas Jefferson, reportedly instituted a profit-sharing plan in 1795 at his Pennsylvania Glass Works out of a belief that such a system was important for the newly developing U.S. democracy (PSCA 1959). Experiments in profit sharing attracted support from eminent scholars in the 1800s, including Charles Babbage, John Stuart Mill, and Stanley Jevons. A pastor and crusader for profit sharing, Nicholas Paine Gilman (1899), documented 34 profit-sharing plans in 1899.[1] Two decades later, the National Civic Federation (1920) documented 46 plans in the United States with worker pay tied to a percentage of profits (and many others with more loosely based elements of profit sharing).

Much of the early support for profit sharing can with fairness be described as ideological. Many proponents viewed profit sharing as a way to integrate workers into the capitalist system by sharing the benefits of capitalism in a more direct and tangible way than allowed by fixed wages. Advocates promoted it as a cure for "unrest" and "irrational agitation" in capitalism, arguing that the "great uplift and inspiration that sharing of profits cultivates in the employee" would lead to "harmony and contentment" (Askwith 1926: 20). It was seen by many advocates as a means to build support for capitalism and to solidify opposition to the competing communist and socialist systems. It was also seen by some as a logical extension of political democracy—Gallatin advocated profit sharing on the grounds that the

> democratic principle upon which this Nation was founded should not be restricted to the political processes but should be applied to the industrial operation (quoted in U.S. Senate 1939: 72).

1

Ideological support for profit sharing has continued in the twentieth century. A U.S. Senate subcommittee (1939) held hearings on profit sharing toward the end of the Great Depression, clearly displaying support for profit sharing as a means of strengthening capitalism. The ideological support is well-exemplified in the title of a 1954 book by John Spedan Lewis, *Fairer Shares: A Possible Advance in Civilisation and Perhaps the Only Alternative to Communism* (1954). As a further illustration, a 1950s comparison of attitudes between employees in profit-sharing and non-profit-sharing companies lamented that profit sharing "doesn't necessarily carry over into strong faith in free market ideas broadly" (Opinion Research Corporation 1957: 16).[2] Short of engendering support for free markets and capitalism, the ideological approach may still be exemplified today by companies that maintain profit sharing in part out of a belief that employees should share in the fruits of company performance (without attempting to change worker or firm behavior).

Much of the support for profit sharing during the twentieth century, however, has shifted from a broad ideological approach to support based on more narrowly construed economic reasons. Undoubtedly the dominant argument for profit sharing in the twentieth century has been the idea that it can motivate employees to work harder for increased profits, primarily through increased productivity. By tying worker pay to profits, the argument goes, the incentives of workers and owners can become aligned so that productivity-reducing conflict is minimized and productivity-enhancing cooperation and innovation are encouraged. This idea (which will be referred to as the "productivity theory" of profit sharing) was one of the arguments for profit sharing among early supporters (Gilman 1899; Askwith 1926), but assumed a larger role in the U.S. Senate hearings in the 1930s, where it was claimed that profit sharing brings the worker into a

> thoroughly cooperative effort to increase profits of the company by stimulating production at lower cost, conserving materials, creating savings of waste, protecting the product of the institution, stimulating greater sales effort, and bringing into harmonious cooperation all the operating and productive factors of the company operation (U.S. Senate 1939: 65).

This theory has received increased attention in the 1980s, stimulated in part by concerns about lagging productivity growth.

A second argument for profit sharing (developed more recently than the productivity theory) is that it can aid economic stability and decrease unemployment. A key concern of market economies has been macroeconomic instability, represented both by business cycles and, in the extreme, by episodes such as the Great Depression in the 1930s. An often-cited culprit in economic recessions is the fixed wage system—if wages adjusted more quickly to equate supply and demand in the labor market, the argument goes, the economy would spend more time in full-employment equilibrium. Making wages more responsive to economic conditions, as profit sharing allows, is seen therefore as one potential solution to economic instability. Simply making worker pay more flexible, however, may not contribute toward macroeconomic stability; as John Maynard Keynes argued, flexible wages may aggravate business cycles through effects on aggregate purchasing power (1964: 257-71).

Martin Weitzman has developed a theory supporting the stabilizing effects of profit sharing that does not rely on claims of increased flexibility in total pay. This theory (which will be referred to as the "stability theory") holds that profit sharing changes the incentives of firms to hire and retain workers. In brief terms, this theory suggests that firms view profit-sharing payments not as a cost of employing labor, but rather as a profits tax. The fact that the "tax" is being paid to the workers is incidental to the firm's short-run demand for labor; what concerns the firm when hiring or laying off workers is the fixed wage that it must pay. If, for example, the fixed wage is $9/hour and the average profit share is $1/hour, the firm will hire or retain workers as long as their output exceeds $9/hour. The $1/hour does not figure into the short-run decision since it is directly related to the company's profits, and the worker will be hired or retained as long as s/he contributes to profits (i.e., has output exceeding $9/hour). This is in contrast to a firm with a fixed wage of $10/hour, which will lay off the worker when the value of the worker's output falls below $10/hour. Assuming, therefore, that profit-sharing payments substitute for fixed wages, average worker pay per hour is similar in the two systems ($10/hour total), but the risk of layoff is different because of the firm's different incentives. In the long run, profit-sharing and fixed-wage economies will have similar levels of compensation and employment, but when short-run shocks occur, the theory predicts that profit-sharing economies will have less unemployment and milder recessions. Unlike the productivity theory, the stability theory provides a strong public policy case for encouraging profit sharing, since the gains from stability accrue to the economy as a whole.

This study will summarize existing evidence on the productivity and stability theories and bring new evidence to bear on both of them. A key question to be answered prior to that is why employers have adopted profit sharing—what leads firms to view it as a useful form of compensation? These three questions—adoption, employment, and productivity effects—are addressed with use of a new panel dataset on 500 U.S. firms, containing up to 21 years of employment and financial data on each firm.

Definition and Types of Profit Sharing

No neat definition of profit sharing covers the variety of plans that can legitimately claim to share profits with employees. One strict definition would be that profit-sharing plans must have a formula specifying a fixed percentage of profits to be divided among employees in a predetermined way.[3] However, this excludes plans that permit a discretionary amount to be added to the fixed percentage. It also leaves open the question of how profits are defined, and what kinds of restrictions may be applied to the formula—some plans provide shares of profits only after a threshold level of profits has been met or make the percentage of profits to be shared depend upon the overall level of profits. Also, it excludes plans where there may be no fixed formula, but where the discretionary contribution, in practice, systematically depends on profits. These and other examples argue against a strict definition of profit sharing, since the productivity and stability theories may easily apply in cases that do not meet the strict definition.

The Profit Sharing Council of America, a nonprofit association representing U.S. companies practicing profit sharing, does not employ a strict definition. It promotes plans that give employees "a direct stake in profits," but notes that "profit sharing is an extremely adaptable and flexible invention" and that "there are many variations among individual plans as to how company contributions are determined, credited to participants' accounts, [and] distributed" (PSCA 1984: 8, 10, 16). The PSCA membership exhibits this diversity in plan types and formulas (PSCA 1989).

This study likewise does not employ a strict definition of profit sharing. Rather, a profit-sharing plan is defined broadly as a plan in which part of employee compensation during a particular period is based substantially on the profitability of the company in that period (without the requirement of a formula).[4]

As used here, profit sharing is distinguished from employee stock ownership. Profit sharing and employee ownership share many attributes as different forms of compensation schemes tied to company performance. Stock ownership, however, is a separate route for sharing company success: the initial contribution of stock is generally not based on company profits, and its value to employees is necessarily tied not only to the company's current but also to its future expected success. Good performance in one period has the primary effect not of increasing employee income, but of increasing wealth through the stock price.[5] It raises significant issues related to asset portfolios of employees, particularly by introducing substantial risk. In addition, the perquisites of stock ownership generally include at least minimal voting rights. For these and other reasons, employee ownership may plausibly have motivational effects different from profit sharing. Also, the stability theory of profit sharing does not apply to employee stock ownership. While the effects of employee ownership will be treated incidentally here, the focus is on the direct sharing of profits with employees, not on affecting their asset portfolios through changes in stock price. (For research on employee ownership, see Blasi 1988; Conte and Svejnar 1990; and Blasi and Kruse 1991).

There are three basic forms of profit sharing in the United States: cash, deferred, and combination cash/deferred plans. In the cash form of profit-sharing plan, employees have their share of the profits added directly to their paychecks (usually at quarterly or annual intervals). It is a deductible business expense for the employer, but taxable to the employee as income. There is no central source of information on all cash plans, since they need not be reported to the government. In the deferred form of plan, the profit share is put into a pension trust for the employee, where it is invested in a pension portfolio and the eventual value is normally received by the employee at retirement. (As such, it is a popular form of "defined contribution" pension plan, in which the employer's obligation is defined at the point the contribution is made, rather than at the point the benefit is received by the employee.) The income is not taxable to the employee until received at retirement. Finally, the cash/deferred profit-sharing plans are simply a combination of cash and deferred contributions.

There are three noteworthy features of deferred profit-sharing plans. The first is that, beyond the direct company contribution, employees may be permitted or required to make contributions in many of these plans. An increasingly popular pension option has been the 401(K) option, in which employers typically match a percentage of employee contributions to a retirement plan. For example, a popular method is for the employer to contribute 50 percent of the value of the employee's contribution, up to a specified percentage of the employee's pay. The 401(K) option has muddied the definition of deferred profit-sharing plans, since many of these plans are technically listed as profit-sharing plans even though the employer contribution is not related to profits but wholly to the employee contribution. Simply having a 401(K) option, however, does not disqualify a plan as profit sharing, since the employer match may be tied to profitability as well as to the employee contribution.[6]

A second noteworthy aspect of deferred profit-sharing plans is that, once the employer contribution is made, it may be largely invested in the employer's own stock. The subsequent performance of the company will affect the employee's account value through the effect on the stock price. As noted, this study distinguishes profit sharing from employee stock ownership, but in practice the two may be combined even in the same plan. Unlike the standard defined benefit pension, in which the employee receives a specified benefit at retirement (usually based on final salary and years of service), deferred profit-sharing plans may be structured so that more than 10 percent of the assets can be invested in the employer's stock. In this way, deferred profit-sharing plans may closely resemble Employee Stock Ownership Plans (ESOPs), and in fact there is overlap between them. ESOPs are pension plans that are required to invest primarily in employer securities, and thereby become a pension vehicle for employee stock ownership of companies (see Blasi 1988; and Conte and Svejnar 1990). Because deferred profit-sharing plans may (but are not required to) invest heavily in employer stock, they can combine profit sharing with a large degree of employee stock ownership.[7] Therefore there is no neat separation between profit sharing and employee ownership, and it may be that investment of profit-sharing funds in company stock can strongly reinforce the link in employees' minds between company performance and personal reward.

A third noteworthy aspect of deferred profit-sharing plans is that, as pension plans, they are subject to regulations governing pension plans. Plan administrators each year must file a form in the Form 5500 series (5500, 5500C, or 5500R), and such information is publicly available. As such, it is a valuable source for research, but contains very little information on firm characteristics.[8]

Growth and Prevalence in the United States

What are the trends in profit sharing? Apart from the theories on its effects, is it a common enough phenomenon to warrant attention and study?

Table 1.1 summarizes a variety of evidence on prevalence and growth of profit sharing in the United States. The longest series of data comes from the U.S. Chamber of Commerce Employee Benefits Survey, which has the percent of companies making profit-sharing payments and the percent of payroll represented by such payments for most of the years since 1955. The percent of companies making profit-sharing payments grew through the later 1950s but has hovered between 19 and 23 percent since 1963. The Survey of Benefits in Medium and Large Firms, by the U.S. Bureau of Labor Statistics (BLS), shows slow growth in the number of employees in profit-sharing companies over 1981-84, though no real trend in employees covered by profit sharing over 1985-91 (taking into account the changed survey coverage in 1988).[9]

These sources refer to both cash and deferred profit sharing. Two additional data sources refer only to deferred profit-sharing plans. A Hewitt panel of 250 large employers showed increased use of profit

Table 1.1 Evidence on Prevalence and Growth of Profit Sharing

Year	COC (hourly employees)[a] cash & deferred	Hewitt (salaried,large firms)[b] deferred	C&S (small firms) cash & deferred	Smith (fast-growing public) cash & deferred	B&S (public computer firms) cash & deferred	Nickel (Fortune 1000) cash	MLL (bus. units, public firms) cash & deferred CL	PR
1991	21							
1990	22							
1989	22					37		
1988	20				41			
1987	23		28				37	38
1986								
1985	22	17[c]		33				
1984	21	23						
1983	20	22						
1982	23	20						
1981		19						
1980		19						
1979	21	19						
1978	21							
1977	20							
1975	20							
1973	20							
1971	19							
1969	22							
1967	21							
1965	19							
1963	21							

Year	Percent of employees who work in companies with plans — BLS (medium & large firms) cash & deferred			Percent of employees in plans — BLS (medium & large firms)[c] cash & deferred				Percent of employees in plans — B&N (union contracts negotiated in given year) cash & deferred		Percent of employees in plans — Kruse (all private sector) deferred		PS contribution/total payroll in firms with plans[d] — COC (hourly employees)[a] cash & deferred
	P/A	T/C	PR	All	P/A	T/C	PR	Manuf.	Non-manuf.	All	Nonthrift	
1991				16			18					2.7
1990				15	16	17	13					4.4
1989				16	15	13	18					3.2
1988				18	20	21	15					
1988				21	23	24	18	12.2	0.0			3.3
1987								18.0	2.1			3.3
1986				22	22	22	22	17.1	2.6	18.4	15.3	5.1
1985				18	19	22	16	12.1	1.8	18.1	14.6	5.1
1984	28	31	23					61.4	2.2	16.7	13.6	5.2
1983	27	31	23					11.5	7.9	16.1	13.2	
1982	25	28	18					36.5	0.4	14.6	12.0	4.8
1981	25	26	17					16.7	0.0	13.5	11.2	
1980								0.7	0.0	13.3	11.4	
1979								41.6	0.2			6.7
1978								0.0	0.0			6.6
1977								0.1	0.5			5.5
1975								0.0	0.0			5.5

Year	Percent of employees who work in companies with plans
1961	17
1959	15
1957	14
1955	13

	Percent of employees who work in companies with plans			Percent of employees in plans										PS contribution/ total payroll in firms with plans[d]
	BLS (medium & large firms) cash & deferred			BLS (medium & large firms)[c] cash & deferred				B&N (union contracts negotiated in given year) cash & deferred		Kruse (all private sector)			COC (hourly employees)[a]
Year	P/A	T/C	PR	All	P/A	T/C	PR	Manuf.	Non-manuf.	deferred	All	Nonthrift	cash & deferred
1973													5.7
1971													5.5
1969													5.2
1967													5.7
1965													5.5
1963													3.9
1961													4.7
1959													5.6
1957													5.4
1955													5.5

NOTES: Employee class: CL = clerical; PR = production; P/A = professional and administrative; T/C = technical and clerical. COC: Chamber of Commerce of the United States (various years); BLS: Bureau of Labor Statistics (various years); Hewitt: Hewitt Associates (1985, 1986); B&N: Bell and Neumark (1993); C&S: Chelius and Smith (1990); MLL: Mitchell, Lewin, and Lawler (1990); B&S: Bradley and Smith (1992); Kruse: Kruse (1991b); Smith: Smith (1988).

a. 1987-91 Chamber of Commerce surveys exclude cash profit sharing and include salaried employees.

b. 1979-84 Hewitt numbers from constant sample of 250 large employers, while 1985 number reflects larger sample of 812 employers.

c. BLS survey coverage changed in 1988: both new and old coverage numbers are presented for 1988. BLS numbers for 1990, unlike other years, are for small private establishments. Survey methodology was changed in 1991, with a redefinition of occupational groups. In the new group of professional/administrative/technical employees, 13 percent were participants, and in the new clerical/sales group, 16 percent were participants.

d. Total payroll includes payroll of nonparticipants.

sharing over the 1979-84 period. The more comprehensive Form 5500 data, which comprise close to the universe of deferred profit-sharing plans in the United States, show steady growth in coverage over the 1980-86 period (Kruse 1991b). The percentage of private wage and salary workers covered by all deferred profit-sharing plans grew from 13.3 percent to 18.4 percent over this period, according to these data. Eliminating the influence of 401(K) options and other "thrift" features (which permit or require employee contributions) shows an increase from 11.4 percent to 15.3 percent over this period.[10]

The prevalence of profit sharing does not appear to differ greatly by occupational group (as shown by the BLS numbers, and the Mitchell, Lewin, and Lawler comparison of clerical and production workers) or by firm size (the Chelius and Smith numbers on small firms show a prevalence only slightly higher than the Hewitt and Chamber of Commerce figures, and the BLS small firm survey in 1990 shows coverage equivalent to that in medium and large firms). The prevalence appears higher in companies with public stock (as indicated by Bradley and Smith, and the Mitchell, Lewin, and Lawler numbers). There is also a difference by union status: Mitchell, Lewin, and Lawler (1990) report that unionized workers were less likely to be covered by profit sharing (among unionized groups, only 15 percent of clerical and 18 percent of production units were covered, while the corresponding numbers for nonunion groups were 42 percent and 46 percent). However, profit sharing became much more prevalent among union workers in the 1980s, particularly in the manufacturing sector, as shown by Bell and Neumark (1993).[11] Much of this was linked to concession bargaining (Zalusky 1986, 1990).[12]

While these numbers indicate substantial portions of employees in some form of profit sharing, many of these plans do not tie profit-sharing payments tightly to company profits. As will be reviewed in chapter 3, most plans also allow a discretionary component by the employer. A recent examination of 10,000 variable-pay plans found 2,200 that "have a clear, preannounced performance-payout link," are more than one year old, cover more than 20 people, and are not fully deferred (McAdams and Hawk 1992).[13]

In summary, data on the prevalence of (broadly-defined) profit sharing in the United States indicate that roughly one-sixth to one-fourth of companies have profit-sharing plans, and roughly the same percentage of private-sector employees are covered. Such coverage does not differ greatly by firm size or occupational group, but is much less common among unionized workers. Several sources point toward slow growth in the prevalence of plans in the early 1980s, even among unionized workers, but no general trend in the later 1980s.

Data on international trends are extremely sparse. The prevalence in Canada appears similar to that in the United States: two surveys indicated profit sharing at 22.2 percent of Canadian firms in 1985, and 17.3 percent in 1989/90 (the difference apparently reflects not a decline in profit sharing, but a tighter definition and different method in the later survey) (Long 1989, 1992). It is clear that profit sharing is a common practice in a number of European countries (Uvalic 1990; Perry and Kegley 1990; D'Art 1992).[14] The PEPPER report (Promotion of Employee Participation in Profits and Enterprise Results) documents the extent of profit sharing and employee stock ownership schemes, and government policies affecting such schemes, among European Community members. One conclusion is that "recently there has been a steady growth of various forms of PEPPER schemes in the majority of EC countries, with widely different relative weight" (Uvalic 1990: 197). The percentage of employees covered by such schemes is estimated as 18 percent in France, 8 percent in the UK, 7.4 percent in the Netherlands, 5 percent in Germany, and 3 percent or less in Ireland, Italy, and Spain (Uvalic 1990: 200).[15]

There has been particularly strong interest in profit sharing in the United Kingdom, spurred in part by its potential to reduce unemployment. Within the United Kingdom, cash profit sharing was found in 20 percent of establishments in 1984, although only 9 percent of private-sector workers reported participating in profit sharing in 1987. Profit sharing was found to be more common in large plants, but just as common for union members as for other employees (Blanchflower 1991: 4-5). Results from a 1988 survey of 180 of the largest publicly held UK companies indicated that 6.1 percent had cash-based profit sharing for all employees (Peel, Pendlebury, and Groves 1991).[16] The prevalence appears to be increasing, spurred largely by tax incentives: Singleton-Green reports that the number of plans and employees covered doubled between 1991 and 1992, so that 700,000 employees are now covered (1992: 38).

Data on profit sharing in non–European countries are difficult to find. Florkowski (1991: 102) reports that 12 non–European countries have some form of mandatory profit sharing in the constitution or statutes, but in several of these countries it is not enforced (the countries are Bolivia, Brazil, Chile, Columbia, Ecuador, India, Mexico, Nigeria, Pakistan, Panama, Peru, and Venezuela). A major effort has been made in Singapore to encourage the use of profit sharing for both productivity and stability reasons, and more than half of the labor contracts in Singapore now contain profit sharing (National Wages Council 1986). The extensive use of bonuses in Japan and Korea has been viewed as a form of profit sharing that may have contributed to the economic success of those countries (Freeman and Weitzman 1987; Kim 1988). While nearly all Japanese firms with more than 30 employees pay bonuses twice a year to regular employees, only 24.6 percent of firms have a formal profit-sharing plan (Jones and Kato 1992a).

Therefore, while the practice of profit sharing may be slowly growing in the United States, it is not clear to what extent this is true outside of the United States. At a minimum, profit sharing is very much a strong topic of interest internationally, as legislation and public policy discussion make clear (Uvalic 1990; Florkowski 1991).

New Data on Profit Sharing in Publicly Held Companies

Available data on profit sharing have important limitations on their usefulness.[17] Among these limitations are one or more of the following: lack of information on both cash and deferred plans, lack of sufficient company performance data, response rate problems common to business mail surveys, or lack of longitudinal information on individual companies to control for firm-specific effects.

This study surveyed 500 companies to collect information for testing the productivity and stability theories of profit sharing. Such tests require longitudinal information on company performance and employment that many companies are unwilling or unable to provide. Companies with publicly traded stock, however, are required to make public a wide variety of company information. These data are packaged in Standard and Poor's CompuStat database. A subset of 500 companies from the 1990 CompuStat (with over 3000 public companies)[18] was surveyed to obtain information on profit sharing and other firm characteristics. Firms with profit sharing were oversampled, in order that they would constitute one-half of the final sample. An attempt was made to pair each firm surveyed in the initial sample with a firm of the opposite profit-sharing status in the same industry.[19] For example, for each profit-sharing food processor, an attempt was made to find a non-profit-sharing food processor to act as a paired control. This could be done for 410 of the surveyed firms (creating 205 pairs). Comparison of characteristics between the within-industry pairs will automatically control for any industry effects on those characteristics. Construction of the dataset is described in appendix 1.

Each company was asked, "Does your company have a profit-sharing plan for employees *other than top management?*" If the response was positive, the company was treated as a profit-sharing company, and a series of questions elicited information on the features and coverage of the plan.[20] The resulting sample of profit-sharing companies may be overinclusive, since it includes whatever type of plan is viewed by the employer as profit sharing (even if there is little or no *de facto* relationship to profits). The advantage is that it allows analysis of what goes under the name of profit sharing in the United States, with additional data to distinguish plans by profit-sharing formulas and features. The lack of a strict definition matches the practice of the Profit Sharing Council of America, as noted earlier in this chapter.

Table 1.2 contains statistics on the prevalence of profit sharing among firms surveyed in the initial sample (prior to the attempt at pairing).[21] As can be seen, 112 of the 275 firms, or 40.7 percent, have a profit-sharing plan for employees other than top management. Collectively the 275 firms employed slightly over 6 million employees in 1990. Profit-sharing firms had an estimated 2.3 million participants, representing 38.2 percent of the total employees among the firms in this sample. Industry distribution shows the highest concentration of profit-sharing participants in durable manufacturing (47.7 percent) and the lowest in utilities (6.3 percent).

The closest comparison for these numbers comes from the Columbia Business Unit Data Set (Mitchell, Lewin, and Lawler 1990), which reports results of a survey of business units among publicly held com-

Table 1.2 Prevalence of Profit Sharing in Sample

	Distribution of companies			Distribution of employees (1990 sum, in 000s)		
	All firms (1)	PS firms (2)	PS as percent of all (3)	All employees (4)	PS participants (5)	PS as percent of all (6)
Mining/construction	12	4	33.3	21.9	2.7	12.4
Nondurable manufacturing	86	35	40.7	1393.1	345.5	24.8
Durable manufacturing	86	40	46.5	3153.4	1503.2	47.7
Communications	11	5	45.5	279.0	44.5	16.0
Utilities	37	6	16.2	172.2	10.9	6.3
Wholesale	9	4	44.4	71.1	13.0	18.2
Retail	15	8	53.3	635.8	187.6	29.5
Finance, insurance, real estate	13	6	46.2	210.2	131.3	62.5
Service	6	4	66.7	85.9	60.2	70.0
Total	275	112	40.7	6022.6	2298.9	38.2

NOTES: These numbers consider only the responses from the primary sample, which was based on a systematic sample of all firms with at least eight years of employment data over the 1980-89 period. Companies contacted to provide matched pairs are excluded from selection rule for pairing. PS = profit sharing.

Table 1.3 Descriptive Statistics on Profit-Sharing Dataset

	PS (1)	NPS (2)	Within-industry paired difference (PS minus NPS) Mean (3)	Within-industry paired difference (PS minus NPS) t-stat. (4)	Percent of PS employees (5)		PS (6)	NPS (7)	Within-industry paired difference (PS minus NPS) Mean (8)	Within-industry paired difference (PS minus NPS) t-stat. (9)
N	253	247	205			Occupational mix				
Percent employees in PS	78.5					Percent production/service	49.5	51.2	-3.7	-1.31
Percent cos. w/unions	65.9	75.9	-7.1*	-1.77		Percent clerical/technical	24.7	21.8	1.8	0.72
Percent of employees in union, if unionized	38.6	35.8	3.2	0.97		Percent prof./admin.	26.6	26.9	2.4	0.98
Majority of U workers are in PS	44.7					Percent employees covered by PS:				
Percent companies with personnel policy:						Percent production/service	75.8			
Surveys	38.0	35.4	0.5	0.11		Percent clerical/technical	86.5			
Suggestion system	57.1	51.7	6.1	1.22		Percent prof./admin.	87.6			
Job enrichment	35.1	25.0	11.4**	2.63		Type of PS:				
Employee involvement	60.7	58.2	1.6	0.33		Cash	37.7			
Autonomous workteams	26.1	22.5	3.7	0.91		Deferred	50.8			
Employment security	16.1	13.6	5.1	1.52		Combination	8.5			

Gainsharing	45.3	39.0	1.1	0.22	
Percent employees covered by personnel policy:					
Surveys	23.3	22.3	0.3	00.8	23.0
Suggestion system	19.1	17.5	2.5	0.90	19.8
Job enrichment	14.5	10.8	4.3*	1.67	13.0
Employee involvement	25.6	24.5	1.6	0.47	24.2
Autonomous workteams	9.5	7.8	1.9	0.99	9.3
Employment security	9.5	7.6	3.1	1.15	8.7
Gainsharing	19.8	16.0	1.3	0.40	19.8
Percent employees provided w/info on:					
Overall co. perf.	85.3	83.4	0.8	0.29	
Bus. plans & goals	61.8	57.5	3.6	0.97	
Competitors' perf.	30.4	24.6	4.6	1.24	

More than one PS plan	24.7			
Age of oldest PS plan				
1-5	21.7			
6-10	17.7			
11-20	22.1			
20+	29.9			
NA	8.7			
Change in other personnel policies when PS adopted				
Yes	17.3			
No	56.7			
NA	26.0			
1990 employment (000s)				
Mean	21.52	18.08	1.275	0.21
Median	5.60	5.40		
Mean of ln(employment)	1.71	1.63	-0.048	-0.29
1990 sales (000,000s):				
Mean	3823.40	3494.06	583.9	0.52
Median	876.55	935.27		
Mean of ln(sales)	6.76	6.81	-0.039	-0.23

NOTES: Except where NA (not answered) is used, reported percentages exclude "don't know" responses. PS = profit sharing; NPS = nonprofit sharing; U = union.

*Statistically significant at p <.10   **p <.05.

panies. Despite differences in the level of analysis and response rates, the results are similar.

Mitchell, Lewin, and Lawler (1990: 76) report that 36 percent of the units have profit sharing for clerical workers, and 37 percent have profit sharing for manufacturing production workers. This is closely in line with the 40.7 percent of companies in this study that report profit sharing for employees other than top management.

Additional sources of data on profit sharing in publicly held companies come from Smith (1988) and Bradley and Smith (1992). Reporting on a survey of 52 of the "INC 100 Fastest Growing Publicly Held Firms," Smith found that 17 (33 percent) reported general profit-sharing plans. Focusing on firms with public stock in the computer (hardware and software) industries, Bradley and Smith (1992) found that 41 percent reported profit-sharing plans. The results from these three data sources on U.S. companies with public stock (consistent with Canadian results from Long 1992) indicate that profit sharing is more prevalent in such companies than among private companies. One reason for this may have to do with information disclosure about profitability: private companies may be more reluctant to give signals of profitability (to competitors or unions) through the size of profit-sharing payments, while publicly held companies must already report profit figures to investors.

Descriptive statistics on the full sample of profit-sharing and non-profit-sharing companies are presented in table 1.3. Columns 1 and 2 contain statistics for the profit-sharing (PS) and non-profit-sharing (NPS) companies. Column 3 contains the paired differences for the 410 companies that could be matched within their industry, which controls for any general differences associated with an industry. As in all sampling, there exists random error from sampling a population. Column 4 presents the t-statistic testing whether random sampling error in the mean paired difference can be ruled out as an explanation of the difference.[22]

Among the profit-sharing companies, an (unweighted) average of 78.5 percent of employees participate in the profit sharing. These companies are less likely to have unions present (the average difference between industry pairs is 7.1 percent, where sampling error can be ruled out at the 90 percent level). If unions are present, a majority of unionized workers participate in profit sharing in 44.7 percent of the companies. A major purpose of the survey is to determine whether profit sharing is accompanied by other personnel policies that may affect productivity and employment stability, either by themselves or by interacting with profit sharing. Of the seven personnel policies that firms were asked about, table 1.3 indicates that profit-sharing firms are generally more likely to have all seven policies and to cover a larger percent of employees. The differences are not large, however, and only for job enrichment programs can one reject sampling error as an explanation for the difference between profit-sharing and non-profit-sharing firms. The same story holds for information-sharing with employees: table 1.3 indicates that profit-sharing firms share three types of information with a larger percentage of employees, but random sampling error cannot be ruled out as an explanation for the paired differences.[23] While the effects of these policies will be analyzed later, the simple differences presented here do not support the idea that profit-sharing companies are more likely to make greater efforts to involve their employees through these other policies.

The occupational mix of profit-sharing and non-profit-sharing firms shows no significant differences. Within profit-sharing firms, production and service workers are somewhat less likely to be covered (75.8 percent) than are clerical/technical (86.5 percent) and professional/ administrative employees (87.6 percent).

Among profit-sharing firms, more than one-third (37.7 percent) have cash plans, and an additional 8.5 percent have combination cash/ deferred plans. One-fourth (24.7 percent) have more than one plan. A majority of the plans (61.5 percent) were begun within the last 20 years, and one-sixth (17.3 percent) report changes in other personnel policies when profit sharing was adopted. Comparisons of 1990 sales and employment levels show no significant differences between profit-sharing and non-profit-sharing companies.

The apparent growth in popularity of profit sharing in the United States over the 1980s, and popular interest in the potential of profit sharing to increase productivity and/or stabilize employment, provide the setting for this study. These data will form the basis of analyses of the productivity and stability theories of profit sharing, and of the factors that predict adoption of profit sharing.

NOTES

1. Although the rate of failure was high, however, In an 1896 survey of 50 plans, many of which were documented by Gilman in an 1891 book, only 12 were fully operating (Monroe 1896). Also, of 299 plans begun in England between 1829 and 1913, only 133 were operating at the end of the period (National Civic Federation 1920: 392).

2. A current example is the hope that profit-sharing plans may help to change negative public opinions about corporate profits (Fosbre 1989).

3. This closely matches a resolution of the International Congress on Profit Sharing in 1889, which defined profit sharing as an "agreement, freely entered into, by which the employee receives a share, fixed in advance, of the profits" (quoted in National Civic Federation 1920: 22).

4. The report on the U.S. Senate hearings on profit sharing regarded "welfare and benefit payments," including a wide array of fixed benefits such as health care and educational benefits, as forms of profit sharing (1939: 53-57). Such fixed benefits, which are not viewed as "profit sharing" by employers, are excluded from the definition used in this study.

5. In some limited circumstances employees may be able to have quick access to the increased wealth by selling the stock or borrowing against it.

6. The use of profit sharing in 401(k) plans appears to be increasing (kertesz 12990).

7. This is supported by two pieces of evidence on investment of profit-sharing funds. An average of 26.4 percent of these funds were invested in company stock in 1991, and the percentage of plans where company stock represents more than 50 percent of plan assets increased from 16 percent in 1980 to 27 percent in 1990 (PSRF 1992b, 1992c).

8. Employers are required to report on deferred profit-sharing plans under the provisions of the Employee Retirement Incomes Security Act (ERISA) of 1974, using the Form 5500 series. Such reports are publicly available either by hardcopy or computer tape. These reports contain a large amount of financial information on reported plans; however, they have the following problems. Most important, while employers may check a box indicating that theirs is a profit-sharing plan, "profit sharing" has no clear definition. Until 1986, the only restriction on what would qualify as a profit-sharing plan for tax purposes was that contributions to the plan could not be made in a year in which employer profits were not positive; in 1986, even this mild restriction was dropped. Employers need not have a clear formula typing worker pay to profits to qualify as a profit-sharing plan, and in fact, in many of these plans contributions are wholly discretionary or a fixed percent of participant pay. Therefore the "profit sharing" label is overinclusive. A second problem with these data is that, while the plan's financial information is detailed, very little information is provided on the employer other than location, industry, and number of employees. For most analyses, these data must be matched to industry data (Cheadle 1989; Kruse 1991c) or other specific company data (Bloom 1985; Kruse 1992).

9. For further evidence from this data source, see Coates (1991). The survey is based on a sample and the numbers are subject to sampling variability. For percentages of this magnitude, the standard error of any one year's estimate is approximately 1.4 percent, implying a 95 percent confidence interval of plus or minus 2.8 percent (BLS 2336, 1989: 145). Year-to-year differences of 2 percent are clearly within the bounds of sampling variability. The changes from 1988 to 1989 could be due to sampling variability; another possible explanation is that there were several large companies that restructured or terminated profit-sharing plans in these years to fund employee ownership of stock, and these may have been included in the survey (Blasi and Kruse 1991: 111-115)

10. These figures constitute the "low" estimates from Kruse (1991b), which count only the largest plan in a company. Smaller plans may cover additional workers, but there is no way to ensure against double-counting of workers covered by more than one plan.

11. The spikes in 1982 and 1984 are primarily due to large autoworker contracts negotiated in those years.

12. Looking at the concession issue, Mitchell, Lewin, and Lawler compare union contracts with and without profit-sharing provisions over the 1981-88 period. Of all contracts with first-year wage decreases, profit sharing appeared in 17.1 percent of them. In the 133 contracts with profit sharing, 36 percent involved a first-year wage decrease, compared to 14 percent of the 1,666 contracts without profit sharing. The prevalence of COLA freezes or eliminations was also higher among contracts with profit sharing (1990: 25).

Bell and Neumark (1993) also report the overlap between profit sharing and wage concessions (defined as a nominal wage freeze or decline in the first year of the contract). The percentages of all manufacturing workers negotiating contracts in a given year in which the contract included both profit sharing and a wage concession, were 0.0 percent through 1980, 1.4 percent in 1981, 33.2 percent in 1982, 8.4 percent in 1983, 0.9 percent in 1984, 1.7 percent in 1985, 16.7 percent in 1986, 4.3 percent in 1987, and 0 percent in 1988. Comparison of these numbers with those reported in table 1.1 reveals that wage concessions existed for a majority of workers in profit-sharing manufacturing contracts only in 1982, 1983, and 1986.

13. Additional recent survey evidence is contained in Markham, Scott, and Little (1992) and Lissy (1991).

14. For an earlier international survey, see Latta (1979).

15. For an earlier analysis of profit sharing and employee stock ownership schemes in Europe, see Latta (1979).

16. For a historical view of profit sharing in the UK between 1865 and 1913, see Hatton (1988) and Lindop (1989).

17. For a comprehensive listing of data sources and research findings, see PSRF (1989).

18. This comprises the "primary, secondary, tertiary, and OTC" files of CompuStat.

19. Such pairing was done within the two-digit Standard Industrial Classification (SIC) definition.

20. For respondents who inquired about the definition, a profit-sharing plan was defined as one in which employer contributions to the plan are based at lest in part on the financial performance of the company.

21. Including the contacts during the attempts at pairing would induce a bias in the representativeness of the firms, due to the stopping rules for pairing.

22. When the absolute value of the t-statistic is greater than 2, one can be confident at the 95 percent level that the within-industry difference between the profit-sharing and non-profit-sharing firms is not due to sampling error (i.e., a difference this large from random sampling error would occur less than 5 percent of the time).

23. These results differ from Peel, Pendlebury, and Groves (1991), who find that British firms with profit sharing or stock ownership are more likely to share information and engage in consultative practices with employees.

2
Prediction of Profit Sharing

Why is profit sharing ever adopted? The simplest model of neoclassical economic theory assumes perfect information and mobility in competitive labor markets, with the conclusion that each worker receives the value of his or her contribution to output (marginal revenue product). In this simple model, where the employer has perfect information on employee effort and output, the form of payment does not matter. In the absence, however, of perfect information on worker behavior, the employer runs the risk of employee "shirking" (substandard performance). Where supervision is costly, the compensation scheme may be set up in one or more of several ways to induce appropriate levels of worker effort.

First, if worker effort is costly to monitor but individual worker output can be easily measured, piece rates may be used (Parsons 1986; Lazear 1986; Brown 1990; Keefe 1991). A compensation system is set up which pegs worker pay to units of well-defined output. (This may be true of only a portion of pay: a base hourly wage may be set, and the piece rate or commission may be on top of this.) This necessitates easily observable quantity and quality of output that can be attributed to an individual. Drawbacks of piece rate systems include the possibility of excessive wear or misuse of capital equipment and difficulty in setting appropriate piece rates, particularly in cases where worker collusion is possible (Levine 1992a).

Second, in the presence of costly monitoring, employers may choose to defer a significant amount of employee compensation to minimize the risk of employee shirking. Even with less than perfect monitoring, employees will not shirk if the consequences of being caught include the forfeiture of deferred compensation. This can be done with a pension plan (through vesting requirements or final pay formulas in defined benefit plans), or by "tilting" the tenure-earnings profile so that employees are paid less than the value of their output early in their tenure, and more than the value of their output later (Lazear 1979).

A third method of motivating employees in the presence of costly supervising is to pay an above-market "efficiency" wage—the wage can be set such that employees will put forth optimal effort for fear of being caught shirking and losing the wage premium (Akerlof and Yellen 1986; Katz 1987).

Finally, collective incentive schemes such as profit sharing are a fourth option in the presence of costly supervising.[1] Bringing employee and employer incentives into closer alignment by tying a portion of pay to a measure of company performance, the employer may be able to lessen the principal-agent problems of costly supervision. Profit sharing may be a better way of doing this than individual piece rates when: (a) output is not easily ascribed to an individual, that is, production is interdependent and/or aided by worker cooperation; (b) setting piece rates is too costly; or (c) potential misuse or abuse of capital equipment is a concern.

Therefore one motivation for profit sharing is to induce higher levels of worker performance, particularly in situations where performance is enhanced by cooperation among employees. The chief liability of profit sharing for productivity purposes is the "1/N problem"—if there are N workers in a profit-sharing plan, the average worker share is only 1/N of any increased profits going to workers. Individual incentives for better quality and quantity of work are diluted by the fact that the economic rewards must be shared with the other members of the profit-sharing plan. This predicts that profit sharing will be more popular in small companies, where the smaller denominator causes a smaller "1/N problem." It also predicts that profit sharing, to have positive productivity effects, will generally need other changes in workplace relations to encourage focus on collective goals, resulting in increased "peer pressure" (Kandel and Lazear 1992) or "horizontal monitoring" (Fitzroy and Kraft 1987). (This and other theoretical issues are discussed in chapter 3.)

A second potential benefit to employers is that profit sharing builds in a degree of compensation flexibility. When exogenous events lower company profitability, profit sharing automatically decreases employee compensation without the need for costly renegotiation of the hourly wage, or worker layoffs that may sacrifice firm-specific skills. This would lead two types of firms to adopt profit sharing as a means of sharing variability with workers. First, profit sharing may be favored by those experiencing increased variability in company performance, where flexibility in labor costs is desired through flexibility in worker pay rather than through layoffs. Second, it may be favored by new firms with uncertain prospects—employees may be attracted by the promise of a share in lucrative profits if the firm does well, without tying the firm to a high fixed wage if the firm does poorly. By accepting profit sharing in this way, an employee in the new firm is essentially buying a lottery ticket as a part of his or her compensation. The flexibility in compensation may be a liability for risk-averse workers who prefer to avoid income variability—this may be mitigated by higher average levels of compensation, or lower probabilities of layoff if the stability theory is correct.

A third potential motivation for employers to adopt profit sharing is to discourage unionization. The reasoning is that by encouraging a focus on profitability, profit sharing may cause employees to identify more closely with employers, thus discouraging the adversarial act of unionizing. While this possibility forms part of the traditional hostility of union leaders toward profit sharing (National Civic Federation 1920: 368-381; Lindop 1989), and unionized employees are less likely to be in profit-sharing plans (Czarnecki 1969; Mitchell, Lewin, and Lawler 1990), no reliable evidence exists on whether it does, in fact, discourage unionization.[2]

Profit sharing is predicted, therefore, in situations where: (1) supervision is costly, group cooperation is valuable, and care of capital equipment is a concern; (2) compensation flexibility is desired by the firm; and/or (3) the firm desires to discourage unionization by increasing employee identification with the company's goals.

Prior Research

The presence of profit-sharing plans has been predicted in several studies, but it is fair to say that this field of research is underdeveloped. Eleven studies will be reviewed here, and are listed in table 2.1.[3] As will be seen, the findings do not support simple conclusions about the factors predicting profit-sharing presence. In contrast to the studies

Table 2.1 Studies on Prediction of Profit Sharing

Study	Data source	Time period	Profit-sharing measures	Main results
Cahuc and Dormont 1992	565 French manufacturing firms (258 w/PS)	1986-89	Profit-sharing income/base wage	Pos. assoc. w/base wage, blue-collar employees, and capital stock Neg. assoc. w/market share
Carstensen, Gerlach, and Hubler 1992	136 German manufacturing firms (45 w/PS)	1989	PS presence (includes several with employee ownership)	Pos. assoc. w/size of firm, workers' councils, and training expenditures Neg. assoc. w/degree of firm competition No assoc. w/unionization
Cheadle 1989	U.S. deferred profit-sharing plans, Form 5500, >100 participants, matched to industry data (n=5998, 2741 w/PS)	1981	PS presence (deferred plans)	Neg. assoc. w/unionization Pos. assoc. w/engineering personnel, and mean age of PS in industry and state No assoc. w/industry variability or w/size of firm
Estrin and Wilson 1989	52 British metalworking firms	1978-82	PS presence	Pos. assoc. w/profits variability, market share, works councils, job evaluation schemes Neg. assoc. w/size of firm, blue/white-collar ratio No assoc. w/unionization
Fitzroy and Kraft 1987	65 West German metalworking firms	1977, 1979	PS income per employee	Pos. assoc. w/ratio of blue-collar to white-collar, and w/age of PS plan
Freeman and Kleiner 1990	364 U.S. firms w/union elections and matched pairs	1981-84	PS presence after union drive	PS plans tend to be dropped after union drive whether union won or not

Study	Sample	Year	Measure	Findings
Gregg and Machin 1988	1,047 British establishments (229 w/ PS)	1984	PS presence	Pos. assoc. w/firm size, rising product demand, supervisor ratio, unionization, industry employment change; Neg. assoc. w/labor costs/sales, and female, manual, and part-time proportions
Jones and Pliskin 1991a	357 Canadian firms	1986-87	Eligibility of nonmanagerial employees, and of production employees, for PS	Nonmanagerial: Pos. assoc. w/voluntary turnover rates, and evaluations of worker performance; Production: Pos. assoc. w/evaluations of worker performance; Neg. assoc. w/ unionization and capital intensity
Kim 1993	183 U.S. business units (107 w/PS)	1986	PS presence, percent covered, and (profit share)/(labor costs)	Pos. assoc. w/age of plan for measures 2 and 3; Pos. assoc. /profitability for measure 3; Neg. assoc. w/union presence for measure 2; Neg. assoc. w/profitability for measure 1
Kruse 1991c	Same as Cheadle, but includes plans w/<100 participants	1980-86	PS adoption (deferred plans)	Pos. assoc. w/industry variability; Neg. assoc. w/avg. size of firm; No assoc. w/unionization
Poole 1989	303 British enterprises		PS presence	Pos. assoc. w/sales, growth in sales, and financial sector; Neg. assoc. w/unionization and capital intensity

NOTES: PS = profit sharing, Neg. = negative, Pos. = positive, Assoc. w/ = associated with (all reported associations are statistically significant).

reviewed, this one will look not simply at the presence of profit sharing, but will use longitudinal data to examine factors predicting the
profit-sharing *adoption decision*.

One of the most comprehensive attempts to predict profit sharing
was made by Cheadle (1989). Using the Form 5500 data tapes from
1981, with data on all pension plans covering 100 or more participants,
Cheadle analyzed the choice between deferred profit sharing and
defined benefit pension plans (using matched industry data as explanatory variables). Some of his findings were that: (1) unionization is negatively associated with the presence of deferred profit sharing; (2) a
high ratio of engineering personnel in the industry is positively associated with deferred profit sharing, "consistent with an incentive
motive"; (3) industry-level variability is generally uncorrelated with
the choice of plan; and (4) size of firm is unrelated to the presence of a
profit-sharing plan. Additionally, the mean dates of establishment of
profit-sharing plans and of defined benefit plans (by industry and by
state) have strong effects on the likelihood of adoption for the two
types of plans: "if pension plans in an industry are (on average) five
years older, the probability of a firm having a profit-sharing plan is
reduced by 13 percent" (p. 395). Cheadle concludes,

> The explanation with the most consistent support is the "customary"
> hypothesis, the idea that the dominant savings plan in an industry/region
> is determined more by past practice than the inherent superiority of one
> plan over the other. (p. 399)

In Kruse (1991c), I report on a similar analysis that uses Form 5500
and 5500C data matched to industry data, but analyzes adoption or termination of the different types of plans over the 1980-86 period.
Within this period, an estimated 185,800 firms in the United States
adopted deferred profit-sharing plans, while 53,300 terminated such
plans. Lower average establishment size and higher variability of
industry employment over the 1970-80 period caused firms without
plans in 1980 to be more likely to adopt defined contribution plans (the
majority of which were deferred profit-sharing plans), rather than
defined benefit plans. This provides some support for the flexibility
argument (that increased variability favors profit sharing) and the productivity argument (that profit sharing will be more likely in small
firms where the 1/N problem is less).

In a study of profit sharing and productivity by Fitzroy and Kraft (1987), data from 1977 and 1979 were analyzed for 65 West German metalworking firms. Predictions were made, not of profit-sharing status but of the profit share income per employee. The two most important variables were the ratio of blue-collar to white-collar workers, and the age of the profit-sharing plan. Similar techniques were used by Kim (1993) on a dataset of 183 U.S. business units in public companies in 1986. The age of the profit-sharing plan was found to positively affect both the percentage of employees covered and the profit-sharing bonus as a percent of labor costs, while union presence was found to negatively affect the percentage of employees covered. While profitability was found to decrease the likelihood of having a profit-sharing plan, it was also found to increase the profit share as a percent of labor costs.[4]

Similarly, a study of French manufacturing firms attempted to predict profit share income as a proportion of the base wage, rather than the simple existence of profit sharing (Cahuc and Dormont 1992). Positive predictors were found to be the base wage level, capital stock, and blue-collar employees as a percent of all employees in the firm, while a negative predictor was the firm's market share in the preceding year.

Profit sharing prevalence in Great Britain has been analyzed in several studies. In Poole (1989), a sample of 1,125 large enterprises, both with and without profit sharing and employee stock ownership schemes, was contacted, resulting in 303 interviews. Several tests of these 303 enterprises revealed that profit-sharing companies were more likely to be in the financial sector, and had higher capital intensity, sales volume, and growth in sales volume. In addition, profit-sharing companies were found to be more likely to have staff associations, but slightly less likely to have unions (1989: 65 116). Based on this sample, Poole and Jenkins conclude that: "our data suggest that an improved profits performance is frequently the trigger mechanism for the adoption of schemes" (1990: 95).

A sample of 52 British metalworking firms, 21 with profit sharing, was analyzed by Estrin and Wilson (1989). The existence of profit sharing in 1978 was positively associated with profits variability and market share, and negatively associated with company size and blue/white-collar ratio. Several industrial relations variables were analyzed; those found to be more prevalent in profit-sharing firms included works councils, formal job evaluation schemes, and managers' perceptions of worker participation, but there was no significant association with unionization.

Using the 1984 Workplace Industrial Relations Survey, Gregg and Machin (1988) analyze a cross-section sample of British establishments. Among the findings were that profit sharing was more likely in firms that were very large (>50,000 employees), had rising product demand, were in industries with smaller employment declines, did not have high labor costs as a percentage of sales, and had smaller proportions of manual, female, and part-time employees but larger proportions of supervisors. The presence of a "strong" union (proxied by whether members were in a closed shop) increased the probability that an establishment would have profit sharing by 2.1 percentage points, while the presence of a "weak" union increased this probability by 7.1 points.

The use of profit sharing in a 1989 sample of 136 German firms (45 of which had profit sharing) was examined by Carstensen, Gerlach, and Hubler (1992). Firm size was found to be a positive predictor of profit- sharing use, as were workers' councils and high training expenditures. Profit sharing was more likely among firms that had little competition in the product market, but equally likely among union and nonunion firms.

Jones and Pliskin (1991a) analyzed results from a 1987 survey of 313 Canadian organizations. Results indicated that the existence of profit sharing for any nonmanagerial employees was associated with higher voluntary turnover rates and higher managerial evaluations of worker performance, whereas profit sharing for production employees was associated with a lower proportion of workers unionized, lower capital/labor ratios, and higher evaluations of worker performance. For the production employees, the difference between 0 percent and 33 percent unionization (where 33 percent was the mean value of union density) was estimated to be associated with only a 1 to 2.5 percent decrease in the probability of being eligible for profit sharing.

On the unionization question, therefore, while Gregg and Machin found a positive effect of unionism on the probability of profit sharing, and Estrin and Wilson and Carstensen, Gerlach, and Hubler found no effect, Jones and Pliskin found a negative effect. Unionists have long had an uneasy and suspicious relationship with profit-sharing plans (see, e.g., National Civic Federation 1920, and Zalusky 1986).[5] The principal complaints against profit sharing from the union perspective have been that profit sharing brings workers into competition with each other, and that it is difficult or impossible for workers to verify that managers are defining and sharing the profits properly (see discussion in chapter 5).

One relevant study concerns the effect of new unionization on profit sharing. Freeman and Kleiner (1990) analyzed data from 203 firms with union elections, and from 161 matched pairs that did not have union drives. They found that profit-sharing plans tended to be dropped after a union organizing drive. The effect was largest where the union had won and signed a contract, which is consistent with the traditional union antipathy toward profit sharing. The effect, though, was also negative where the union had lost, or won but had not signed a contract. However, sampling error could not be rejected as an explanation of the differences, so it is uncertain whether new unionization does affect profit-sharing status.

These 11 prior studies have not provided clear answers on what factors predict profit sharing. There have been contradictory findings on even basic variables such as unionization and firm size. Employee composition, firm growth, capital intensity, and industry variability are other variables that have been highlighted as potentially important by previous research.

It is worth noting that most of the prior research has relied on cross-sectional data, meaning that causality is a particular concern. The characteristics associated with profit sharing may be valid predictors of profit sharing, or may be (at least partially) consequences of profit sharing or of other factors related to profit sharing. This study employs panel data, enabling analysis not only of the presence of profit sharing, but of the factors predicting profit-sharing adoption. By examining how changes in particular variables are related to subsequent decisions to adopt profit sharing, one can have heightened confidence about the causality between these variables and profit sharing.

Motives for Maintaining Profit-Sharing Plans

The profit-sharing firms that were surveyed for this study were asked to rate the importance of several factors in *maintaining* profit-sharing plans. (They were not asked why such plans had been adopted, since many survey respondents were not involved in the adoption.) The responses are summarized in table 2.2. There it can be seen that "providing a source of retirement income" is the predominant expressed reason for maintaining profit sharing, with "recruiting and retaining personnel" and "motivating existing employees" the next most important reasons. The remaining reasons received a majority of 1's or 2's on the 5-point scale.

The lower half of table 2.2 disaggregates the answers by whether the firm maintains any cash plans or not. As would be expected, "providing a source of retirement income" is much more important for the firms that maintain only deferred plans.[6] For the remaining motives, those maintaining any cash plans gave slightly higher importance to motivating existing employees, and lower importance to recruiting and retaining employees, and to reducing the likelihood of unionization.[7]

These results are broadly consistent with the expressed opinions of Profit Sharing Council of America (PSCA) members (PSRF 1992a), and with the stated objectives of British respondents in Poole (1989). In a 1990 PSCA survey with 197 respondents, the most-cited objectives for profit-sharing plans were employee retention (95.4 percent), increasing employee interest (94.9 percent) and sense of partnership (90.4 percent) in the firm, motivating for higher productivity (83.8 percent), and recruiting key personnel (80.2 percent). Other objectives listed by more than half of the respondents were: increasing or stabilizing profits (71.1 percent) enhancing employee job security (61.4 percent), and providing supra-wage benefits without a fixed commitment (57.4 percent). For each of these objectives, more than three-fifths of those listing it stated that the plan had great or moderate success in meeting the objective. From the British data reported in Poole (1989: 69), the three most highly-rated objectives of profit-sharing schemes, according to executive respondents in the companies, were "to make employees feel they are part of the company," "to make employees

Table 2.2 Expressed Motives for Maintaining Profit-Sharing Plan

Question: Each of the following are reasons for maintaining the profit-sharing plan.
Please use the 5-point scale to indicate how important each is for maintaining the profit-sharing plan(s) in your company.

	Not important 1	2	3	4	Very important 5	Mean	n
			(percent)				
Providing a source of retirement income	14.1	1.7	6.6	14.1	63.6	4.12	121
Recruiting and retaining personnel	2.5	10.0	25.0	38.3	24.2	3.72	120
Motivating existing employees	3.3	4.1	26.5	40.5	25.6	3.81	121
Reducing likelihood of unionization	37.8	25.2	16.0	16.8	4.2	2.24	119
Reducing the probability or size of layoffs	59.0	24.8	12.0	3.4	0.9	1.63	117
Stabilizing corporate cash flow	39.8	29.7	17.0	6.8	6.8	2.11	118
Breakdown of answers by presence of cash plan:							
Providing a source of retirement income Any cash	29.8	3.5	8.8	8.8	49.1	3.44	57
Deferred only	0.0	0.0	4.8	19.1	76.2	4.71	63
Recruiting and retaining personnel Any cash	5.4	12.5	28.6	32.1	21.4	3.52	56
Deferred only	0.0	7.9	22.2	44.4	25.4	3.87	63
Motivating existing employees Any cash	1.7	1.7	25.9	44.8	25.9	3.91	58
Deferred only	4.8	6.5	27.4	37.1	24.2	3.69	62
Reducing likelihood of unionization Any cash	42.9	23.2	17.9	12.5	3.6	2.11	56
Deferred only	32.3	27.4	14.5	21.0	4.8	2.39	62
Reducing the probability or size of layoffs Any cash	58.2	25.5	7.3	7.3	1.8	1.69	55
Deferred only	59.0	24.6	16.4	0.0	0.0	1.57	51
Stabilizing corporate cash flow Any cash	40.0	29.1	20.0	7.3	3.6	2.05	55
Deferred only	38.7	30.7	14.5	6.5	9.7	2.18	52

more profit conscious," and "to increase sense of commitment to the company."

Predicting Adoption of Profit Sharing

The results from prior research provide no firm guidelines on the variables and specifications that should be used to predict profit sharing. Therefore a variety of variables and techniques was used in attempting to predict the adoption of profit sharing (discussed in appendix 2). The adoption decision is presumably influenced by changes that the firm is undergoing. To examine this, most variables were specified as the change in values in the two years preceding the adoption decision (from t - 2 to t - 1, if t is the current year).[8] (The current year's values are not included since these could reflect the effects of profit sharing, rather than causes of the decision.) The variables examined here as possible predictors of profit-sharing adoption include union status, firm size, and changes in the profit margin, sales, stock price, capital intensity, research and development spending, firm and industry compensation levels, debt levels, interest expenses, and variability in sales and the profit margin.

A summary of significant results is provided in table 2.3 (based on the logit specifications presented in tables A2.2 and A2.3 in appendix 2). Only four variables helped predict the adoption of profit sharing.

The first was an increase in the profit margin in the preceding two years. As noted in column 2, the within-industry paired results show that a 1-point increase in the profit margin (e.g., from 11 percent to 12 percent of sales) is associated with an increase of 5 to 7 percent in the probability of adopting profit sharing in any year. This appears to be important for the adoption of cash plans (row 4), but not for the adoption of deferred plans.

The variable that most consistently predicts the adoption of profit sharing is a change in the stock price. As shown in column 3 of table 2.3, a 10 percent increase in stock price in the preceding two years is associated with a 4 to 9 percent increase in the probability of adopting any profit sharing, and this variable appears important for both cash and deferred plan adoption. Note that stock prices should reflect inves-

Table 2.3 Summary Results on Prediction of Profit-Sharing Adoption

All figures based on logit specifications reported in appendix tables A2.2 and A2.3.

	Baseline yearly probability of adoption in year t^a (1)	Percentage change in adoption probability from:[b]			
		1 percentage-point increase in profit margin (from t-2 to t-1) (2)	10 percent increase in stock price (from t-2 to t-1) (3)	Union presence (4)	Inter-quartile range of increased variability in profit margin (5)
Adoption of any profit sharing	.019				
1. Nonpaired values		n.s.	8 to 9	31 to 39	0.6
2. Within-industry paired differences		5 to 7	4	n.s.	n.s.
Adoption of cash plan	.008				
3. Nonpaired values		n.s.	8 to 9	126 to 167	n.s.
4. Within-industry paired differences		8 to 9	n.s.	60 to 83	n.s.
Adoption of deferred plan	.007				
5. Nonpaired values		n.s.	9 to 10	n.s.	0.5
6. Within-industry paired differences		n.s.	7 to 9	n.s.	n.s.

Variables never found significant in predicting adoption

Change from t - 2 to t - 1 in:	Variance of change in ln(sales) over t-5 to t-1
Labor expenses per employee (natural log) (both firm- and industry-level)	Debt/asset ratio
Sales (natural log)	Advertising/sales
Debt/equity ratio	Depreciation/assets
Interest payments/sales	Current ratio
Employment level (natural log)	Productivity
Capital intensity (natural log of gross assets/employment)	Research and development/sales

NOTES: n.s. = no estimates were significantly different from zero.

a. The baseline probability of adoption is the probability that, if a company does not have a profit-sharing plan already, one will be adopted in the current year. These numbers represent the population probabilities (after the sample estimates were weighted to account for oversampling of profit-sharing firms).

b. Percentage change in adoption probability = (New prob.-Baseline prob.)/(Baseline prob.).

tors' evaluations of the long-term prospects for profitability, while the profit margin may only reflect short-term performance. This would indicate that expectations of better long-term performance influence the decision to adopt profit sharing. By its very nature, profit-sharing-compensation may be easily decreased if the expected better performance does not materialize, while a wage increase may be seen as an obligation that is more difficult for the company to rescind.

A strong note of caution on the interpretation of this result, however, is in order. Stock prices are affected by news about the expected future profits of the company, and the announcement of profit sharing may be taken as a positive sign of higher expected profits. Profit sharing may have been announced in the year preceding adoption, and therefore may have affected the stock price change prior to adoption. The announcement of profit-sharing provisions in union contracts was found to be associated with stock price increases by Florkowski and Shastri (1992).[9] For this dataset, whether the profit-sharing adoptions were announced, and if so, when, is not known. It is likely that most were not announced, as is the case with most employee ownership transactions (Blasi and Kruse 1991).[10] Announcements are more likely in union negotiations, and the influence of stock price changes was found to be very similar between plans that covered a majority of union members and those that did not. Whether this result reflects a cause, or an effect, of profit-sharing adoption cannot, however, be known for certain. Eliminating this variable from the equations produced no noteworthy differences in the estimates for other variables.[11]

A third variable that predicts adoption of profit sharing is union presence. A union trend variable was included based on Bell and Neumark's (1993) finding, reproduced in table 1.1, that profit sharing in union contracts has been prevalent in the 1980s (after being nonexistent in the major contracts of 1975). Having a union strongly increased the probability of cash plan adoption during this period (by 60-167 percent), but had no significant effect on deferred plan adoption.

To test the possibility that a need for flexibility prompts firms to adopt profit sharing, two variables were constructed to represent the variance of the yearly changes in sales and the profit margin.[12] Increased variability in the profit margin was weakly significant in two of the equations. The magnitude as well as the significance was weak: firms at the 75th percentile of this variable were only 0.6 percent more likely to adopt profit sharing than were firms at the 25th percentile, while firms at the 90th percentile were only 4.3 percent more likely to adopt than were firms at the 10th percentile.

Therefore the best predictors of profit-sharing adoption are improvements in company performance (increases in profit margin and stock price) and union presence. The former result is consistent with the observation by Poole and Jenkins (1990) that profit sharing may be an effect of better performance as well as a potential cause. This clearly draws into question the studies that use simple statistical comparisons between profit-sharing and non-profit-sharing companies on profitability and other performance measures (to be reviewed in chapter 3). More generally, it calls into question the studies that use only cross-sectional data. If higher profits and profit expectations precede the adoption of profit sharing, it is not surprising that profits and other performance measures will on average be higher after the adoption.

Just as notable are the variables that were not significant in predicting profit-sharing adoption. The ability of firms to structure deferred profit-sharing plans so that a substantial amount of the assets can be invested in employer stock suggests that firms with need for capital will adopt such plans. The variables used to test for this possibility are the total value of interest payments (as a percentage of sales) and the debt/equity and debt/asset ratios (long-term debt over total invested capital, and over gross assets), but none attracted a significant estimate.

Capital intensity was included as a potential predictor since it is a complement to worker skill levels, and changes in this variable may reflect changes in desired skills by the company. Using cross-section data, Jones and Pliskin (1991a) found this to be a significant predictor of profit sharing, but changes in capital intensity were not found to influence profit-sharing adoption here.

A research and development (R&D) variable was tested based on the idea that innovative activity plausibly involves costly supervision and the importance of group cooperation, which the productivity theory predicts will be associated with profit sharing. Recent changes in R&D expenditures, however, did not appear as significant predictors of the adoption of profit sharing. The same was true of the within-company mean of R&D levels.[13] The idea that R&D activity is not associated with profit sharing is also supported by a recent compensation survey which found that most R&D workers are not covered by profit sharing (only 17-37 percent of various specialties are so covered) (Morkes 1991).

The 1/N problem suggests that profit sharing will be most effective in small firms, and prior research (Poole and Jenkins 1990) suggests that fast-growing firms are more likely to adopt profit sharing. Neither idea was supported here. The employment level in the year preceding adoption, and recent changes in employment and sales, were not significant predictors of adoption.

It might be expected that companies facing pressure from rising compensation levels would turn to profit sharing as a way of increasing compensation without obligating the firm to a higher wage level. However, recent trends in labor costs per employee, both at the firm and industry levels, were not significant predictors of adoption.

A variety of other financial variables was tested with no significant findings. These included: alternative measures of the debt/equity ratio, advertising/revenues, current ratio, depreciation/assets, return on equity, and return on assets.

Prediction of Union and Occupation Participation

Profit sharing is not always extended to all employees within a company. Under the productivity, stability, or union avoidance theories, it may be targeted toward particular occupations or locations where it is felt to be most useful. Among the profit-sharing companies in this survey, only two-fifths (40.5 percent) include 100 percent of the employees in the profit sharing. As can be seen in table 1.3, in only 44.7 percent of the unionized profit-sharing companies do more than half of the union members participate. An average of 75.8 percent of production and service workers are covered within profit-sharing companies, compared to 86.5 percent of clerical and technical and 87.6 percent of professional and administrative employees.

For the firms that adopt profit sharing, what determines the participation of union members and the different occupational groups? Table 2.4 presents the results predicting participation in profit sharing among all employees, and among these four groups (based on the full results in appendix table A2.4). Since these estimates of participation are

Table 2.4 Summary Results on Union and Occupational Participation in Profit Sharing

All figures based on specifications reported in appendix table A2.4.

Dependent variables	Mean (s.d.)	Effect of			
		10 percentage-point increase in union percentage in firm	10 percentage-point increase in prof./adm. share in company	10 percentage-point increase in prdn./service share in company	10-year increase in age of oldest PS plan in company
1. Probability of having majority of union members participate in profit sharing[a]	43.5 (50.0)	6.5	n.s.	n.s.	n.s.
2. Percent of all workers who participate in profit sharing	80.4 (26.0)	-2.2	4.4	n.s.	4.2
3. Percent of clerical/technical workers (nonexempt) who participate in profit sharing	85.4 (28.6)	n.s.	n.s.	4.0	n.s.
4. Percent of professional/administrative (exempt) workers who participate in profit sharing	71.0 (38.6)	-1.9	6.4	5.6	4.7
5. Percent of production/service workers (nonexempt) workers who participate in profit sharing	87.3 (26.8)	-3.8	10.5	4.9	n.s.
Indep. variable mean (s.d.) for line 1		37.9 (24.5)	26.0 (14.1)	40.2 (20.0)	13.5 (11.6)
Indep. variable mean (s.d.) for lines 2-5		24.9 (26.9)	25.4 (13.6)	48.1 (22.2)	15.9 (12.2)

Variables never found significant in predicting participation in profit sharing by union and occupational status:

Employment level (natural log) Interest payments/sales
Capital intensity (natural log of gross assets/employment) Selling, general, and administrative expenses/sales
Profit margin Research and development expenses/sales
Debt/equity ratio

NOTES: n.s. = estimates were not significantly different from zero.
a. Probability effect in row one is based on mean values of variables from probit in column 1 of appendix table A2.4.

restricted to profit-sharing firms (and to unionized profit-sharing firms for the union participation estimates), they should be seen as conditional on a prior decision to adopt profit sharing.[14]Unlike the previous estimates in this chapter, these do not attempt to predict the adoption of profit sharing. Rather, they employ 1990 data in attempting to describe the characteristics of profit-sharing companies that predict current coverage of different employee types.[15]

In what unionized companies are union members more likely to be included in profit sharing? As seen in row 1 of the summary in table 2.4, the only significant predictor of having a majority of union members participate in profit sharing is the percentage of the firm's employees who are unionized. An increase of 10 percentage points in the percent unionized is associated with a 6.5 percent increase in the probability of having a majority of union members participating in profit sharing.[16] The range of percentage unionized in this sample is 1 percent to 80 percent. For profit-sharing firms with only 1 percent of employees unionized, there is only a 21 percent probability that more than half will be covered by profit sharing; whereas the probability rises to 71 percent if 80 percent of all employees are unionized. The occupational composition, capital/labor ratio, total employees, profit margin, and age of the oldest profit-sharing plan are not significant predictors of union participation in profit sharing.

What predicts the percentage of employees covered by profit sharing within the firm? Row 2 of table 2.4 shows that the share of professional/administrative employees in the company is a strong predictor: a 10 percentage-point increase in the share of these employees is associated with an increase of 4.4 percent in employees covered (while doubling this share from its sample average of 25 percent is associated with 11 percent higher profit-sharing coverage) for the firm as a whole.[17] Also, a higher percentage unionized is associated with lower profit-sharing coverage: each increase of 10 points in unionization is associated with 2.2 points lower profit-sharing coverage (consistent with the results of Kim 1993). (While unionization tends to decrease overall coverage, it increases the likelihood that union members will be covered, as described above.) The age of profit sharing in the company is also a strong positive predictor: each 10 years of age is associated with an additional 4.2 percent of coverage within the firm.

What predicts profit-sharing coverage of different occupational groups? The results in rows 3 to 5 indicate that the occupational composition of the company does make a difference in profit-sharing coverage by employee groups.[18] A 10 percentage-point increase in the professional/administrative share in the company is associated with a 6.4 percent increase in the profit-sharing coverage of professional/administrative employees and a 10.5 percent increase in the profit-sharing coverage of production/service employees. A 10 percentage-point increase in the production/service share is associated with significant increases in the coverage of each occupational group. The influence of the clerical/technical share is not accounted for separately since (as defined) it is simply the remainder after the other two occupations have been measured.[19] Therefore an increase in the clerical/technical share can be viewed as coming at the expense of the other two occupational shares, indicating that companies with higher shares of clerical/technical workers are likely to have lower profit-sharing coverage of all employees and of each occupational group.

In line with the results on profit-sharing coverage of all workers, the percent unionized is found to exert a significant effect on coverage of professional/administrative and production/service workers. A 10 percentage-point increase in unionization is found to reduce coverage of these groups by, respectively, 1.9 percent and 3.8 percent. Finally, the age of profit sharing in the company is associated with higher coverage for each group, although sampling error can be ruled out only for professional/administrative employees. The magnitude indicates that an extra 10 years of age is associated with 4.7 percentage points higher profit-sharing coverage for this group.

To briefly summarize, this chapter has found four principal variables predicting the adoption of profit-sharing plans: two reflecting company performance (increases in the profit margin and increases in the stock price), one reflecting variability (the variance of the change in the profit margin), and the other representing union presence. The results indicating that improvements in performance help predict plan adoption (consistent with Poole and Jenkins 1990) cast serious doubt on cross-sectional comparisons of profit-sharing and non-profit-sharing companies. Unionization is associated with lower percentages of all employees covered, though a higher probability of having union members covered. The occupational composition of profit-sharing companies shows that higher proportions of professional/administrative and production/service employees are associated with greater coverage of each occupational group, meaning that firms with a higher proportion of clerical/technical employees will have lower profit-sharing coverage among each occupation. A fuller summary is presented in chapter 5.

NOTES

1. As discussed in chapter 1, employee stock ownership is another variety of collective incentive scheme, and it has some important differences from profit sharing. Employee stock ownership and other schemes such as gainsharing (group bonuses tied to cost or productivity measures) are distinguished from profit sharing, but their separate influences will be analyzed in chapter 3.

2. Czarnecki (1969) examines the union win rate over the 1961-66 period in companies with deferred profit-sharing plans in 1965. He finds the union win rate in profit-sharing companies to be 44.3 percent, compared to 59.8 percent among other union elections. The conclusion that profit sharing hurts union win rates is, however, subject to a serious question of causality: almost all of the elections took place prior to the measurement of profit sharing. The lower prevalence of profit sharing where unions won reflects the effects of collective bargaining in a context of union hostility toward profit sharing. The principal conclusion to be drawn is that profit sharing is less prevalent in workplaces which have been unionized.

3. This review is based on all published studies that could be located in books or in economic, personnel, and business journals (using searches up through June 1993 of the Business Periodicals Index and the computerized databases ABI/INFORM, UNCOVER, ProQuest, and Business Dateline), and on unpublished studies made available by colleagues.

4. These estimates were made in the context of a simultaneous system, in which both profit sharing and profitability (return on assets) were treated as endogenous.

5. See Cardinal and Helburn (1986) for a comparison of management perceptions of profit sharing in union vs. nonunion firms.

6. The difference is statistically significant at the 95 percent level.

7. However, these differences were not statistically significant at the 95 percent level.

8. The models were estimated only on the years in which firms did not have profit sharing already.

9. The effects of employee ownership announcements on stock prices have been more extensively studied and are reviewed in Blasi and Kruse (1991: 181-183).

10. An indication that such announcements are rare comes from their absence in several years of searches on the Dow Jones newswire (Joseph Blasi, personal communication).

11. Also, use of the percentage change in stock price between $t - 3$ and $t - 2$, which is more likely to be fully exogenous, showed coefficients of negligible magnitude and significance.

12. Specifically, these are the variance of annual changes in ln(sales) and ln(profit margin) over $t - 5$ to $t - 1$. Note that, since these represent the variance of the *changes* in logarithms, they effectively represent variance around a growth trend—in other words, simple straight growth in sales or profits will not result in increased values of these variables. (Such straight growth is separately tested by sales and profit margin variables.) Note also that the current period is not included in the calculation of the variance ($t - 5$ to $t - 1$) so it does not include any possible effects of the adoption of profit sharing.

13. Results for this measure are not presented in appendix tables A2.2 and A2.3 since it is not reported for utilities and most financial companies. Its inclusion therefore substantially restricts

the sample. The mean value of R&D/sales was close to identical between new adopters and non-profit-sharing firms (.014), but was significantly larger for old profit-sharing firms (.019).

14. Results including the non profit sharing firms did not produce noteworthy differences.

15. Ideally, one would have year-by-year data on which employees were covered, so that one could analyze employee coverage at the time of adoption, as well as changes in coverage as the plan matured. For this study, the benefits of such detailed data were judged to be outweighed by the reduced response rate entailed in asking for such data. Therefore only current coverage by employee type is analyzed here.

16. For example, the mean union density is 38 percent, and the mean probability of having a majority of union members participate in profit sharing is 43.5 percent. Increasing the union density by 10 points (e.g., to 48 percent) is associated with an increase in this probability of 6.5 percent (e.g., to 50 percent).

17. This is based on column 6 of appendix table A2.4, using only profit-sharing firms. These results may therefore be seen as exploring the question of how firms, conditional on having decided to use profit sharing, choose to extend coverage to various employees.

18. The small sample size prevents the use of detailed industry controls. The regressions include seven broad industry controls to partially account for industry differences; nonetheless, the results will reflect both within-industry and between-industry effects.

19. Its inclusion in the regressions will therefore produce perfect multicollinearity among the three occupational shares.

3
The Productivity Theory

Profit sharing has long been promoted as a way to improve company performance by tying the incentives of the employees more closely to those of the owners and managers. Such incentives are theorized to encourage employees to put forth extra effort ("working harder"), or to develop ways to reduce costs or improve quality ("working smarter"). As a group incentive, profit sharing is designed to encourage such activity in cooperation with other employees. Such cooperation can be productive in itself, and can encourage "peer pressure" or "horizontal monitoring," so that employees encourage better performance by their fellow employees.

The productivity theory of profit sharing relies on the idea that supervision is costly. If it were costless, the behaviors that are desired under profit sharing could be directly measured and rewarded.[1] As noted in the previous chapter, several methods have been identified in economic theory to deal with the problem of costly supervision.

1. Piece rates. Where quantity and quality of output are easily observable and can be directly attributed to an individual, worker pay can be directly tied to output. Costly monitoring of quality and quantity, the possibility of misuse of capital equipment, and difficulty in setting the rates are drawbacks.[2] In addition, piece rates do not encourage cooperation among employees, which may be important for performance in certain kinds of jobs.

2. Deferred compensation, in the form of a pension or an earnings profile in which workers receive less than what they produce early in their tenure and more than what they produce later in their tenure. Better worker performance may be motivated by the fear of being fired and losing the deferred portion of compensation. This fear can motivate higher performance even under incomplete monitoring. In return, to induce workers into such arrangements, total compensation over the working life needs to be higher than where compensation is not deferred.

3. Efficiency wage. Rather than changing the type or timing of compensation to deal with problems of costly supervision, employers may choose to pay an above-market "efficiency wage." This can motivate higher effort even under imperfect monitoring.

Profit sharing may be used as a substitute or complement for these methods when monitoring is costly. Relative to a fixed wage, profit sharing does provide more of a link between an individual's performance and pay by allowing the worker to share in the extra value generated by his or her performance. This extra value, however, is shared with all other workers in the plan. If workers share profits equally, and there are N workers, each one will receive only 1/N of any increased profits going to workers. Clearly the individual incentive becomes weak, even negligible, as N grows large.

Other conditions must be present, therefore, for profit sharing to act as a spur to better performance. One of these conditions may be that group cooperation increases performance. By tying the economic reward to group performance, individuals have incentives not only to improve their own performance, but also to improve fellow workers' performance. This may be done in straightforward ways, such as by sharing ideas, or in subtle ways, through encouraging co-workers and ostracizing those who do not work hard. It may be much less costly and more effective to have "horizontal monitoring" done by co-workers, rather than monitoring by supervisors.

> Employees engaged in the routine day-to-day fulfillment of a task are usually in a position to detect inefficiencies in operations that diminish productivity. They are also likely to acquire important information concerning the actual productive contributions of their co-workers. ... The information derived from such activity... is potentially very valuable to the firm as an input to production. Yet such information transfers will not be induced under an individual performance-based rewards system since it does not affect his own performance measures. . . .

> But under the group system, the appropriate incentives are much more likely to be present. If there are indeed positive externalities associated with these information inputs and all the relevant group members are subject to the same incentives, then there is reason for the employee to identify his own interests with those of the firm and to furnish the inputs requisite to the firm's success (Nalbantian 1987: 26).

While the possibility of information-sharing and horizontal monitoring may slightly mitigate the 1/N problem through enlarging the individual's range for affecting group performance, this problem would still seem to be a strong deterrent to individual incentives. The 1/N problem may be seen as a classic "prisoner's dilemma" from game theory. If one worker puts forth better performance which increases profits while other workers maintain a constant baseline performance, the workers all share in the increased profits from the one worker's better performance; however, the one worker is likely to be worse off (assuming the extra effort is personally costly and exceeds 1/N of the increased profits). Therefore, predicated on a lack of increased effort by other employees, the individual incentive for increased effort is likely to be outweighed by the costs of that effort. If, however, the "game" is repeated in an ongoing relationship (or if the continuation of the game is uncertain), workers can collectively establish an agreement to work harder, and the financial rewards from sharing in the increased profits might outweigh the individual costs from participating in the agreement. Among the many potential equilibria that may result in this situation, one is that the workers might establish a "cooperative equilibrium" in which performance and profits are higher (see, e.g., Axelrod 1984; Fudenberg and Maskin 1986; Tomer 1987).

A cooperative equilibrium is clearly one solution to prisoner's dilemma situations. Two major questions are: How does one get established, and how is one maintained? Neither question has a clear-cut answer, and in fact there may be many answers to each. Factors such as group size, history, criteria for membership, personal connections, task interdependence, communication system, and physical environment may be important in establishing a willingness to cooperate for higher performance. The same factors may be important in maintaining the cooperative agreement, since after one is established there would continue to be an individual incentive to "defect" from the cooperative solution—to share in the higher profits without putting forth the extra effort that other workers are putting forth. The "shirkers" from the cooperative agreement may be punished by fellow workers through nonpecuniary sanctions such as social ostracism, or by personal guilt or shame (Kandel and Lazear 1992; Bashir 1990). Laboratory experiments on prisoner's dilemma situations show that cooperation is more common than would be predicted by simple models of self-interest, and is more likely when participants can begin to form a group identity by talking with each other before making their choices (summarized in Dawes and Thaler 1988; also see Kahneman and Thaler 1991). The empathy with co-workers that may be built through communication can help develop and enforce worker norms that support higher performance (Kandel and Lazear 1992; Lazear 1992).

These considerations make it clear that a profit-sharing plan cannot simply be installed and expected to improve performance. "To get the productivity-enhancing effects, something more may be needed— something akin to developing a corporate culture that emphasizes company spirit, promotes group cooperation, encourages social enforcement mechanisms, and so forth" (Weitzman and Kruse 1990: 100). This is echoed by those who set up group incentive plans: Gross and Bacher (1993: 55) note the importance of a "supportive culture" in which "teamwork, trust, and involvement at all levels are important."

An additional consideration is that the direct financial stake in the group incentive may not be as important as a perception that the fruits of greater effort are being shared with employees. If implemented in the right way, group incentive schemes can provide a psychological as well as financial stake in group success.[3] "Theories that suggest that workers' productivity is related to their sense of fair treatment imply that profit-sharing plans may still lead to an increase in productivity even when the individual's own effort has a negligible effect on profits" (Stiglitz 1987: 66). Put another way, workers may directly value the *existence* of a pay-performance link (and possibly the group cohesion it may foster) apart from the *size* of that link.[4]

Profit sharing also raises the issue of managerial incentives to monitor workers. Alchian and Demsetz (1972) argued that the optimal level of monitoring within an enterprise requires that the monitor receive the residual income (profits) from the activity being monitored. If profits are shared with workers, the incentive for monitoring workers is diluted, and both owners and workers are hurt by the lower efficiency that results. Therefore, owners should receive the full amount of profits in order that they (and their agents, the managers) will have the correct incentives for monitoring.

This argument relies on several assumptions, including that there are no principal-agent problems between owners and managers, and that the decrease in monitoring by management will not be accompanied by an increase in workers monitoring each other.[5] As noted by Bonin and Putterman,

> Alchian and Demsetz's hypothesis is limited to the effects of a particular specification of property rights on *incentives to monitor* but not on the ability to observe accurately. ... It is possible, for example, that while concentrated residual claimancy creates heightened incentives to monitor, this factor could be partly or wholly offset by reduced efficacy of monitoring when much information concerning workers' real productivities cannot be easily observed from "above" (1987: 48).

One part of the argument for the importance of central monitoring is that more monitoring induces more optimal labor effort. Putterman and Skillman (1988) show how this is sensitive to the compensation scheme, workers' risk preferences, and the informational content of monitoring. In particular, monitoring may produce either an accurate or a "noisy" signal of effort. When the signal is accurate, increased levels of monitoring will generally produce positive incentive effects. When, however, the signal is "noisy"—that is, there is some error in measuring a worker's true effort—increased monitoring may increase or reduce worker effort (depending on worker risk preferences and the compensation scheme). Putterman and Skillman conclude that

> closing the story which says that a particular assignment of residual rights will best elicit the desired monitoring effort remains a difficult challenge, especially if monitoring is itself difficult to observe and there are reasons why the monitor or monitors might want to misrepresent their information (1988: 118).

An additional issue concerns the relationship between profit sharing and capital investment (Summers 1986; Estrin, Jones, and Svejnar 1987; Weitzman 1986). If employees collectively receive a predetermined fixed share of profits, they will naturally share in any increase in profits from new capital investments, thereby decreasing the return on investment for the firm's owners.[6] This decreased return would decrease the incentives for investment, implying that profit sharing would inhibit company growth. While the gains to employees, and losses to owners, may be dissipated through the attraction of new employees to the company, the adjustment lags may still represent a disincentive for owners to invest. This disincentive would be a function of having the profit share strictly tied to profits; as will be seen, this is rare in the United States. The discretionary component of most profit-sharing formulas in the United States (often in addition to a fixed percentage) adds a substantial amount of flexibility that may mute this disincentive.

A final issue addressed here is employee self-selection. The type of compensation system that a firm employs will clearly affect the type of employee it attracts and retains. If profit sharing attracts higher-quality employees, a finding that profit-sharing firms have higher productivity may have nothing to do with the incentive effects of profit sharing, but may simply reflect the higher labor quality of the firm.[7] A priori, it is not clear that profit sharing would attract high-quality or low-quality workers. Employees who desire to be paid according to performance are more likely to be more productive persons and should be attracted to firms that have performance-dependent compensation systems. Profit sharing may be a form of compensation that attracts higher-quality workers. However, such workers may instead be attracted to compensation systems that are highly sensitive to individual performance, while lower-quality workers may be attracted to group-based systems in which the costs of shirking are shared with co-workers. An additional factor that would affect self-selection of employees is the degree of risk aversion—those who are averse to income variability will presumably tend to avoid compensation systems like profit sharing that have variable payments.[8]

There is very little evidence on the self-selection of workers into group incentive systems. One piece of evidence on this issue strongly suggests that self-selection favors workers of average quality. Studying a company in which workers started with an individual incentive system and moved into a group incentive system within several months, Weiss (1987) found that both the initially high and low performers were more likely to quit the company after their pay became tied to group incentives. Among those who stayed, the performance of the best and worst workers moved toward group averages, suggesting co-worker influence upon performance. This study shows that employee self-selection is a relevant concern in group incentive systems, but suggests that labor quality imparts no general upward or downward bias to estimates of the effects of group incentive systems.

Prior Research: Noneconometric Evidence

The relationship between profit sharing and economic performance has been addressed in a variety of studies. These range from employee and employer attitude surveys, to comparisons of simple statistics, to formal econometric studies that control for a variety of influences on productivity.

The attitude surveys and simple statistical comparisons will only be briefly reviewed here.[9] When employees in profit-sharing plans are asked for general opinions of profit sharing, or about the effect of profit sharing on individual and company performance, they strongly tend to respond favorably (Bell and Hanson 1987; Colletti 1969; Jehring 1956; Opinion Research Corporation 1957; Industrial Participation Association 1984; Poole and Jenkins 1990). Comparing expressed opinions between employees in profit-sharing plans and those who were not, the profit sharing employees were more likely to agree that employees "get their share of company growth," "get credit for company progress," and "gain from cost-cutting" (Opinion Research Corporation 1957). On the negative side, Bell and Hanson (1987) found that 42 percent of respondents from 12 British profit-sharing companies felt that profit sharing "can cause disappointment or resentment because profits can go down." Also, Blanchflower (1991) found that worker attitudes about the quality of industrial relations were no more favorable among profit-sharing participants than among all private sector workers in the United Kingdom.

Employers who have adopted and maintained profit-sharing plans, not surprisingly, strongly tend to view it favorably. When asked about the general success of profit sharing in their companies, strong majorities view it as successful (Brower 1957; Knowlton 1954; Metzger 1966 1975; New York Stock Exchange 1982; Nightingale 1980; Wider Share Ownership Council 1985; O'Dell and McAdams 1987; Smith 1986; Nickel 1990). Among managers familiar with flexible compensation plans, Mitchell and Broderick (1991) found that 43 percent agreed that cash profit sharing increases productivity, 51 percent agreed that it increases loyalty, 44 percent agreed that it creates demands for participation, and 50 percent agreed that it is difficult to administer (each of these percentages was slightly lower for deferred profit-sharing plans).

Asked to compare profit sharing, ESOPs, gainsharing, and simple incentives, 28 percent (48 percent) saw profit sharing as the best alternative for raising productivity (loyalty).

Employees and employers in profit-sharing companies, therefore, have generally favorable views of profit sharing and its effects on performance measures. Among the many biases in attitude surveys, the respondent selection bias is strong here: employees who have chosen to work in profit-sharing companies and employers who maintain profit-sharing plans are clearly likely to view it positively.

Two studies used regression analysis of employer opinions about economic performance, and one study used a path analysis of employee support for profit sharing. In a sample of 343 unionized Wisconsin firms, Voos (1987) found that profit sharing had positive effects on employer opinions of firm performance, particularly on product quality and productivity. Using data on employer attitudes from 1,266 British establishments in 1984, Blanchflower and Oswald (1988) use profit sharing and other variables to predict whether the company's financial performance was reported as "better than average." In two estimates they find that profit sharing was a positive predictor, but sampling error could not be ruled out.[10] They also note that there are no differences associated with profit sharing in tabulations of managers' opinions of the "general state of relations between management and workers at this establishment." The study of employee support for profit sharing (Florkowski and Schuster 1992) found that perceptions of performance-reward contingencies and pay equity, but not of influence on decisionmaking, were significant determinants of support for profit sharing among 160 employees in three U.S. profit-sharing companies.

Simple comparisons of performance statistics between profit-sharing and non-profit-sharing companies in the United States and the United Kingdom have been done in six studies (Bell and Hanson 1987; Howard and Dietz 1969; Howard 1979; Jehring and Metzger 1960; Metzger and Colletti 1971; Metzger 1978). These cross-sectional comparisons strongly favor profit sharing, with profit-sharing firms having higher mean or median values on substantial majorities of the performance measures. In a longitudinal comparison, Bell and Hanson (1987) found that companies that adopted profit sharing had relative improvement in seven of nine measures (compared to non-profit-sharing firms). A more intensive examination of the Bell and Hanson data is reported in Hanson and Watson (1990), who focus on four performance measures: return on equity, return on sales, sales growth, and annual investor returns. Cross-sectional comparisons accounting for industry membership show that the profit-sharing companies had higher mean values of these measures over the 1978-85 period, while the longitudinal comparisons show improved performance for the first three measures but not for investor returns.[11]

Several case studies of British enterprises that had either profit-sharing or employee-shareholding schemes are reported by Poole and Jenkins (1990). In examining behavioral measures, they find no clear evidence that these schemes reduce strikes or absenteeism, although they might reduce turnover (1990: 50). Examining case study material on economic performance, they conclude

> [T]here is almost certainly a positive relationship between company profitability and whether or not a firm has adopted profit-sharing schemes. However, there remains considerable doubt about the direction of this relationship. In particular, our data suggest that an improved profits performance is frequently the trigger mechanism for the adoption of schemes. This, in turn, enables a company to continue an onward advance in terms of profitability. . . .
>
> *Ceteris paribus*, firms introducing schemes can expect positive financial consequences, though these may well be indirect and mediated through organizational commitment and identification. But there is not a direct linear relationship here or any certainty that firms introducing schemes will inevitably reap substantial financial benefits. (1990: 95)

The simple performance comparisons are clearly consistent with the idea that profit sharing can improve economic performance, although other explanations are clearly plausible. Poole and Jenkins note the possibility of reverse causality: profit sharing may be causing higher performance, but may also be partially caused by higher performance. This possibility is reinforced by the finding of chapter 2 that increases in profits or expected profits helped predict the adoption of profit sharing.

Prior Research: Econometric Studies

The relationship of profit sharing to productivity has been addressed by studies using formal econometric techniques only within the last 12 years. Common to these studies is the use of an objective productivity measure (such as value-added per employee), a measure of profit sharing as an explanatory variable (such as a dummy, dollar figure, or percent of compensation), and several other explanatory variables that may be important for productivity (particularly capital intensity). Most of the studies reviewed here use a production function to model the basic determinants of productivity.[12] Common problems of these studies include standard statistical difficulties of proper specification, the influence of other variables on the profit-sharing measures, the omission of variables that may themselves affect productivity and be associated with the profit-sharing variable, and possible bias from the use of financial rather than physical output measures (Gerhart and Milkovich 1992).

Table 3.1 briefly describes 26 econometric studies that include a profit-sharing independent variable in a regression predicting productivity.[13] Six of these studies (numbers 10, 11, 16, 17, 19, 20) were of worker cooperatives, in which the authors attempted to separate the effects of profit sharing from other cooperative features (e.g., ownership of assets, membership on boards of directors). One study combined U.S. cooperatives with profit-sharing and ESOP firms (number 8), while the remaining studies were of capitalist firms in the United Kingdom (numbers 1, 4, 8, and 26), France (number 6), West Germany (numbers 3, 5, 7, 12, 13, and 14), Japan (18), Korea (23) and the United States (numbers 2, 9, 15, 21, 22, 24, and 25). Six studies report corrections for potential statistical bias from the factors that predict the presence of profit sharing (numbers 6, 10, 11, 12, 13, 20, and 25), with generally similar results to those found in the other studies.[14] Several studies measured not just the direct effect of a profit-sharing variable on the productivity measure, but also the effect of profit sharing interacted with capital, labor, and other variables (numbers 2, 4, 5, 9, 14, 18, 19, and 26).

Overall, the prior results from econometric studies strongly indicate positive relationships between productivity and profit sharing. There are 265 reported estimates on profit-sharing variables when interactions or lags are not included. Of these 265 estimates, 8.7 percent take negative values, and nearly all of these are within the range of sampling error,[15] while 57.4 percent take positive values where random sampling error can be ruled out as an explanation.[16] If the true relationship between profit sharing and productivity is zero, and these estimates represent an unbiased sample of estimates of this relationship, the odds are infinitesimally small of finding such positive estimates (as indicated by a variety of meta-analyses) (Weitzman and Kruse 1990: 138). There is clearly no guarantee that this is an unbiased sample of such estimates: as noted by Card (1990), both the stopping rules for specification search (Leamer 1978) and publication bias (Berlin, Begg, and Louis 1989) may favor positive results where sampling error can be ruled out.[17] While providing no guarantee of unbiasedness, the wide range of data sources and empirical techniques employed, plus the fact that profit sharing was not the primary focus of several of the studies, makes it unlikely that the positive results are *purely* an artifact of stopping rules and publication bias.

These studies indicate that profit sharing may be associated with increased productivity, but provide very little information on the causality and the mechanisms through which profit sharing may affect productivity. Most of these studies are cross-sectional, raising the possibility that profit sharing is reflecting rather than causing better performance. Concerning the mechanisms, the idea that profit sharing enhances the value of labor's contribution to output is supported by the productivity specifications of Shepard (1986). Positive effects on worker behavior are also reported by Wilson and Peel (1991), who find that absenteeism and quits are significantly lower in firms with profit-sharing plans than in other firms. The idea that worker participation in decisions may increase the positive effects of profit sharing is supported by Cable and Fitzroy (1980) (who find a significant positive estimate on profit sharing only in "high-participation" firms) but not by Jones and Pliskin (1991) (who find no positive interactions between profit sharing and worker membership on boards of directors). The idea that it may be most productive in small companies is supported by Bradley and Smith (1991).[18] Cooke (1993) finds that profit sharing appears to have much greater effects in nonunion than in unionized settings. (Among other possible explanations, he suggests that due to

56

Table 3.1 Econometric Studies of Profit Sharing

Authors of the studies	Source of data	Productivity measure	Profit-sharing measure	Number of coefficients reported	Percent of coeffs. <0	Percent of t-stats. >+2
1. Bhargava 1991	150 British firms with public stock, 1978 to 1989	Profits defined as rate of return on fixed capital	Dummy for firms with profit sharing, current and lagged	10 current / 10 lags	0.0 / 100.0	40.0 / 0.0
2. Bradley and Smith 1991	86 U.S. firms in computer industry with public stock, 1986-88	Revenues	Dummy for profit-sharing firms, plus interactions w/labor	2 main effects / 3 interactions	0.0 / 33.3	100.0 / 33.3
3. Cable and Fitzroy 1980a, 1980b	42 West German firms members of the AGB from 1974 to 1976	Value-added	Total profits distributed to workers	3	33.3	33.3
4. Cable and Wilson 1989	52 U.K. firms in engineering, from 1978 to 1982	Value-added	Dummy for profit-sharing firms, interacted with firm characteristics	a	a	a
5. Cable and Wilson 1990	61 West German firms in 1977; 62 West German firms in 1979	Value-added	Dummy for profit-sharing firms, interacted with firm characteristics	a	a	a
6. Cahuc and Dormont 1992	565 French manufacturing firms, 1986-89	Value-added	Profit-sharing payments divided by base wage	12	0.0	83.3
7. Carstensen, Gerlach, and Hubler 1992	136 German manufacturing firms in 1989	Value-added, profits per employee, and return on capital	Dummy for profit sharing, profit share/ profits, profit share per employee	21[b]	61.9	14.3

Study	Sample	Dependent variable	Profit-sharing measure	Number	0.0	Positive
8. Conte and Svejnar 1988	40 U.S. firms (period not reported)	Value-added	Dummy for firms with profit sharing	6	0.0	33.3
9. Cooke 1993	1,173 U.S. manufacturing firms, 1989	Value-added per employee, and sales per employee	Dummy for profit sharing/gainsharing, interacted with union status and work teams	8 interactions[a]	0.0	100.0
10. Defourney, Estrin, and Jones 1985	440 French cooperatives in 1978; 550 French cooperatives in 1979	Value-added	Profits distributed to workers per head	14	0.0	64.3
11. Estrin, Jones, and Svejnar 1987	Cooperatives in France (550 in 1978-79), Italy (150 in 1976-80), and Britain (50 over 1948-68)	Value-added	Profits distributed to workers per head	11	0.0	81.8
12. Fitzroy and Kraft 1986	61 West German firms in 1977; 62 West German firms in 1979	Profits defined as cash flow divided by assets	Profits distributed to workers per head	2	0.0	100.0
13. Fitzroy and Kraft 1987	Same as above	Total factor productivity (residual of a Cobb-Douglas estimation)	Profits distributed to workers per head	2	0.0	100.0
14. Fitzroy and Kraft 1992; Kraft 1991	Same as above	Value-added	Dummy for profit sharing, alone and interacted with capital and employment	6 main effects / 3 interactions[a]	0.0 / 33.3	83.3 / 0.0

Authors of the studies	Source of data	Productivity measure	Profit-sharing measure	Number of coefficients reported	Percent of coeffs. <0	Percent of t-stats. >+2
15. Florkowski 1988	3 U.S. profit-sharing companies (monthly data)	Value-added per worker	Intercept and slope effects before and after the plan introduction or modification	6	16.7	16.7
16. Jones 1982	From 46 to 30 British cooperatives over the period 1948-68	Value-added	Individual bonus to labor	52	5.8	40.4
17. Jones 1987	50 British cooperatives in the retail sector in 1978	Gross margin	Surplus distributed to workers as dividend	2	0.0	0.0
18. Jones and Kato 1992b	100 Japanese firms over 1973-80 period	Value-added	Profit-sharing bonus per employee, and divided by base wage, alone and interacted with capital, labor, and ESOP presence	15 main effects / 59 interactions[a]	0.0 / 45.8	73.3 / 32.2
19. Jones and Pliskin 1991b	70 firms in clothing, footwear, and printing over the period 1923 to 1968	Real sales	Size of bonus and dummy for bonus, alone and interacted with capital, labor and employees on board	12 main effects / 27 interactions[a]	8.3 / 55.6	50.0 / 3.7
20. Jones and Svejnar 1985	316 Italian cooperatives from 1975 to 1978; 315 Italian cooperatives from 1975 to 1980	Value-added	Profits distributed to workers per head	6	0.0	100.0

Study	Sample	Performance measure	Profit-sharing measure	Number	%	%
21. Kim 1993	183 U.S. companies with public stock, 1986	Return on assets	Dummy, percent of workers covered, and bonus/labor costs	15	6.7	20.0
22. Kruse 1988, 1992	2,976 U.S. companies with public stock, 1971-85	Sales per employee	Dummy for firms with profit sharing; percent of employees covered by profit sharing	76	5.3	68.4
23. Lee and Rhee 1992	Industry data from South Korea, 1972-89	Index of industrial production/total labor hours	Profit-sharing bonus divided by wage	7	0.0	85.7
24. Mitchell, Lewin, and Lawler 1990	495 U.S. business units, 1983-86	Sales per employee; return on investment; return on assets	Dummy for firms with profit sharing	12	0.0	83.3
25. Shepard 1986, forthcoming	20 U.S. chemical firms from 1975 to 1982	Value-added	Dummy for firms with profit sharing; profits distributed to workers per head; ratio of profit sharing to fixed compensation	16	0.0	81.3
26. Wadhwani and Wall 1990	96 U.K. firms from 1972 to 1982	Real sales	Dummy for firms with profit sharing, and interaction w/capital	1 main effect 1 interaction[a]	0.0 0.0	0.0 100.0
Total main effects, where no interactions or lags appear[a]				265	8.7	57.4

a. For the study using lags (number 1), all 10 specifications indicate positive effects of adopting and maintaining profit sharing. For the eight studies using interactions, six (numbers 4, 5, 9, 14, 19, 26) indicate that profit sharing is associated with higher performance at mean values of the interacted variables (the productivity difference is 3 to 8 percent in study 4, 20 to 30 percent in study 5, and 1.4 to 28.3 percent in study 14). Study 2 reports positive associations only for small firms, and study 18 reports positive effects only when profit sharing is associated with employee stock ownership.

b. Estimates with industry controls.

lower base pay in nonunion settings, the profit share may be a better motivator since it is a larger portion of total compensation.)

Finally, a study that does not measure productivity directly, but measures stock price response, is Florkowski and Shastri (1992).[19] They report on a study of 45 announcements of union contracts that included profit sharing over the 1979-88 period. These announcements were found to be associated with positive abnormal returns to shareholders. Such positive returns could reflect expectations of better overall economic performance, a shareholder premium for sharing future income risk with employees, or simply a transfer from employees to shareholders if the profit sharing comes in lieu of higher wages or benefits (Abowd 1989). The positive returns were not found to be significantly higher when the contract included wage reductions or signalled the end of a strike, but were significantly higher when the firm was reported to be facing bankruptcy or plant shutdowns. The fact that returns were not significantly higher when wage reductions were announced points against a simple story of profit sharing signalling wealth transfers, but it is still very possible that profit sharing was viewed as substituting for more costly wage and benefit increases. This evidence is clearly consistent, however, with the proposition that profit sharing improves overall performance.

Prior research thus indicates a good likelihood that profit sharing is positively related to productivity, but the causality has not been well disentangled (most studies share a weakness of not analyzing productivity before and after the adoption of profit sharing, leaving open the possibility that more successful firms are more likely to adopt profit sharing). In addition, these studies provide very little evidence on the mechanisms by which this may happen. This study will build upon this research by intensively analyzing the effects of profit-sharing adoption and presence, and the role played by different plan types, formulas, firm sizes, and information-sharing and personnel policies.

Simple Comparisons on Productivity Levels and Growth

To examine the productivity effects of profit sharing, two measures of productivity are employed in this study: sales per employee, and value-added per employee. The first measure is calculated in a straight-forward way, while the second is not straightforward because it requires data on labor costs, which are not reported by most publicly held companies. Where labor cost data were not available, the value was imputed using industry compensation levels, sales, and employment levels.[20]

Table 3.2 presents simple statistical comparisons on productivity levels and changes. Mean levels of the productivity measures for 1975 and 1990 are at the top, with the within-industry comparisons on lines 3 and 6. There it can be seen that profit-sharing firms had 4.0 percent to 7.4 percent higher average productivity in 1975, and 1.0 percent to 3.5 percent higher productivity in 1990, but random sampling error cannot be ruled out as an explanation of the differences.[21]

Comparisons of productivity *growth* are reported on lines 7 to 13.[22] Over the sample period the average yearly growth rates for non-profit-sharing companies in the two measures were approximately 8.1 percent and 7.6 percent. The growth rates for profit-sharing companies were slightly lower: 7.3 percent and 7.1 percent for the companies that adopted profit sharing before 1975, and 8.0 percent and 7.3 percent for those that adopted it after 1975.[23] (Note that the numbers on lines 7 to 9 reflect inflation as well as pure productivity increases—the inflation rate averaged 6.0-6.2 percent.)[24]

Comparisons of productivity growth between within-industry pairs will automatically control for any general productivity trends in an industry in a given year. The comparisons of non-profit-sharing companies with pre-1975 ("old") adopters are reported on line 10, while lines 11 to 13 answer the question, "How did average yearly productivity growth compare between profit-sharing adopters and their non-profit-sharing pairs prior to the adoption (line 11), during the year of adoption (line 12), and after adoption (line 13)?"

The old profit-sharing firms had slower productivity growth than their pairs in the 1970s and 1980s. Line 10 shows that the average yearly productivity growth of old adopters was less than that of their pairs by 0.7 percent for sales/employee and 0.5 percent for value-added/employee.[25] This is not so for the new adopters. Productivity growth was, on average, slightly and insignificantly lower in the pre-adoption period (line 11), but higher in the year of adoption (line 12). When profit sharing was adopted, average sales/employee increased

Table 3.2 Simple Statistical Comparisons on Productivity

	N (1)	Sales per employee		Value-added per employee	
		(2)	(3)	(4)	(5)
Productivity levels (means)					
1. 1975 No PS in 1975	357	73,318		32,355	
2. PS in 1975	99	69,617		33,479	
3. Paired difference	76	7.4%	(1.23)	4.0%	(0.83)
4. 1990 No PS in 1990	250	213,110		96,700	
5. PS in 1990	211	182,510		87,590	
6. Paired difference	169	1.0%	(0.23)	3.5%	(1.06)
Yearly productivity growth, $t - 1$ to t (trimmed means)[a]					
Nonpaired values					
7. NPS	4,678	8.1%		7.6%	
8. PS adopted before 1975	1,962	7.3%		7.1%	
9. PS adopted after 1975	2,004	8.0%		7.3%	
Paired differences between PS and NPS					
10. Pre-1975 adopters	1,417	-0.7%	(1.69)	-0.5%	(1.14)
Post-1975 adopters					
11. Preadoption	1,172	-0.1%	(0.22)	-0.3%	(0.59)
12. Year of adoption	98	4.1%	(2.34)	2.3%	(1.11)
13. Postadoption	699	-0.7%	(1.17)	0.0%	(0.00)

Paired differences between cash PS and NPS

14.	Pre-1975 adopters	365	0.0%	(0.00)	0.4%	(0.42)
	Post-1975 adopters					
15.	Preadoption	2,341	-0.3%	(0.94)	-0.3%	(1.10)
16.	Year of adoption	45	4.7%	(1.61)	0.8%	(0.22)
17.	Postadoption	240	-2.8%	(2.66)	-1.4%	(1.22)

Paired differences between deferred PS and NPS

18.	Pre-1975 adopters	684	-0.9%	(1.54)	-1.1%	(1.78)
	Post-1975 adopters					
19.	Preadoption	2,242	-0.5%	(1.46)	-0.3%	(0.82)
20.	Year of adoption	61	4.3%	(2.14)	4.1%	(1.67)
21.	Postadoption	466	0.4%	(0.56)	1.0%	(1.15)

NOTES: NPS = no profit sharing; PS = profit sharing. N = 247 for NPS companies, N = 103 for pre-1975 PS adopters, N = 128 for post-1975 adopters. Paired differences represent value for PS company minus the value for its same-industry NPS pair for that year. Absolute values of t-statistics in parentheses.

a. Trimmed means were calculated after removing the upper 1 percent and lower 1 percent of values.

4.1 percent, and value-added/employee increased 2.3 percent, relative to the industry pairs; sampling error can be ruled out for the former difference. Once adopted, average yearly growth in sales/employee is 0.7 percent lower, and in value-added/employee is equal, between the adopters and their pairs. While the 0.7 percent difference is not significantly different from zero, the point estimate indicates that the 4.1 percent jump in sales/employee when profit sharing is adopted is dissipated within six years (perhaps indicating a positive "honeymoon" effect that dies over time).

These results may clearly differ by type of plan. In this period, 45 cash or combination plans were adopted and 61 deferred plans were adopted. The remainder of table 3.2 presents similar comparisons by type of plan (where cash plans include combination plans, since they both have cash components). The initial patterns are similar to those described above: the preadoption comparisons indicate lower productivity growth for the adopters, while productivity jumps up during the year of adoption (with these jumps being statistically significant at the 90 percent level for deferred plans, but not for cash plans). The postadoption growth comparisons are negative for cash plans (significantly so for the sales/employee measure, indicating that the initial upward jump is dissipated in two years), but insignificantly positive for deferred plans. The "honeymoon" effect may therefore be more important for cash plans than for deferred plans.

Productivity growth among profit-sharing adopters (compared to their industry pairs) appears, therefore, to be slightly lower prior to adoption, to jump up during adoption, and to be flat or declining after adoption. This upward jump apparently exists for both cash and deferred plans, but the subsequent decline is apparent only for cash plans. These simple comparisons control for industry and year effects, but do not control for other important influences on productivity, most notably capital intensity. The comparisons would be biased if, for example, capital intensity tended to dramatically increase when profit sharing is adopted, indicating that the upward jump in sales/employee is due to forces other than profit sharing. These influences can and will be accounted for in the analysis that follows.

Estimating the Productivity Effects of Profit Sharing

Following most prior econometric work, this study investigates the relationship between profit sharing and productivity using a production function framework. The framework will be briefly outlined here (with technical detail in appendix 3). Labor and capital are viewed as the two most important inputs to the production process, and the levels of these factors and their relation to each other are expected to be key influences on output. With longitudinal data on each firm, such as exists in this database, *changes* in capital and labor can be related to *changes* in output per worker, which subtracts out any constant unobserved features that may make one firm more productive than another (such as particularly strong market placement, or high quality management).

The potential effects of profit sharing and other company policies on output per worker are accounted for after controlling for the effects of changes in labor and capital stocks. In this analysis, with up to 20 years of data on any firm, there may also be general time trend effects or industry growth effects; these are accounted for by the addition of time and industry variables to the unpaired estimates, or by looking at differences between paired firms within the same industry and year.

Two possible ways in which profit sharing may affect productivity are examined here. First, profit sharing may have a simple effect on the productivity level, implying an upward or downward jump in productivity when profit sharing is adopted. Second, profit sharing may have an effect on productivity growth after adoption—possibly a positive effect if employees gradually learn how better to cooperate and improve performance, and possibly a negative effect if workers' initial optimism is unfulfilled and they gradually return to preadoption levels of performance. Both the initial adoption effect and subsequent trend effect are reported here.

The potential effects of several other firm characteristics are included in all specifications. ESOPs, defined benefit pensions, and unions may all have independent effects on productivity, and their omission could lead to biased estimates of the effect of profit sharing.[26]

A serious problem in estimation involves potential statistical bias from self-selection of profit-sharing status by companies. A classic experiment would randomly assign firms to profit-sharing or non-profit-sharing status, and then compare their performance to obtain unbiased estimates of the productivity effect of profit sharing. Random assignment of profit sharing in a classic experiment, as desirable as it may be for a researcher, is obviously not possible. In a field study, when the subjects have been able to select themselves into or out of the condition being studied, there is a strong possibility that the selection rule is itself related to the outcome being measured.[27] For example, if profit-sharing companies are found to have better performance, it may be that these companies would have had high performance even in the absence of profit sharing (suggested by Poole and Jenkins 1990).

Statistical bias from self-selection may be manifested in many ways. Four broad types of statistical bias from self-selection will be described here, and appendix 3 describes a variety of statistical methods to control for several of the biases. The simplest and clearest form of statistical bias from self-selection is when companies with pre-existing high productivity are more likely to select profit sharing. If this is the case, a cross-sectional comparison of profit-sharing and non-profit-sharing companies will show higher productivity among the profit-sharing group, but the profit sharing is not causing the higher productivity—rather, the causality may be reversed. This simple form of statistical bias from self-selection is controlled by comparing preadoption and postadoption productivity levels, as is done here with the panel data.

Several forms of statistical bias from self-selection may exist even in comparing preadoption and postadoption outcomes. One is that the companies selecting profit sharing may have been on an upward growth path in productivity, and profit sharing may have played no role in stimulating the higher growth.[28] This is a particular problem if there are only single observations before and after the adoption; however, with multiple observations (as exist in this dataset) the preadoption and postadoption trends can be checked.

A third form of statistical bias from self-selection is that companies may be undergoing other changes at the time profit sharing is adopted, and any productivity changes may be due to these other changes rather than to profit sharing.[29] Without controlling for these other changes, profit sharing may statistically reflect the productivity effects of these changes. This potential bias is partially addressed in this study by asking the firms about the existence and duration of other policies that may affect productivity, and by analyzing responses to an open-ended question about any significant changes in other policies that accompanied profit-sharing adoption. There nonetheless remains the possibility that, at the time of profit-sharing adoption, the company was undergoing other changes in financial and organizational structure that were responsible for any changes in productivity.

These three forms of statistical bias from self-selection, therefore, address ways in which profit sharing may mistakenly be concluded to have a true effect on productivity. A fourth broad form of statistical bias from self-selection addressed here posits that profit sharing may in fact have a true effect on productivity, but that this effect varies across firms. The incentive to adopt profit sharing is clearly strongest where it is expected to have the most impact—reflecting, perhaps, a particular organizational structure, culture, or history into which profit sharing meshes well. This implies that, even though profit sharing may have helped fuel a productivity increase in some companies, the result cannot be generalized (i.e., the effect would be much smaller or nonexistent in other companies). This bias is made more plausible by the fact that these companies have continued to maintain profit sharing, whereas it may have been terminated before the survey date by companies in which the profit sharing made little difference.[30] If this were the case, it would nonetheless be of interest that profit sharing helped productivity in some companies, and investigation of the circumstances that created this effect would be valuable to study.

The first two forms of statistical bias from self-selection are easily addressed with panel data, while the second two are not. A variety of techniques were employed to statistically correct for such bias (discussed in appendix 3), using the factors that help predict profit-sharing adoption from chapter 2. There were no substantial differences in conclusions reached by any of these techniques (reflecting in part the difficulty in finding variables that predicted profit-sharing adoption). For the two performance variables that appeared to predict adoption (change in stock price and change in profit margin in the two years preceding adoption), the profit-sharing effects on productivity were calculated separately for those experiencing positive and negative changes in stock price and profit margin, and the results were equivalent. From a variety of sources, therefore, statistical bias from self-selection does not appear to be strongly influencing these results.

The results that are presented are restricted to the years 1977 to 1991. Exclusion of 1970-76 observations was done for two reasons: (1) use of a selection term to correct for statistical bias, based on the variables predicting profit-sharing adoption (removing the first several years of the panel); and (2) substantial concern about the accuracy of data on adoptions reported this long ago (in particular, there are sharp upward spikes in reported ages of "15" or "20" years, which are likely to represent convenient targets for those who are not certain). Results employing the entire 1970-91 panel, without the selection term, were similar to those reported but indicated slightly lower and more dispersed effects of profit-sharing adoption (as would be expected if measurement error is greater for the adoption dates of these earlier plans).[31]

Do Profit-Sharing Adoption and Presence Affect Productivity?

A summary of the profit-sharing estimate from the productivity regressions is on lines 1 and 2 of table 3.3 (based on results in appendix table A3.2). As shown in the first column, the adoption of profit sharing was accompanied by an estimated 4.4 percent increase in sales per employee, and random sampling error can be ruled out at a 99 percent level of confidence.[32] The within-industry comparison, in column 2, is almost identical for this productivity measure.[33] Columns 3 and 4 measure productivity as value-added per employee, where it can be seen that the unpaired results are stronger for profit sharing (an estimated 5.0 percent increase) and weaker for the within-industry pairs (3.5 percent, where sampling error can be ruled out only at the 90 percent level).

The subsequent trend after profit sharing was adopted is estimated as slightly positive but not significantly different from zero in all four columns. Therefore one cannot confidently say that there is either a positive or negative trend effect associated with profit sharing. A simple trend effect may, however, be a misleading guide to the postadoption effects of profit sharing. The productivity effects may be nonlinear and may grow either stronger or weaker during the first several years after adoption. They may grow stronger if it takes time for employees to develop the cooperative effort that is theorized to lie behind a positive effect of profit sharing. There may be a negative effect, however, if initial enthusiasm for profit sharing is not maintained; perhaps the innovation raised hopes that were not fulfilled. The preadoption growth path should also be examined; it is possible that the firm was simply on an upward growth path when profit sharing was adopted, and profit sharing may have played little or no role in this.

To examine this, for the firms that adopted profit sharing within the sample period, estimates were made of the productivity effects in each of three preadoption and postadoption years. The productivity path revealed by such estimates is illustrated in figure 3.1 for each of the four productivity measures.[34] This figure illustrates the consistent finding of an upward jump in productivity in the year that profit sharing is adopted, which is maintained above the levels predicted for nonadopters in subsequent years.

Figure 3.1
Predicted Productivity Path of Adopters

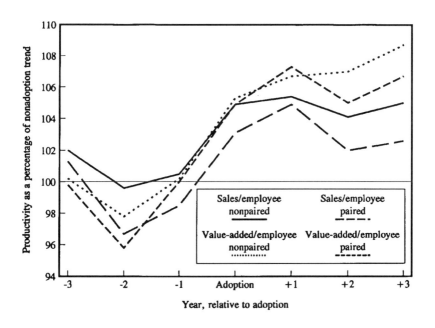

Year, relative to adoption

Table 3.3 Summary Results on Productivity Growth and Profit Sharing

Productivity measure	Yearly growth in sales per employee		Yearly growth in value-added per employee		Based on results from appendix table
	Unpaired (1)	Within-industry pairs (2)	Unpaired (3)	Within-industry pairs (4)	
	Estimated productivity effects (percent)				
All profit-sharing plans					A3.2
1. Year of adoption	4.4***	4.3**	5.0***	3.5*	
2. Subsequent trend	0.2	0.8	1.0	1.9	
Cash vs. deferred plans					A3.3
Cash profit sharing					
3. Year of adoption	3.5**	6.5**	3.6**	4.3	
4. Subsequent trend	0.5	-0.4	-0.3	0.8	
Deferred profit sharing					
5. Year of adoption	1.8	0.9	1.4	-1.1	
6. Subsequent trend	0.2	2.5	3.6***	2.7	
Plan formulas					A3.4
Percent-of-profits plan					
7. Year of adoption	4.8	2.2	7.9**	1.4	
8. Subsequent trend	-0.2	3.7	-2.5	0.5	
Discretionary plan					
9. Year of adoption	7.7**	3.8	9.2**	10.5**	
10. Subsequent trend	-0.4	3.5	2.1	5.0*	

Percent-of-pay plan				
11. Year of adoption	2.2	3.3	-1.6	4.4
12. Subsequent trend	-1.7	2.4	-2.8	-5.1*
Other plan formula				
13. Year of adoption	1.6	2.9	0.7	1.6
14. Subsequent trend	-0.1	-0.9	-0.4	-1.2

NOTES: Results based on coefficients from regressions listed in last column. All regressions include controls for capital and labor ratios, adoption and presence of defined benefit plans and ESOPs, and union presence. The unpaired results (columns 1 and 3) contain controls for broad industry trends and year effects. The paired results (columns 2 and 4) are paired differences between profit-sharing and non-profit-sharing companies within industry and year.

*Significantly different from zero at 90 percent level   **95 percent level   ***99 percent level.

This figure has two other findings of interest. First, each measure indicates a decrease in productivity two years prior to adoption, followed by an increase in the preadoption year. This raises the possibility that profit sharing was adopted during a rebound from poor performance, but leaves open the question of causation—profit sharing may have helped cause the upward jump in productivity, or it may simply reflect a policy which happens to have been adopted during normal recovery from poor performance. If profit sharing were purely a symptom of rebounding from poor performance, however, one would not expect performance to remain high in subsequent years.[35]

Second, while each measure indicates continued productivity growth in the year following adoption, three of the four measures in figure 3.1 indicate a productivity decrease in the second year. If profit sharing is in fact a key cause of the productivity trends, such a decrease in the second year may indicate problems in maintaining an initial increase in worker performance.[36] However, none of these decreases is statistically significant, and they are all followed by further increases in productivity in the third year.

Does every adopter of profit sharing experience a productivity increase? This is certainly not the case. While the average productivity increase in the year of adoption is about 4 percent, between one-fourth and one-third of the adopters had no productivity increase beyond that predicted by the other factors in the equation.[37]

Adoption of defined benefit pensions and ESOPs are both associated with small productivity increases (about 0.9 percent to 2.7 percent for defined benefit pensions, and 0.3 percent to 1.4 percent for ESOPs), but these estimates are not significantly different from zero (results in appendix table A3.2). Union presence is estimated to decrease growth in sales per employee by about 0.4 percent to 0.8 percent per year, but this effect is also not significantly different from zero.[38] The capital and labor terms of the production function were strong predictors of productivity changes.[39]

Additional tests were made measuring profit sharing as proportion of employees covered (columns 5-8 in appendix table A3.2). If profit sharing does have a positive productivity effect, one would expect this effect to be larger as a greater proportion of employees is covered. The practicality of estimating this effect, however, is limited by its low variance: over 50 percent of the profit-sharing companies include 90 percent or more of their employees in profit sharing. Results from measuring profit sharing in this way were similar but slightly weaker.[40]

The finding from table 3.2, that sales/employee jumps upward when profit sharing is adopted, is replicated here when controlling for capital, labor, deferred benefit plans, ESOPs, union presence, and the sample selection term. The adoption effect is slightly weaker when profit sharing is measured as proportion covered. It is notable that the estimated increase in productivity when profit sharing is adopted—an average of 4.3 percent across the four estimates—is remarkably close to the 4.4 percent median estimate of effect sizes from other studies. The studies surveyed in Weitzman and Kruse (1990) were analyzed for the estimated productivity differentials associated with profit sharing—the median estimate was 4.4 percent (with a mean of 7.4 percent, and lower and upper quartiles of 2.5 percent and 11.0 percent). As noted there, "Such estimates strike us as reasonable—they are neither so small as to be negligible, nor so large as to be implausible when adjustment costs are considered" (1990: 138-9).

Do Cash and Deferred Plans Have Different Effects?

It is often theorized that cash plans will be more effective motivators for employees, since they provide more immediate rewards. This is supported by the expressed motives in table 2.1, where the average expressed importance of "motivating existing employees" was slightly higher for firms maintaining any cash plans than for firms maintaining only deferred plans.[41]

This theory is supported by the results summarized in table 3.3 (based on results from appendix table A3.3), that separate profit sharing into cash plans and deferred plans.[42] The adoption of cash profit sharing is predicted to increase sales per employee by 3.5 percent and 6.5 percent in the first two estimates (line 3), both effects being significant at the 95 percent level. The estimated adoption effects are similar in size (3.6 percent and 4.3 percent) when productivity is measured as value-added/employee, but sampling error cannot be ruled out for the latter result. The postadoption trend effects are close to zero, and cannot be statistically distinguished from zero.

None of the estimates on adoption of deferred plans indicate a significant change in productivity. The first three columns indicate positive effects of 0.9 percent to 1.8 percent from adopting deferred profit sharing, while the fourth column indicates a small decrease; the trend effects are all positive but sampling error can be ruled out for only one of them (column 3).[43]

Does the Profit-Sharing Formula Matter?

There is no set formula among profit-sharing plans for how the company's profit-sharing contribution should be tied to profits. Several common formulas follow, along with the percentage of respondents using these formulas from the Profit Sharing Council of America (PSCA 1989), and the percentage of participants in deferred plans that use these formulas (BLS 1990):

	PSCA	BLS
Specific percentage of profits	17%	10%
Specific percentage of profits in excess of amount reserved for return on stockholder equity	11%	
Sliding percentage based on profits, sales, or return on assets		18%
Percentage of participants' pay	12%	
Specific percentage of profits plus a discretionary amount	7%	
Discretionary amount	46%	40%

Tying the formula to a specific percentage of profits is clearly the most straightforward way to link employee rewards to the performance of the firm and should, therefore, have the greatest effect on employees.

The lack of a formula—where the employer can simply determine a discretionary amount—is popular, and is not straightforward to analyze. There is no guarantee that higher profits will result in higher profit-sharing payments, so that the incentive effect would appear very weak. In any given period, a firm maximizing short-run profits for investors would clearly have an incentive to provide no profit-sharing payment to employees. The fact that these plans are maintained, however, clearly indicates that firms see them as useful and do make contributions to them. There may be a strong relationship between profits and contributions to these plans, so that these may clearly be *de facto* profit-sharing plans even if there is no formula tying payments to profits. As will be discussed, it may be that the discretion allows managers to provide a better reward for employee performance (subtracting out influences on profits from other sources).

The formula that appears least consistent with profit sharing is making profit-sharing payments a fixed percentage of participants' pay. Taken literally, this implies that "profit-sharing" payments have the same relationship to profits as do fixed wages, so that there is nothing distinctive about them as a form of compensation. Presumably these are called "profit-sharing" payments so that they may be cut more easily than wages when the company is undergoing financial difficulties. This implies, however, only a very weak relationship to profits. Any productivity effect would therefore be expected to be much weaker or nonexistent.

Profit-sharing firms in the survey being analyzed here were asked for the method by which profit-sharing payments were determined. The breakdown of methods (for 163 plans in 124 companies reporting) was the following:

1. Specific percentage of profits	19.6%
2. Specific percentage of profits in excess of amount reserved for dividends or retained earnings	3.7%
3. Fully discretionary	22.1%
4. Specific percentage of profits plus discretionary amount	4.3%
5. Specific percentage of participants' pay	30.1%
6. Other	34.4%

(Total exceeds 100 percent because more than one method could be listed for each plan)

These responses were classified into four categories so that the relationship to productivity could be analyzed: (a) payments linked to specific percentage of profits (1, 2, and 4 from above); (b) payments that are fully discretionary (3 from above); (c) payments that are a specific percentage of pay (5 from above); and (d) "other" methods (6 from above, where the variety prevented any neat classification).

Of the profit-sharing firms, 90 provided data on yearly profit-sharing contributions as a percentage of participants' pay. The mean value across all reported years was 7.4 percent, with a median of 4.0 percent. Correlations between year-to-year changes in contributions and changes in profits per employee were calculated. As expected, this correlation was close to zero when a percent-of-pay plan was in place ($r = -.001$). Also as expected, the correlation was positive when a percent-of-profits plan was in place ($r = .102$); somewhat unexpectedly, the correlation was higher for discretionary plans ($r = .220$).[44] Therefore discretionary plans do appear to operate as *de facto* profit-sharing plans.

The results of estimating separate productivity effects for different formulas are summarized in table 3.3 (based on results presented in appendix table A3.4).[45] These are based on: 30 companies that maintained percent-of-profit plans (15 adopted in sample period), 20 companies that maintained discretionary plans (11 adopted in sample period), 23 companies that maintained percent-of-pay plans (12 adopted in sample period), and 46 companies that maintained plans based on other formulas (27 adopted in sample period). Clearly the small number of plan adoptions in the sample period limits the ability to obtain consistent estimates.

Plan adoption tends to be positively related to productivity for all methods (rows 7, 9, 11, and 13), with the only negative estimate appearing for percent-of-pay plans (in row 11, column 3). However, sampling error cannot be ruled out for most of the estimates. The most favorable results appear for discretionary plans: in three of the estimates, the adoption of discretionary plans is associated with significant increases in productivity (of 7.7 percent to 10.5 percent). The only other statistically significant estimate is for the adoption of percent-of-profits plans (an estimate of 7.9 percent in row 7, column 3). Adoption of plans with percent-of-pay or other formulas, and the postadoption trends, are never associated with significant productivity changes.

With the small number of observations for any plan formula, the results are somewhat sensitive to different specifications. In particular, expanding the sample slightly by deleting the selection terms for the different plan formulas produces results somewhat more favorable to percent-of-profits plans.[46]

The pattern of results suggests that percent-of-pay plans do not have positive effects on productivity, since there is one negative estimate and no significant positive estimates. This is consistent with theory on a positive motivational role for profit sharing, since a fixed percent-of-pay has little or no relationship to profits. There are stronger indications that adoptions of percent-of-profit plans and discretionary plans have positive productivity effects. The results are most favorable, somewhat surprisingly, for discretionary plans. The lack of a specific formula may seem to represent a strong drawback for profit-sharing plans, since it leaves open the possibility that firms will share very little with employees even when employees may have contributed to high profits. It is nonetheless possible that the employer's discretion may be used to more accurately reward employee efforts, in an atmosphere of high trust. As argued by Baker, Gibbons, and Murphy (1993), almost every objective performance measure is subject to contamination from influences other than the performance it is designed to measure. In the case of profit sharing, company profits are clearly influenced by a large variety of factors other than employee performance, such as capital investment, imports, managerial decisions, and regulations. Baker, Gibbons, and Murphy note that while

> an ideal performance measure would reflect an employee's contribution to firm value, . . unfortunately, for most employees, contribution to firm value is not objectively measurable. ... [I]t sometimes can be subjectively assessed by managers and supervisors who are well placed to observe the subtleties of the employee's behavior and opportunities. . . [A]n implicit contract based on subjective performance assessments may augment or replace an explicit contract based on objective performance measurements (1993: 2).

If payments are at the discretion of the employer, there is no written contract that can be legally enforced. Noting that "trust between workers and supervisors is essential if subjective performance assessment systems are to be successful," Baker and his colleagues show how an implicit contract based on subjective assessments can be enforced by the firm's concern about its reputation in the labor market. In the context of profit sharing, this implies that companies with high employee trust may be able to use discretionary payments to encourage and maintain high employee effort and commitment. The high effort and employee trust would be threatened if the employer took advantage of the discretion to, for example, pay very little in a year when employees have contributed to higher profits.[47]

This raises two opposing interpretations of the strong upward jump in productivity when profit sharing with discretionary payments is adopted (before employees have had a chance to observe the company's pattern of profit-sharing contributions). A first possible interpretation is that, since profit-sharing plans with no formula should not be good motivators, it is likely that the profit-sharing variables are simply reflecting productivity increases that are due to other factors (as is clearly possible with all estimates reported in this chapter). A second possible interpretation is that, in a company where there is an atmosphere of trust between employees and employers at the time of adoption, the lack of a profit-sharing formula may not be a hindrance to positive effects on employee behavior and relations (i.e., the announced profit sharing may build on past trust to make employees optimistic about the company's use of profit sharing to reward employees for better performance).

Does Company Size Matter?

The effect of a group incentive system such as profit sharing is strongly predicted to depend upon the size of the group. As described earlier, such systems have a 1/N problem (with N representing group size), in which the direct individual reward from better individual performance becomes more diluted as the work group grows larger. For the group incentive to have a positive effect on group performance, some form of cooperative solution to this problem, relying on increased monitoring of co-workers and group identification, would appear to be necessary. Game theory is silent on how such a solution may be established; in a business, it plausibly involves changes in personnel policies, information-sharing, and employee relations to increase employee identification with co-workers and the company.

The establishment of such a cooperative solution may be easier in a small company, in which any one employee is more likely to have personal contact with top managers and with a greater proportion of the workforce. Personnel policies may be more quickly established and adapted to maintain employee identification with co-workers and the company. In combination with the 1/N problem, this consideration predicts that profit sharing is more likely to have a positive effect on performance in small companies.

To the extent that personnel policies and information-sharing have large fixed costs, the establishment and maintenance of such policies may be done more easily and costlessly in a large company. In addition, larger companies may have more experienced employee relations staffs who are better able to coordinate profit sharing with other personnel policies. Finally, to the extent that worker behavior is affected not by the size of the performance-pay link, but instead by the existence of such a link, company size may not be a crucial variable—large size may not be a strong disadvantage as predicted by the 1/N problem.

To examine the relationship of profit sharing and work group size, the sample of profit-sharing adopters was split into five groups. These groups were defined by employment size at the time of profit-sharing adoption, for which the lowest decile, lower quartile, median, and upper quartile were, respectively, 775, 1681, 4599, and 17,600. These four cut-offs were used to create five groups, and the adoption and presence of profit sharing were interacted with group membership. In addition, the terms of the production function were interacted with group membership, to allow different production functions by group size. Because there were very few cases in which paired firms fell into the same employment size class, reliable results for the paired sample could not be obtained.

The employment size class results are summarized in table 3.4 (based on results in appendix table A3.5). In the smallest size class, the productivity effect of profit-sharing adoption is large and highly significant (11.1 percent and 17.2 percent, where sampling error can be ruled out at the 99 percent level). The subsequent presence of profit sharing, however, is not estimated to have any significant effect on productivity growth. The second and fourth size classes show no significant estimates of profit-sharing adoption or subsequent trend, while the third size class shows a weakly significant estimate of a 4.2 percent increase in sales per employee when profit sharing is adopted, and a 2.2 percent trend in value-added per employee. The fifth and largest size class

Table 3.4 Summary Results on Profit-Sharing Effects by Company Size and Profit-Sharing Contribution

Size class	Yearly growth in sales per employee Unpaired (1)	Yearly growth in value-added per employee Unpaired (2)
	Estimated productivity effects (percent)	
Empl. < 775		
Year of adoption	11.1***	17.2***
Subsequent trend	-0.7	0.1
775 <= Empl. < 1681		
Year of adoption	-1.5	6.2
Subsequent trend	-0.3	1.1
1681 <= Empl. < 4599		
Year of adoption	4.2*	-3.3
Subsequent trend	0.2	2.2*
4599 <= Empl. < 17,000		
Year of adoption	2.2	2.9
Subsequent trend	0.1	1.2
Empl. >= 17,000		
Year of adoption	6.9***	5.8***
Subsequent trend	0.1	0.8

Contribution size	Yearly growth in sales per employee Unpaired (3)	Yearly growth in sales per employee Within-industry pairs (4)	Yearly growth in value-added per employee Unpaired (5)	Yearly growth in value-added per employee Within-industry pairs (6)
	Estimated productivity effects (percent)			
PS plans with low mean employer contributions				
Year of adoption	1.4	-1.9	2.1	-1.9
Subsequent trend	0.8	-1.4	0.8	-3.2
PS plans with high mean employer contributions				
Year of adoption	13.1***	10.7*	7.3*	10.0
Subsequent trend	4.4**	-0.3	2.9	-1.1*

For those reporting profit-sharing contribution as a percentage of participant payroll, the mean figure for each company was calculated. The median of these figures was 3.62 percent. A mean contribution less (greater) than 3.62 percent was designated as a "low" ("high") mean employer contribution.

NOTES: All regressions include controls for capital and labor ratios, adoption and presence of defined benefit plans and ESOPs, and union presence. The unpaired results (columns 1, 2, 3, 5) contain controls for broad industry trends and year effects. The paired results (columns 4, 6) are paired differences between profit-sharing and nonprofit-sharing companies within industry and year. Paired results could not be computed for size classes due to inadequate observations. For regression results, see appendix tables A3.5 and A3.6.

*Significantly different from zero at 90 percent confidence **95 percent confidence level ***99 percent confidence level.

shows significant effects of profit-sharing adoption of 6.9 percent and 5.8 percent.

The result that profit-sharing adoption is estimated to have the strongest productivity effects in the smallest size class is consistent with the above considerations about the 1/N problem and the relative ease of establishing a cooperative solution in a small work group. The result that smaller, but still highly significant, productivity effects are estimated in the largest size class is not consistent with these considerations. It may be that, as noted above, there are fixed costs in establishing and maintaining personnel policies conducive to a positive effect of profit sharing; therefore large companies may be more likely to have these in place or be able to adopt them along with profit sharing. In addition, the larger companies may have more experienced employee relations staffs. Finally, as discussed above, it may be that the existence of profit sharing creates a psychological stake in the company apart from the direct financial stake, so that increased employer size may not be a strong liability. It is possible that these productivity jumps may be traced to profit-sharing adoption. Nonetheless, given the minute contingency between employee effort and profit share in large companies, and the small proportion of fellow workers with whom an employee would interact, it is somewhat difficult to believe that adoption of profit sharing would cause productivity to increase by over 6 percent in such very large firms.

Does Size of the Profit Share Matter?

The size of the profit share in relation to other employee compensation should clearly be an important factor in the impact of profit sharing upon workplace relations and performance. A profit share that, for example, averages less than 1 percent of employee compensation is unlikely to be taken seriously by employees as an incentive for increased effort, monitoring, and cooperation with co-workers.

What size of profit share is necessary to improve employee performance is an open question. For this study, profit-sharing firms were asked to provide the size of the employer's profit-sharing contribution as a percentage of participant payroll for the years 1975-90. Of respondents, 71 firms provided three or more years' worth of data. The average contribution was calculated for each of these 71 firms. Of these 71 average contributions, the mean was 4.95 percent, the median was 3.63 percent, and the upper and lower quartiles were 1.98 percent and 7.35 percent.

To examine the relationship between productivity and bonus size, one could simply enter the yearly bonus size as an explanatory variable in the productivity equation. This approach, however, would be strongly plagued by a statistical bias of simultaneity (reflecting reverse causality): an increase in productivity will clearly lead to larger bonuses in a given year, whether or not the bonus size has any direct effect on productivity. What is desired is a measure of company *policy* regarding size of contributions—does the company intend profit shares to be a large chunk of employee compensation? To minimize the simultaneity bias, profit-sharing firms were divided into two groups: those with "high" and "low" *average* contributions (as percentages of payroll, with separate selection terms for these two groups). The cutoff between these two groups was defined as the median average contribution of 3.63 percent—i.e., a high-contribution firm was defined as one that provided, on average, profit-sharing contributions exceeding 3.63 percent of participants' payroll. By not focusing on each year's bonus size and by using separate selection terms for the two groups, the simultaneity bias is minimized, and the membership in high- or low-contribution groups comes closer to a measure of company policy on size of profit shares in relation to compensation.[48]

If profit sharing does positively affect productivity, the effect is clearly expected to be larger where it represents a higher percentage of pay. The results summarized in table 3.4 (based on estimates in appendix table A3.6) are consistent with this expectation. The adoption of a low-contribution plan is never estimated to have a significant association with productivity change, while the adoption of a high-contribution plan is estimated to have significant associations with 7 percent to 13 percent increases in productivity in columns 3 to 5 (and a nonsignificant 10 percent increase in column 6). A strong positive postadoption association with productivity growth is found in column 3, but not in the other columns (in fact, a significant negative trend is found in column 6).

Therefore the limited available data on size of profit-sharing contribution is consistent with the expectation that a policy of larger contributions will have more positive productivity effects. No significant effects were detected for either the adoption or presence of a low-contribution plan, and the signs of several of these estimates were negative. In contrast, the adoption effects were all large and positive for high-contribution plans.

Is Profit Sharing a Proxy for Other Company Policies?

A serious problem with nonexperimental data is that the variable of interest may be strongly correlated with, and may act as a proxy for, other variables that affect the observed outcome. Firms that adopt profit sharing may also adopt a variety of other policies designed to improve company performance. There are two fundamental ways in which these other policies may affect company performance, by having: (1) direct effects on performance, or (2) interactive effects with profit sharing.

If profit-sharing firms adopt other policies that have direct effects on performance but are not measured in the equation, profit sharing may act as a proxy for these variables and attract a positive significant estimate *even if* profit sharing itself has no effect on performance. (The estimated profit-sharing effect may be unduly high because of bias from the omitted variables.) In addition, profit sharing may be associated with differences in managerial quality, representing another possible omitted variable. This potential bias is a standard criticism of the positive results for profit sharing represented by the studies in table 3.1.

This section will address whether profit sharing is simply reflecting other company policies or management changes that may in fact be the important influences on productivity, while the following sections will address whether such policies *interact* with profit sharing to influence performance.

The use of longitudinal data to analyze yearly changes in productivity levels will automatically control for the effects of any company characteristics, such as constant high-quality management, that affect productivity levels but do not change over time. The obvious case in which managerial quality may not be constant is where there is a significant change in management personnel. Profit-sharing firms in this study were asked, "Was the profit-sharing plan adopted following a change in management personnel?" Of the 122 respondents, four (3.3 percent) answered affirmatively. This makes it highly unlikely that the profit-sharing adoption variable is measuring significant changes in managerial quality.

The policies identified here as being particularly likely to compete or interact with profit sharing are those that seek to increase involvement of the employee in the company by tapping employee ideas, opinions, and decisionmaking skills. There has been substantial experimentation with such policies over the 1970s and 1980s (see, e.g., Lawler, Ledford, and Mohrman 1989; and Eaton and Voos 1992). Such policies may improve company performance both directly—through making use of employee information and skills—and indirectly—by increasing employee identification with the company, which may reduce turnover and improve both quality and quantity of work.

Survey respondents were asked about the presence, age, and coverage of seven company policies. Two policies that solicit employee ideas and opinions are employee surveys and suggestion systems. Three policies that seek to change the structure of work are job enrichment, self-managed work teams, and employee involvement programs such as quality circles.[49] Gainsharing plans represent an alternative group incentive system, typically increasing employee involvement in production decisions and tying employee bonuses not to overall company performance but to more narrowly-defined group performance.[50] Finally, a formal policy of employment security attempts to increase employee identification with the company and willingness to share information.[51] The definitions provided to survey respondents of these seven policies were based on the General Accounting Office's 1987 survey of employee involvement efforts in Fortune 1000 firms. These definitions are presented in table 3.5, with the percentages of profit-sharing and non-profit-sharing firms who maintain these policies in table 1.3.[52]

Tests of the effects of the adoption and presence of these policies are presented in appendix table A3.8 (with descriptive statistics in appendix table A3.7).[53] Results are presented both with simple measures of

Table 3.5   Definitions of Personnel Policies

The term in capital letters is the one used in the tables presented here, followed by the term presented to survey respondents, and the definition made available to respondents. (Definitions are based largely upon the 1987 General Accounting Office survey of employee involvement in Fortune 1000 companies.)

SURVEY: Attitude survey feedback. Use of employee attitude survey results, not simply as an employee opinion poll, but rather as part of a larger problemsolving process in which survey data are used to encourage, structure, and measure the effectiveness of employee participation.

JOB ENRICHMENT: Job enrichment and redesign. Design of work that is intended to increase worker performance and job satisfaction by increasing skill variety, autonomy, significance and identity of the task, and performance feedback.

EMPLOYEE INVOLVEMENT: Employee involvement groups, such as Quality Circles or other formal committees. Structured type of employee participation groups in which groups of volunteers from a particular work area meet regularly to identify and suggest improvements to work-related problems. The goals are improved quality and performance: there is no direct reward, group problemsolving training is provided, and the groups' only power is to suggest changes to management.

AUTO. WORKTEAM: Self-managed work teams. Also termed autonomous work groups, semi-autonomous work groups, self-regulating work teams, or simply work teams. The work group (in some cases acting without a supervisor) is responsible for the whole product or service, and makes decisions about task assignments and work methods. The team may be responsible for its own support services such as maintenance, purchasing, and quality control, and may perform certain personnel functions such as hiring and firing team members and determining pay increases.

EMPLOYMENT SECURITY: Company policy designed to prevent layoffs.

SUGGESTING SYSTEM: Company system of soliciting employee suggestions for improved performance.

GAINSHARING: Productivity-related Group Bonuses. Plans based on a formula that shares some portion of gains in productivity, quality, cost effectiveness, or other performance indicators. The gains are shared in the form of bonuses with all employees in an organization (such as a plant). It typically includes a system of employee suggestion committees. It differs from profit sharing or an ESOP in that the basis of the formulas is some set of local performance measures, not company profits. Examples include the Scanlon Plan, the Improshare Plan, the Rucker Plan, and various custom-designed plans.

For each policy, survey respondents were asked about its presence and age, as well as percentage of corporate employees and (for profit-sharing companies) of profit-sharing participants who participate. The percentage figures were categorized as None (0 percent), Some (1-40 percent), About half (41-60 percent), Most (61-99 percent), or All (100 percent). "Proportion covered" for table 3.16, and columns 5-8 of tables 3.13 and 3.14, were computed from these five categories as, respectively, .00, .20, .50, .80, and 1.0.

each policy's existence (in columns 1-4), and with proportions of employees covered by each policy (in columns 5 to 8).

The results are not summarized in a separate table because they are so easily summarized in text: the profit-sharing estimates change negligibly with the addition of the other policy variables.[54] Estimates on the personnel policies are of interest in themselves. Across the eight columns, there are no estimates indicating a significant positive effect of adoption or presence of these seven policies. One negative estimate attains the standard level of significance at which sampling error is ruled out (adoption of job enrichment in column 4), but in the absence of a clear pattern this is very weak evidence.[55] There is no clear evidence of productivity effects for these individual policies.[56]

Does Information-Sharing Enhance Profit-Sharing Effects?

While sharing sensitive business information with employees may have positive or negative consequences for the firm (see, e.g., Kleiner and Bouillon 1988, 1991), it is commonly believed that profit-sharing plans have more positive effects when the companies make extra efforts to share information with employees. Such information-sharing is a plausible part of establishing and maintaining worker norms in the cooperative solution to the problem of diluted individual incentives.

Survey respondents were asked, "About how many corporation employees, excluding top management, are routinely provided with: a. Information about the company's overall operating results; b. Information on business plans and goals; and c. Information on competitors' relative performance?"[57] From this the approximate proportions of employees provided with such information were constructed.[58] As can be seen in table 1.3, profit-sharing companies, on average, provided more of this information to their employees (85.3 percent compared to 83.4 percent for operating results, 61.8 percent compared to 57.5 percent for business plans and goals, and 30.4 percent compared to 24.6 percent for competitors' performance), but none of the paired differences indicated that sampling error could be ruled out.

The key question examined in this section is whether information-sharing interacts with profit sharing in affecting company performance.[59] The three information-sharing variables are interacted with profit sharing and added to the standard productivity equations. The results, in appendix table A3.9, include profit-sharing adoption and presence without the interactions; therefore the interaction estimates represent productivity effects on top of the "main" (noninteracted) effect.[60]

As with the personnel policy results, a summary can easily be presented in text. Interactions of the first two types of information-sharing with profit sharing have no significant associations with productivity growth. The third type of information-sharing—on competitors' performance—has an intriguing interaction with profit-sharing adoption in significantly increasing sales per employee, but no significant relationship with value-added per employee. This is the type of information that is least likely to be shared with employees by any firms, and with which there is the largest association with profit sharing—as noted in table 1.3, the average percentage of employees provided with this information is 4.6 percent higher for profit-sharing than for non-profit-sharing firms. There is greater dispersion on this variable than on the first two types of information-sharing: of the firms that adopted profit sharing in the sample period, 96 percent shared each of the first two types of information with at least some employees, while only 70 percent shared information on competitors' performance with at least some employees. The results here provide some weak evidence that the productivity increases are greater for the profit-sharing adopters that share information with employees on competitors' performance. Given that this result is strongly significant in only one of the four estimates, and that the estimated effect sizes vary considerably, it should not be taken as strong evidence.[61]

The lack of strong evidence that sharing these three types of information enhances the effects of profit sharing can be interpreted in several ways. First, and most obviously, it may be that information-sharing does not enhance the effects of profit sharing. Second, it is possible that the information measured here is superfluous; the size of the profit share is an important signal of company performance, and there are many informal ways in which employees gain company performance information in their daily work (through news reports, union negotiations, existence and severity of layoffs, etc.). Third, it is clearly possible that more detailed measures of information sharing—including not only different types of information but also different mechanisms for its distribution—would produce different results.

Does Profit Sharing Interact with Other Personnel Policies?

Profit sharing may need to be combined with other personnel policies to create group cooperation for improved company performance. Theory suggests the need for other policies to counteract individual disincentives in a group incentive plan, and case study material often emphasizes the importance of combining profit sharing with such policies (see, e.g., Gross and Bacher 1993; Doherty, Nord, and McAdams 1989 for gainsharing case studies; more generally, see Huselid 1992 and Ichniowski 1992 on synergy among human resource policies). In general, the prescribed policies seek to tap the ideas and skills of employees, thereby increasing the involvement and identification of the employee in the workplace and company. The results of Fitzroy and Kraft (1987) support the idea that worker participation in decisions may enhance the productivity effects of profit sharing, while Quarrey and Rosen (1986), U.S. GAO (1987), and Rooney (1992) suggest that such participation may enhance the performance of ESOP companies.

Two types of data are used here to address the possibility of interactions between profit sharing and other policies. First, the seven personnel policies that were earlier analyzed as potential "omitted variables" in the productivity equations are tested for interactions with profit sharing in affecting performance. Second, profit-sharing companies were asked what other changes in personnel policies and compensation were made when profit sharing was adopted.

Profit-sharing companies were asked, for each of the seven personnel policies, what approximate percentage of the profit-sharing participants were covered by this policy. The mean percentages covered (including zeros for those without the policy) are presented in table 1.3 (e.g., among profit-sharing companies, an unweighted average of 21.6 percent of profit-sharing participants are covered by employee surveys). The proportion covered was interacted with the presence of both profit sharing and the personnel policy for each company in each year, and this was used to create variables for both the adoption and trend effects of combining profit sharing with a particular policy.[62] For example, the adoption of the interaction between employee surveys and profit sharing indicates that both were present in the given year, while at least one was not present in the preceding year. In addition to these interactions, the simple profit-sharing adoption and presence variables were included in the specifications.[63]

Results on personnel policy interactions with the profit-sharing variables are presented in appendix table A3.10. Once again, these are not separately summarized in a table because the bottom line is simple: there is very little support for the idea that these policies interact with profit sharing in affecting company performance. The simple (non-interacted) profit-sharing adoption estimates are similar in magnitude and significance levels to the results without personnel policy interactions, and the majority of estimates do not indicate that these policies add to, or subtract from, the main effect. Employee involvement is the only policy that may interact positively with profit sharing, since it shows one weakly significant estimate (in column 2) and the other estimates are all positive (in columns 1, 3, and 4, unlike the pattern for all other interactions).

Positive effects of such an interaction is consistent with case study material and prescriptive literature emphasizing the importance of drawing workers into decisionmaking, but the results here must be regarded as very weak. There are two negative estimates of adopting profit sharing with an employment security policy, probably indicating that these policies were adopted when the firms were undergoing financial stress.

A finding reported earlier is that the positive adoption effects of profit sharing are concentrated among the very smallest and very largest firms. What personnel policies were in effect in these firms at the time of adoption? A comparison revealed no strong differences among the different size classes, with the exception that employee involvement programs were somewhat more prevalent among the largest adopters.[64] This again suggests that the 1/N problem may be overcome in large companies through a combination with other policies to gain greater employee input; however, the general lack of differences in policies among firm sizes casts further doubt on the idea that these policies have important interactions with profit sharing.

The presence of error in measuring the age or substance of these policies will bias the estimates toward zero. If there were a "true" positive effect of the interaction of profit sharing with a particular policy, though, it is likely that the pattern of estimates would remain positive. This pattern remains positive only for the employee involvement estimates; none of the others are uniformly positive across all four estimates, suggesting it is unlikely that a true positive effect is being mismeasured.[65]

The second method for testing interactions between profit sharing and personnel policies relied on the survey question to profit-sharing respondents:

> When the profit-sharing plan was established, were any significant changes made in personnel policies or other compensation? (If yes: Please describe these changes.)

As shown in table 1.3, one-sixth (17.3 percent) of the profit-sharing respondents replied yes, one-fourth (26.0 percent) could not answer, and the remainder (56.7 percent) replied no.

The profit-sharing adoption and presence variables were interacted with two dummy variables indicating "yes" and "no" responses to the above question (excluding those who could not answer). The resulting variables were used in the productivity specifications in place of the standard profit-sharing variables, and the results are summarized in table 3.6.

Estimated productivity growth is higher for profit-sharing adoption when significant changes had been made in personnel policies or other compensation. When such changes were made, the initial productivity effect of profit sharing is estimated as 6.1 percent to 7.5 percent (all significantly different from zero at 90 percent level), while the corresponding estimates when such changes were not made were 0.8 percent to 3.7 percent (only two of which were significantly different from zero). All estimates for postadoption trends in productivity were estimated as positive for both groups, though were not strongly significant.

It appears that the productivity increase is higher when profit-sharing adoption is accompanied by other significant changes. What is the

Table 3.6 Summary Results on Significant Changes Accompanying Profit Sharing

Profit-sharing companies were asked, "When the profit-sharing plan was established, were any significant changes made in personnel policies or other compensation?" "Yes" and "no" answers are interacted with profit-sharing adoption and subsequent trend.

Productivity measure	Yearly growth in sales per employee		Yearly growth in value-added per employee	
	Unpaired (1)	Within-industry pairs (2)	Unpaired (3)	Within-industry pairs (4)
	Estimated productivity effects (percent)			
Significant changes made when profit sharing adopted				
Year of adoption	6.1**	7.5**	7.3***	7.5*
Subsequent trend	0.7	6.5*	1.0*	6.9*
Significant changes not made when profit sharing adopted				
Year of adoption	3.7**	2.2	3.5**	0.8
Subsequent trend	1.9	2.5	3.8	3.1

NOTES: All regressions include controls for capital and labor ratios, adoption and presence of defined benefit plans and ESOPs, and union presence. The unpaired results (columns 1 and 3) contain controls for broad industry trends and year effects. The paired results (columns 2 and 4) are paired differences between profit-sharing and nonprofit-sharing companies within industry and year. Based on regressions presented in appendix table A3.11.
*Significantly different from zero at 90 percent confidence level   **95 percent confidence level   ***99 percent confidence level.

nature of these other changes? The 37 open-ended answers that were solicited from the respondents were coded in the following categories:

Change in incentive plans
    1. Replaced a different incentive plan   7
    2. Added another incentive plan   2
    3. Combined or extended existing incentive plans   6
Changes in wages or benefits
    4. Replaced pension plan   2
    5. Established in lieu of wage increase   2
    6. Part of effort to reduce fixed costs   3
    7. Improvement in other benefit   1
    8. Technical changes in other benefits   6
    9. Part of labor negotiations   3
Other
    10. Part of new training program   1
    11. Part of new "working smarter" philosophy   1
    12. Company went public   1
    13. Company recovering from bankruptcy   1
    14. Part of a merger   1

This distribution of responses provides no clear pattern concerning the types of changes that may enhance the effectiveness of profit sharing. Changes in existing incentive plans were reported by 15 of the respondents (categories 1, 2, and 3 above). Changes in wages or benefits were reported by 17, with four of these changes representing unambiguous sacrifices by employees (categories 4 and 5). The combination of profit sharing with changes in noncompensation policies is clear only for the two companies in categories 10 and 11. While these responses provide a useful portrait of the circumstances under which profit sharing is adopted, there is no clear answer to the question of what types of policies may enhance the performance of profit sharing.

Summary and conclusions regarding the productivity theory will be presented in chapter 5.

NOTES

1. If worker effort is public knowledge, profit sharing that is proportionate to individual effort can produce excess incentives (Sen 1966; Israelsen 1980). For further discussion of alternatives under costly supervision, see Parsons (1986), Calvo (1987), Baker, Jensen, and Murphy (1988), and Lazear (1992).

2. See Lawler (1971) for a summary of studies showing the development of adversarial relations between system designers and employees when piece rate systems are put into place.

3. "[I]n the absence of any relationship between the success of the organization and the pay of individuals, an important part of the business experience for the individual is missing. Everything known about motivation clearly points out that it is greatest when people have both a psychological and a financial stake in the organization's success" (Lawler 1987: 85).

4. An additional perspective on the dilution of individual incentives through the 1/N problem concerns the perception of the actual performance-pay link. Brickley and Hevert (1991) use prospect theory to argue that employees may systematically overweight the likelihood that their actions will affect firm value. While this may mitigate the 1/N problem in small groups, it would seem less plausible in groups of thousands of employees.

5. Alchian and Demsetz mention the "public good" benefits of loyalty and "team spirit," but these play no role in their analysis.

6. This problem is in some respects parallel to the theorized disincentive for investment within a labor-managed firm (Furubotn and Pejovich 1970; summarized by Bonin and Putterman 1987). In such a firm, if workers cannot receive the capitalized value of the firm's investments upon leaving the firm, there will be a tendency to favor investments with a short-run payoff. Such a labor-managed firm may underinvest because the investment returns would be shared with future employees, while the capitalist profit-sharing firm may underinvest because the investment returns are shared with current employees.

7. If the higher labor quality can be traced to the profit-sharing plan, this may be a strong argument for individual firms to adopt profit sharing, though the advantage would clearly decline as other firms adopted profit sharing.

8. An employee's calculation of income risk would include not only the risk from variability of profit-sharing payments, but also the risk of layoff. If profit-sharing companies are less likely to close, or are otherwise less likely to lay workers off in the face of demand shocks (as predicted by the stability theory, to be explored in the following chapter), then risk-averse workers may instead be attracted to profit-sharing companies. For a discussion of compensation and risk, see Parsons (1986).

9. See Weitzman and Kruse (1990) for a summary of findings. For additional research findings see Profit Sharing Research Foundation (1989). For a more general review of employee attitudes under profit sharing, employee ownership, quality circles, and autonomous work groups, see Kelly and Kelly (1991).

10. Their regression controls for size, industry demand, percent labor costs, and unionism. The t-statistics on the profit-sharing variables were 1.4 and 1.6.

11. The authors note that average investor returns were significantly higher for the preadoption group than for other non-profit-sharing companies, and suggest that the "market may have anticipated a positive productivity effect" (though there is no information on when profit sharing was announced) (1990: 180).

12. Such as Cobb-Douglas, constant elasticity of substitution (CES), or translog functions.

13. This table is updated and adapted from table 4 in Weitzman and Kruse (1990). It does not include studies of productivity-gainsharing plans such as Scanlon and Rucker plans (Schuster

1983, 1984), and IMPROSHARE (Fein 1981, 1983; Globerson and Parsons 1987; Kaufman 1992). For gainsharing case studies see the meta-analysis in Bullock and Tubbs (1990), as well as Robertson and Osuorah (1991), Markham et al. (1992), Masternak (1991/92), Masternak and Ross (1992), Gowen (1990), and Hansen and Watson (1990). This review is based on all published studies that could be located in books or in economic, personnel, and business journals (using searches up through June 1993 of the Business Periodicals Index and the computerized databases ABI/INFORM, UNCOVER, ProQuest, and Business Dateline), and on unpublished studies made available by colleagues.

14. These studies used instrumental variable techniques to account for the endogeneity of profit-sharing status. Several studies used instrumental variables for the labor and/or capital stock, although not for profit sharing (numbers 1, 4, 18, and 25).

15. Only two negative coefficients have t-statistics lower than -2, as found by Carstensen, Gerlach, and Hubler (1992) in their estimates with industry controls, when they use profit share divided by profits in predicting value-added. The authors note that this measure is contaminated by the influence of productivity on the denominator of the measure, and the opposite result is obtained (with significant positive coefficients) when profit sharing is measured as profit share per employee.

16. Each of these coefficients have t-statistics greater than 2, indicating that there is less than a 5 percent chance that the true coefficient is zero and the estimate is due to random sampling error. The overall positive results are also reflected in the specifications with interactions and lagged values (see note at bottom of table 3.1).

17. Of the 26 studies, 16 had been or are being published.

18. Additional evidence comes from Smith (Forthcoming), who examines financial performance of Italian cooperatives and finds it to be higher among firms which stress production knowledge of employees, high quality products, and specialized corporate alliances.

19. Stock market reactions have often been studied in announcements of managerial compensation plans (see, e.g., Brickley, Bhagat, and Lease 1985, and Tehranian and Waeglenin 1985).

20. Standard and Poor's CompuStat reports labor expenses for less than one-fourth of the companies. Value-added is the value of final output minus the value of nonlabor inputs. CompuStat reports "cost of goods sold" which includes labor and rental expense as well as material inputs. Since labor and rental expense are part of value-added, these data were required for calculation of value-added as Sales - (cost of goods sold - labor costs - rental expense). Labor costs were imputed in the following way. Average compensation per employee for the industry was calculated from National Income and Product Accounts (NIPA) data. For the firms reporting labor costs, independent variables used to predict ln(total labor costs) in the firm in year t were the logarithm of average industry compensation in t and $t - 1$, logarithm of sales in t and $t - 1$, logarithm of employment in t and $t - 1$, and eight industry dummies. This regression used 3283 observations, and had an R-squared of .982. The coefficients on these variables were then used to predict labor costs in the firms for which labor costs were not reported. This number was used in the above equation for the calculation of value-added.

21. None of the t-statistics indicate statistical significance at even a 90 percent level. It is clearly possible that profit-sharing plans existed in 1975 that were terminated before the survey date and were therefore not recorded in this survey. Thus either the non-profit-sharing or profit-sharing groups may be misclassified as not having profit sharing in earlier years. While this introduces measurement error in the comparisons, it is not likely to produce any systematic biases. Data on terminated plans were not collected due to a substantial concern about the quality of the data. It is unusual for respondents to the phone survey to have been in their positions for more than a few years; therefore their direct knowledge about earlier-terminated plans would be sus-

pect, and a request to look up old records on terminated plans would have resulted in greatly diminished response rates.

22. These values represent trimmed means, where the highest 1 percent and lowest 1 percent of values have been excluded so that the means are not unduly influenced by these outliers.

23. A 1975 cut-off point was chosen for the comparisons since it allows a comparison of several preadoption and post- adoption values for the adopters.

24. Average yearly growth in the GNP deflator was 6.0 percent, and in the Consumer Price Index was 6.2 percent.

25. Though only the former difference is statistically significant at the 90 percent level.

26. For research on the productivity effects of ESOPs see Conte and Svejnar (1990), of pensions see Allen and Clark (1987) and Gustman and Mitchell (1992), and of unions see Hirsch (1991). All specifications account for the adoption and subsequent trend effects of defined benefit pensions and ESOPs, and the trend effects of unions. The variables representing defined benefit plans and ESOPs were constructed from the 1988 Form 5500 pension tapes, which include both the beginning year and the number of participants in these plans. The proportion covered by each plan is projected back to the beginning dates of the plans—an assumption which will result in some downward bias of the coefficients if there is mismeasurement of the true proportion covered, but is unlikely to produce systematic error. Companies were only asked about union status at the survey date; the gains from identifying changes in union status were felt to be very small.

27. Treatments of selection bias in economic studies include Heckman (1976, 1979, 1990), Maddala (1983), Heckman and Robb (1985), Manski (1989), and Heckman and Hotz (1989).

28. This is known as a selection-maturation interaction (Cook and Campbell 1979).

29. Referred to as an interaction between selection and history, or "local history" (Cook and Campbell 1979).

30. The survey did not ask about terminated plans and policies, due to substantial concern about biases and inaccuracies in reporting on benefits and policies that no longer exist (particularly if they were not terminated recently and the respondent may not have been with the company or in a position to know of the policy). Future survey data from these companies can, however, be used to create a more reliable database that includes terminated plans.

31. Taking all reported ages as accurate, the estimated adoption effects range from 2.3 percent to 4.1 percent (to be compared with row 1 of table 3.3). Removing plans with reported ages of 15 or 20 years produces a wider range of estimates: 3.0 percent to 5.5 percent (all statistically significant at p <.05).

32. The value of using panel data, which subtracts out constant firm factors that may affect productivity, is illustrated by comparing these results with simple cross-sectional estimates. Using the same explanatory variables specified as levels rather than as yearly changes, cross-sectional regressions for each year produce an average productivity difference of 6.0 percent between profit-sharing and non-profit- sharing firms, representing an upward bias due to the effect of constant firm factors.

33. For the paired results, the value of each variable for the non-profit-sharing firm was subtracted from the value for the profit-sharing firm, so that a positive value indicates that the profit-sharing firm exceeds its pair on this variable. This technique was also employed by Freeman and Kleiner (1990) in their study of union drives.

The sample size is substantially smaller for the paired regressions, primarily because each observation represents a pair of firms rather than a single firm.

34. This figure is based on the variables and samples used in regressions 1 to 4 of appendix table A3.2, but with separate dummy variables for each of the three preadoption and postadoption years.

35. The statistical regression threat to validity is that outliers will tend to return to mean values over time, and policies adopted when performance is especially high or low may have no role in the return to mean values. Such a threat is unlikely in this case, since the productivity jump is not returning the adopter to mean values, but is putting the adopter at a higher-than-predicted level which does not subsequently return to low levels. It is nonetheless possible that profit sharing was adopted along with other changes that keep productivity at high levels.

The regression threat is also discounted by the finding that the especially poor performers in year $t - 2$ did not have especially high productivity jumps in the adoption year; in fact, the adoption-year productivity increases were similar between those adopters above and below the median productivity change in $t - 2$.

Productivity changes in years $t - 2$ and $t - 1$ were used to explain profit-sharing adoption with the other independent variables in the specifications of chapter 2 and were never statistically significant predictors.

36. This could possibly indicate a "Hawthorne effect," in which changes in performance are due to the novelty of a new treatment rather than to its substance.

37. The basic productivity specifications were run without the profit-sharing variables, and the residuals were analyzed for years in which profit sharing was adopted. In the four specifications, the percentages of profit-sharing adopters with positive residuals were, respectively: 69.5 percent, 72.7 percent, 60.0 percent, and 68.2 percent. Of the adopters, the lower quartile of residuals at the time of adoption ranged from -1.1 percent to -3.7 percent, while the upper quartile ranged from 10.2 percent to 12.2 percent. In other words, approximately one-fourth of adopters had productivity increases exceeding 10 percent, while one-fourth had productivity changes worse than -2 percent.

The dispersion of the residual was equivalent between the entire sample and the observations representing profit-sharing adoption. For regression 1, the standard deviation of the residual for the entire sample was .101, and the inter-quartile range was .103 (from -.051 to .052), compared to figures of, respectively, .115 and .126 for the profit-sharing adoption observations. This technique has the advantage of providing a conservative estimate of the effect of profit sharing, since any collinearity between profit-sharing and other variables is attributed to the other variables. The mean residuals for profit-sharing adopters in their year of adoption were: 3.9 percent, 4.0 percent, 4.0 percent, and 3.4 percent.

38. Hirsch (1991) finds that slower growth in productivity among unionized firms in the 1970s and 1980s is mostly due to industry differences; he concludes that "we cannot reject the hypothesis that unions, on average, have little direct effect on productivity and productivity growth" (1991: 111).

39. Coefficients on the terms including labor will be somewhat biased if there is measurement error in employment levels, since employment also appears in the denominator in the dependent variable. This does not, however, bias the profit-sharing coefficients; results for the variables of interest were equivalent when employment levels were not in the denominator of the dependent variable.

40. This contrasts with my results for deferred plans in Kruse (1992), in which proportion covered resulted in higher coefficients than did simple dummies. This difference may be partly explained by the much smaller variance in proportion covered in this sample: the mean proportion covered in the plans analyzed in Kruse (1992) was 40.7 percent, with very few firms having 100 percent coverage, while the firms in this sample have a mean proportion covered of 78.5 percent and nearly half report 100 percent coverage. The smaller variance in this sample allows for less precise estimates; also, the data are based on self-reports rather than administrative records, introducing a downward bias due to measurement error. It is also possible that, in firms with less than total coverage, profit sharing has been extended to key employees whose participation is expected

to affect firm performance, so that total coverage is not needed for strong effects. Nonetheless this result is at variance with my past research and the expectation that, if the productivity theory is correct, broader coverage should produce larger effects.

41. See Wray (1993) for an overview of cash plans in the United States.

42. As in table 3.2, combination plans are included with cash plans since they both contain cash elements which provide immediate rewards to employees. The reported regressions include separate inverse Mill's selection terms for cash and deferred plans.

43. These magnitudes are lower than those from my previous analysis of deferred plans using administrative data and similar specifications (Kruse 1992), in which the estimated effects of plan adoption were in the range of .025 to .028. The results presented here are based on a smaller sample size, and are more prone to a downward bias from measurement error.

The difference between results for cash and deferred plans may reflect in part the stronger relation to profits among the former. For companies reporting the profit share as a percentage of participant payroll, the correlation between the change in profit share and the change in company profits per employee is .191 for cash plans (n = 203), and .063 for deferred plans (n = 281).

44. The sample sizes are, respectively, 105, 152, and 92. If contributions were closely tied only to profits/employees, the correlation should be close to 1.0. The existence of other factors in the formula, and the use of other measures of profitability (including thresholds that must be met before contributions are made), account for the low correlations. When profit margin rather than profits/employees is used, the correlation for percent-of- profits plans is .124, for discretionary plans is .096, and for percent-of-pay plans is .061.

45. The regressions contain separate inverse Mill's selection terms for each of the plan formulas. None of the coefficients on these terms was statistically significant.

46. None of the selection terms attracted significant coefficients. Without these terms, three regressions show estimated effects of 5.7 percent to 8.1 percent (significant at p <.10), with only one significant coefficient for discretionary plans (10.4 percent), and a significant negative coefficient for percent-of-pay plans (-6.6 percent).

47. As noted earlier, an advantage of discretionary plans to employers is that profits due wholly to other factors (e.g., new capital investment) can be excluded from consideration. A percent-of-profits plan has the risk of discouraging new capital investment, since some of the gains will have to be shared with employees.

48. As noted in appendix 3, the simultaneity bias can also be addressed through instrumental variables. As before, however, instrumental variables estimates produced implausibly large estimates of profit-sharing's effect.

49. For reviews of theory and research on worker participation experiments, see Gershenfeld (1987), and Levine and D'Andrea Tyson (1990). For their relationship to unions see Eaton (1992) and Eaton and Voos (1992). For research on higher-level employee participation in the form of workers' councils, see Freeman and Rogers (Forthcoming) and Addison, Kraft, and Wagner (Forthcoming).

50. For studies of gainsharing see the meta-analysis in Bullock and Tubbs (1990), as well as Schuster (1983 1984), Robertson and Osuorah (1991), Markham et al. (1992), Masternak (1991/92), Masternak and Ross (1992), Gowen (1990), and Hanson and Watson (1990).

51. For a general discussion of employment security strategies, see Dyer, Foltman, and Milkovich (1985). For discussion of the relationship between employment security and firm performance, see Osterman (1987) and Ichniowski (1992).

52. The percentages in table 1.3 exclude "don't know" responses. Those who responded "don't know" for the existence of the policies were: 2.4 percent for attitude survey feedback, 5.6 percent for suggestion system, 5.2 percent for job enrichment, 3.8 percent for employee involvement groups, 4.0 percent for self-managed workteams, 2.0 percent for employment security, and 4.2

percent for productivity-related group bonuses. Also, the percentages of those responding that they had the policy but did not know its age were, respectively, 3.6 percent, 6.6 percent, 4.0 percent, 4.4 percent, 3.0 percent, 1.2 percent, and 5.4 percent.

53. While the rates of response on the individual policy questions were high (see previous note), a substantial number of the respondents answered "don't know" on the existence or age of at least one of the policy questions. Excluding these respondents greatly diminishes the sample size for the regressions. Given the earlier-noted dispersion in outcomes for profit-sharing adopters, changes in the sample size can have substantial effects on the profit-sharing coefficients (with much higher or lower coefficients, due not to the added variables but to the change in sample). To maintain the sample size for comparability with previous results without providing bias to the reported coefficients, the "don't know" responses were coded as separate dummy variables for the regressions reported in appendix table A3.5. The coefficients on the "don't know" variables, which are not reported here, were uniformly small and statistically insignificant. An additional complication is that the reported ages of the personnel policies showed sharp spikes at 5 and 10 years, undoubtedly representing convenient focal points for those who are not sure about the age. Regressions were run treating these alternatively as valid values, and as missing values; results between the two sets of regressions were similar, and the latter results are presented here.

54. F-tests reveal that there were no significant changes in profit-sharing coefficients from the results presented in appendix table A3.2.

55. With 112 coefficients across the eight regressions, it is expected that about six would be randomly "significant" at the 95 percent level. In the absence of a clear pattern, very little importance should be attached to one "significant" coefficient.

56. Clearly the attempt to measure the effects of these policies is limited by error in measuring the age, coverage, or substance of the policies. To focus on respondents who would be more knowledgeable about these policies, the sample was restricted first to Vice-Presidents of Human Resources, and then expanded to include Directors of Employee Benefits, with a similar lack of noteworthy patterns for the personnel policy coefficients. Even among this more knowledgeable group, it is clear that the substance of the policies may differ greatly among firms, creating substantial measurement error.

These results cast doubt on the idea that any one of these policies in isolation can be expected to have an impact on productivity. However, it remains possible that some combination of these with other human resource policies may have consequences for firm performance. For evidence that such a combination may improve company performance, see Ichniowski (1990) and Huselid (1992). For discussion of how human resource policies can interact for better labor-management relations and higher performance, see Ichniowski (1992).

57. These questions were taken directly from the GAO survey of employee involvement in Fortune 1000 firms.

58. The answer options were "none" (0 percent), "some" (1-40 percent), "about half" (41-60 percent), "most" (61-99 percent) or "all" (100 percent). The proportions assigned to each of the five categories were, respectively, 0, .20, .50, .80, and 1.0. While the use of categories produces some measurement error, this should not be systematic error. Following the GAO survey, categories rather than "exact" percentages were used to encourage a higher response rate.

59. This is separate from the question of whether information- sharing itself affects company performance. Kleiner and Bouillon (1991) find that sharing of sensitive information is associated with lower profitability. The information- sharing measures in this study had no significant direct relationship with level or growth of either productivity measure.

60. When the three types of information-sharing are interacted with profit sharing and included in the same regression, there is obviously high multicollinearity among these variables, which raises standard errors and makes estimates less precise. To reduce the multicollinearity

bias, each information-sharing interaction was entered separately in regressions. The results were very similar.

61. To reduce multicollinearity, the interaction terms for the first two types of information were removed. The regression coefficients for the competitors' performance interaction term were .054, .150, .033, and .065, with the second of these being significant only at $p<.10$. Reducing multicollinearity therefore weakens the case that sharing this type of information has strong interaction effects with profit sharing.

62. The interaction was first-differenced, so that the "adoption" of this interaction may signify either the adoption of profit sharing when the policy is present, or the adoption of the policy when profit sharing is present (separate tests on these situations produced no noteworthy differences in results). The trend effect of the interaction simply indicates that both profit sharing and the policy were in effect in that year. Note that the personnel policy variable is defined as the proportion of profit-sharing participants covered by this policy at the time of the survey—the technique employed here extrapolates this proportion back through the time that both profit sharing and the policy were in effect. The measurement error thereby created will bias the coefficients toward zero. Concerns about data quality and response rate precluded asking for detail on personnel policy coverage of profit-sharing participants in earlier years.

63. In addition, tests were made using separate inverse Mill's ratios for the presence of each interaction in each year, but these provided consistently negligible coefficients and were dropped in the final specifications.

64. Among the adopters in the largest size class, an average of 24.5 percent of profit-sharing employees were covered by employee involvement programs which existed at the time of profit-sharing adoption, compared to 12.5 percent among adopters across the other size classes (and compared to 12.6 percent of employees covered in non-profit-sharing firms in the largest size class). Interaction terms revealed that the large adopters using employee involvement programs for profit-sharing employees did have larger productivity increases, but the statistical significance was weak for most of these interactions, and the estimated productivity increases were still significant for the adopters that did not use employee involvement.

65. The multicollinearity of these variables will increase the standard errors of the coefficients. To reduce multicollinearity, the interactions were entered individually in the specifications, and the results were very similar.

4

The Stability Theory

Economic instability is a problem of modern capitalist economies. While simple neoclassical economic models predict that market economies will always be at or close to full employment of all resources, underutilization of resources in market-based economies has been apparent both in business cycles and in more severe episodes such as the 1930s depression. A major aim of government economic policies in Western economies in the twentieth century has been to stabilize the economy and avoid the economic and social costs of unemployment. A variety of policies have been employed for this purpose, ranging from broad monetary and fiscal stimuli to labor market policies such as unemployment compensation and support for job training.

A key element of the simple economic models that predict full employment is mobility and price flexibility for all factors, including labor. If there are unemployed workers, they should be able to bid down wages until all are employed. If the unemployment is prolonged, one culprit may be "sticky wages" that do not decrease to encourage additional hiring.[1] According to this logic, forms of compensation that provide downward flexibility—such as profit sharing—should encourage employers to retain and hire workers. This flexibility has been one of the arguments for profit sharing.[2] Downward flexibility in wages was, though, not part of the "Keynesian revolution" in economic policy that developed in the 1930s depression—Keynes in fact warned that wage decreases could work against economic recovery by decreasing aggregate purchasing power (1964: 257-71).

Profit sharing may have stabilizing potential apart from downward flexibility in compensation. Martin Weitzman developed the theory of the "share economy," in which widespread use of profit sharing would help inoculate the economy against instability and unemployment (1983, 1984, 1985, 1986). The key element of this theory is that firms will essentially ignore the profit share when making employment decisions in the short run—rather, they will base such decisions only upon the fixed wage that must be paid to each worker. The conclusion is that firms with substantial profit sharing will not only have a strong incentive to retain workers when business shocks occur, but also an incentive in equilibrium to snatch up any unemployed workers who may appear in the labor market.

This theory received wide attention in the business press and academic publications and conventions in the 1980s. After reviewing the theory and several objections, this chapter will review existing empirical work and present new evidence.

The fundamentals of this theory will be described here, with a fuller explanation in appendix 4. Employment decisions of firms are based on the value of the worker's output in relation to the cost of the worker. A profit-maximizing firm will employ labor up to the point where the value of the last labor hour (the marginal revenue product) is no less than the wage that must be paid. For a fixed-wage firm with a wage of $10/hour (representing the marginal cost of a labor hour), a firm will employ such labor only if the value of the worker's output exceeds $10/hour.[3] When a negative business shock reduces the value of the worker's output below $10/hour, workers will be laid off or their hours reduced.

The stability theory of profit sharing posits that the view of labor's cost is different in a profit-sharing firm. A profit-maximizing firm with a profit-sharing plan is interested in retaining and hiring workers as long as the value of the worker's output exceeds the base wage, rather than the worker's total remuneration (base wage plus profit share). The profit share is essentially ignored by the employer when making the employment decision, since profits are maximized by employing workers whenever the value of their output exceeds the base wage. This can be seen through the following example. Say that workers are paid a base wage of $9 per hour, and the employer pays 25 percent of profits to the workers representing, on average, an extra $1 per hour in profit share for each worker (so that average pay is $10 per hour). Initially, the company's product demand is high enough that the value of each labor hour is at least $10/hour. If the company's product demand drops so that the value of the last labor hour is only $9.60, a firm that paid a wage of $10 per hour would lay some workers off, or reduce hours. But the profit-sharing firm would retain workers since the last labor hour still contributes $.60 to profits (i.e., $9.60 minus the $9 base wage, with 15 cents of the difference going to workers under the profit-sharing plan). Because of the reduced product demand, both the company and the workers are earning fewer profits than previously, but employment has remained stable.

The same incentive that impels the firm to retain workers in bad times will also cause it to look hard for workers during normal times. Under the example here, while a fixed-wage firm paying $10/hour will hire new workers only if the value of their output exceeds $10/hour, a profit-sharing firm will want to hire new workers if the value of their output exceeds $9/hour. Profit-sharing firms will have this incentive in the short run, but such excessive hiring will not be possible in the long run. While employers ignore the profit share in their short-run employment decisions, workers do not. As more workers are hired, the profit share established by the employer must be divided among a larger number of workers, decreasing its value to any one worker. Workers base their labor supply decisions not on the base wage, but on total compensation. When the total compensation falls below the market level, profit-sharing firms will have difficulty attracting and retaining workers. These firms in the long run will adjust their base wage and profit share so that the expected total compensation paid to workers will equal the value of the last worker's output, but the firms maintain an incentive in the short run to hire any worker as long as the worker's output exceeds the base wage.

The different incentives for fixed-wage and profit-sharing firms are illustrated in figure 4.1 (adapted from Nordhaus 1986). The curve labeled Demand represents the value of worker output from an additional labor hour (the marginal revenue product, or MRP, which is assumed to be the same in the two types of firms). A conventional fixed-wage firm, in the top left diagram, will hire workers up to the point where the MRP equals the fixed wage, with L_0 workers hired. Compare this with a profit-sharing firm, in the top right diagram, which has the same average compensation, but pays half of this in a base wage and half as a profit share. The demand curve is identical, and the profit-sharing firm has an incentive to operate at point B, where the MRP equals the base wage and L_1 workers are hired.[4] Under full employment, however, the firm must operate at point A, with L_0 workers, due to the lack of labor availability when compensation is below the market level. While the profit-sharing firm has no incentive in equilibrium to change the compensation parameters, it would like to hire more labor at the current compensation parameters.

Figure 4.1
Employment Incentives for Fixed-Wage and Profit-Sharing Firms

Labor Demand in Equilibrium

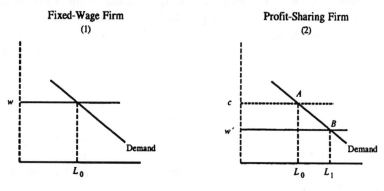

Labor Demand Under Negative Demand Shock

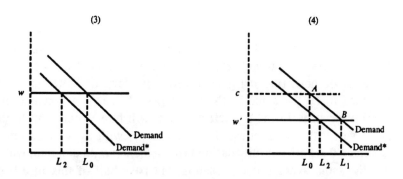

L_0 = initial employment levels
L_1 = desired employment by profit-sharing firm
L_2 = desired employment levels after negative shock
Demand = labor demand curve (marginal revenue product of labor)
Demand* = new labor demand curve after decline in product demand
w = wage in a fixed-wage firm
w' = base wage in a profit-sharing firm
c = total compensation in a profit-sharing firm

This incentive to hire more workers is the driving force in the share economy theory. If new workers enter the labor market, the fixed-wage firm would be indifferent about hiring them until the new workers could bid wages down sufficiently. However, the profit-sharing firm, desiring more than L_0 workers, would quickly snatch them up:

> A share system looks very much like a labor-shortage economy. Share firms ever hungry for labor are always on the prowl—cruising around like vacuum cleaners on wheels, searching in nooks and crannies for extra workers to pull in at existing compensation parameter values (Weitzman 1984: 98-9).

Therefore, in full-employment equilibrium, compensation and employment levels of the two types of firms are similar. The behavioral differences occur when there is reduced demand for the company's products (shifting the labor demand curve inward). A key result of this theory is that profit sharing induces greater employment and output stability than does a system with short-run fixed wages. If wages remain fixed, a negative demand shock (shifting the labor demand curve inward to Demand* in the bottom two diagrams of figure 4.1) leads to layoffs in a fixed-wage firm, with a resulting employment level of L_2 (in the bottom left diagram). However, the similar shock does not lead to layoffs in a profit-sharing firm, where the new desired L_2 is still greater than the old L_1. Layoffs will occur only if the new L_2 is less than the old L_0, and even then they will be smaller than layoffs by the fixed-wage firm. Employee compensation in the profit-sharing firm is decreased, but this decrease is not driving the incentive to retain workers; rather, the lower fixed cost of labor hours perceived by the firm is driving this incentive.

While this theory predicts that profit sharing will be associated with fewer layoffs, one must also consider voluntary labor turnover. By decreasing employee compensation, a negative demand shock may cause workers to seek work elsewhere or drop out of the labor force. In the case of an idiosyncratic demand shock that affects only one or a few firms, the short-run employment change is likely to be less in a profit-sharing firm than in a fixed-wage firm. Due to the lowered compensation in the affected firm, some workers will seek work elsewhere at the market compensation level, and the firm's compensation level will gradually increase to the market level as workers leave and the firm adjusts its base wage or profit-sharing rule. It is likely that voluntary turnover will occur more slowly than would layoffs (due to worker mobility and information costs), so that the short-run change in employment is likely to be less for profit-sharing firms. (The adjustment path of employment and compensation also depends on the speed of readjustment of pay parameters.)

In the case of a general negative demand shock, the short-run employment changes are also likely to be smaller for profit-sharing firms. As explained above, the profit-sharing firms are likely to have fewer or no layoffs. In the extreme case of an equal demand shock among all firms in a share economy, the decrease in average compensation would be the same across all firms, and there would be no incentive for workers to voluntarily switch firms (although some may leave the labor force). In the case of an unequal demand shock, however, workers will choose to switch from the harder-hit firms to the firms that are less hard hit, due to the relatively higher average compensation in the latter. The former will experience an employment decrease, and the latter an employment increase, with near-full employment being maintained. For the individual firm, any decrease in employment under profit sharing is likely to be less than under the wage system since there will be fewer layoffs in the former, and the lowered average compensation in the former reduces the extent to which workers can gain through voluntary job-switching. (Again, the timing of the change would depend on the speed of turnover and readjustment of pay parameters.)

How do the systems respond to a positive demand shock? In the case of a positive demand shock starting from full employment, the behavior would be similar. Additional hiring by any type of firm is only possible if employee compensation is increased, luring new workers into the workforce. Intuitively, a positive demand shock creates a temporary excess demand for labor in a fixed-wage economy to match the permanent excess demand for labor in a profit-sharing economy, so that the employment behavior is similar. If the positive demand shock represented a recovery from a previous negative demand shock, the theory's prediction is that profit-sharing firms would hire back fewer workers than would fixed-wage firms, simply because profit-sharing firms laid off fewer to begin with.

The stability theory therefore predicts that a profit-sharing economy will have more employment stability with negative shocks and recovery from negative shocks than will a fixed-wage economy, and similar behavior under new positive shocks. In a mixed profit-sharing/fixed-wage economy this conclusion should remain true, since the microeconomic incentives for each type of firm remain the same. The issue is complicated by the possibility that, given a general negative demand shock, some workers may leave profit-sharing firms to search for jobs at the fixed-wage firms that maintain higher compensation in the short run; this would be mitigated, however, by the increased unemployment from the fixed-wage firm layoffs. Also, in this situation a profit-sharing firm may be more likely to see an employment increase, since it would stand willing to hire the workers laid off by the fixed-wage firms.

This theory has engendered a substantial amount of debate. There have been five major objections. First, employed workers will resist the hiring of new workers, since the pay of employed workers would be decreased (Summers 1986). Second, as mentioned in chapter 3, employers may be reluctant to invest in new capital since some of the resulting profits would have to be shared with workers (Summers 1986; Estrin, Jones, and Svejnar 1987). Third, if labor productivity depends on worker compensation, as predicted by some efficiency wage theories, the excess demand for labor property would be lost since hiring new workers would lower the productivity of all workers (Levine 1987, 1989). Fourth, if tax incentives are granted for profit sharing, employers and employees may design "cosmetic" schemes to gain tax advantages without the desirable properties of "true" profit-sharing (Estrin, Jones, and Svejnar 1987). Finally, in full-employment equilibrium firms may regard average compensation as the cost of an extra labor hour (due to the labor supply constraint), which would eliminate excess demand for labor (Nordhaus 1988). (For responses to several of these criticisms see Weitzman 1986 and 1988.)[5]

There are two key propositions that emerge from the theory of the share economy:

1. Firms do not view profit-sharing payments as part of the short-run marginal cost of labor in making their employment decisions; and

2. Firms that pay part of their compensation in the form of profit shares will have greater employment stability than non-profit-

sharing firms, particularly with regard to negative demand shocks.

Prior Research

Research on these two propositions of the stability theory is not as extensive as research on the productivity theory. The fifteen empirical studies are summarized in table 4.1.[6] In the studies that use firm or aggregate data (except Gerhart 1991; and Kraft 1991), the level or change in employment is used as the dependent variable. Tests of proposition 1 have used the profit-sharing bonus/wage ratio (B/W) as an explanatory variable, whereas tests of proposition 2 have used the simple existence of profit sharing, or percent of workers covered, as explanatory variables.

Proposition 1, that profit shares are not viewed as part of the marginal cost of employing labor, has been addressed in two studies with aggregate data on the Japanese bonus system (with favorable evidence provided by Freeman and Weitzman 1987, and unfavorable evidence from Estrin, Grout, and Wadhwani 1987). Also, six studies have employed firm-level datasets from Great Britain, France, and the United States (with favorable evidence from Bradley, Estrin, and Taylor 1990; Estrin and Wilson 1989; and Kruse 1991b; unfavorable evidence from Wadhwani and Wall 1990; and Fitzroy and Vaughan-Whitehead 1989; and mixed evidence from Jones and Pliskin (1991a).

Proposition 2, that profit-sharing firms will have greater stability, has been addressed in nine studies. Bell and Neumark (1993) analyze profit sharing in U.S. union contracts, finding that the adoption of a profit-sharing provision is associated with higher employment growth and lower variability than previously, though the possibility of no change in behavior cannot be rejected. Chelius and Smith (1990) find that in response to sales decreases, U.S. profit-sharing small businesses have smaller employment decreases than do comparable non-profit-sharing firms. Also, they find that workers who were in a profit-sharing plan were less likely to report having been laid off in the previous year, controlling for individual characteristics and industry employment trends. Kraft (1991) finds that West German firms with profit-sharing

Table 4.1 Profit Sharing and Employment Stability Studies

Study	Data source	Unit of analysis	N	Time period	Profit-sharing measures	Main results
Disaggregated data						
Bell and Neumark 1993	U.S. publicly traded firms with union contracts	Firm	204	1978-87	Dummy for PS negotiated in union contract	Weakly favorable: adoption of PS in union contract associated with higher employment growth and lower employment variability, though effects not statistically significant
Bradley and Estrin 1990	Large British retail chains (one with PS)	Firm	5	1971-85 (balanced)	PS dummy and B/W	Mixed: PS firm had higher employment than others, and E/W positively related to employment changes, but similar employment changes over the business cycle
	(1) U.S. small businesses	Firm	2997	1987	PS dummy and B/W (cash and deferred plans)	Generally favorable: PS firms have smaller employment decreases when sales decline; result is stronger for PS dummy than for B/W
Chelius and Smith 1990	(2) Quality of Employment Survey	Persons	404	1977	PS dummy	Favorable: workers in PS plans were less likely to be laid off in previous year
Estrin and Wilson 1989	British firms in metalworking and engineering	Firm	52	1978-82 (balanced)	PS dummy and B/W	Generally favorable: authors reject hypothesis that PS payments are part of the marginal cost of labor

Study	Data source	Unit of analysis	n	Time period	Profit-sharing measures	Main results
Finseth 1988	U.S. publicly traded firms in manufacturing	Firm	132	1971-85 (balanced)	PS dummy and B/W (both cash and deferred plans)	Mixed: B/W more responsive than W to changes in profits, mixed results on stability (PS increases employment when profits/L is used as demand measure)
Fitzroy and Vaughan-Whitehead 1989	French manufacturing firms	Firm	116	1983-85 (balanced)	PS dummy and profit share per worker	Mixed: profit share per worker negatively related to employment, but cash PS firms maintain higher employment in downturn
Florkowski 1991	U.S. publicly traded firms	Firm	516	1971-87 (balanced)	PS dummy	Mixed: pre/post comparisons for profit-sharing adopters found greater postadoption stability only in 5- and 6-year comparisons
Gerhart 1991	Exempt employees, U.S. business units	Firm	156	1981-85 (unbalanced)	B/W, net of human capital and job factors	Favorable: higher B/W associated with lower variability of exempt employment, controlling for variability of firm performance
Jones and Pliskin 1989	British firms in printing, footwear, and clothing	Firm	127	1890-1975 (unbalanced)	PS dummy and B/W	Mixed: PS dummy associated with lower employment, but B/W coefficient sensitive to whether measures of worker part. are included
Kraft 1991	West German firms	Firm	62	1977, 1979	PS dummy	Favorable: PS firms had lower dismissal rate

Study	Data	Level	Period	Measure	Findings
Kruse 1991a	U.S. publicly traded firms	Firm	1383 1971-85 (balanced)	PS dummy, and percent of workers covered (deferred plans)	Generally favorable: PS associated with more stability in the face of negative demand shocks in manufacturing, but not in nonmanufacturing
Kruse 1991b	U.S. publicly traded firms	Firm	568 1980-86 (unbalanced)	B/W	Generally favorable: PS payments, unlike wages and defined benefit payments, do not appear to be treated as part of marginal cost of labor
Wadhwani and Wall 1990	British publicly traded firms	Firm	101 1972-82 (balanced)	PS dummy and B/W	Unfavorable: Both PS measures statistically insignificant, but magnitudes indicate B/W depresses employment more than wages do
Aggregate data					
Estrin, Grout, and Wadhwani 1987	Japanese aggregate data	Aggregate economy	1959-83	B/W	Unfavorable: wages and bonuses have slightly positive, insignificant coefficients, when controlling for capital and not output (in contrast to Freeman and Weitzman)
Freeman and Weitzman 1987	Japanese aggregate and industry-level data	Aggregate economy and manuf.	1959-83	B/W	Favorable: Bonus appears to have profit-sharing components, and unlike wages, relates positively to employment (controlling for output changes)

NOTES: PS = profit sharing, B/W = profit-sharing bonus/wage, W = wage.

plans in 1977 and 1979 had lower dismissal rates. Mixed evidence is provided by Finseth (1988), using a sample of U.S. publicly traded manufacturing firms, while unfavorable evidence is provided by Bradley, Estrin, and Taylor (1990), who study one British profit-sharing firm relative to four competitors. Smaller employment decreases in economic downturns were detected by Fitzroy and Vaughan-Whitehead (1989) for French firms with cash profit-sharing plans. Looking at employment changes in relation to aggregate and industry measures of economic activity, reveals a similar pattern of smaller decreases during downturns (Kruse 1991a) for U.S. publicly traded manufacturing firms, although not for nonmanufacturing firms. This data source was examined (using a repeated ANOVA technique) by Florkowski (1991), comparing firm stability before and after the adoption of a deferred profit-sharing plan; his findings were that greater postadoption stability was detected only for the five- and six-year comparisons, concentrated among firms that adopted profit-sharing between the two recessions of the period. Finally, Gerhart (1991) used data on exempt employees from 156 business units over the 1981-85 period. Organizations that had a higher average ratio of bonus to base pay for exempt employees had lower variability for exempt employment (controlling for variability in profits, sales, total assets, and stockholders' equity).

Prior research produces no clear conclusion on the relationship of employment and profit sharing. While the productivity theory lends itself to fairly standard tests using a production function, there has been a much greater variety of techniques used to examine the stability theory. Almost all of the studies that directly measure stability find some evidence of profit sharing being associated with greater stability, though the studies on how the profit share is treated in employment decisions are more mixed. Whether these differences in employment behavior are in fact due to profit sharing, or to other company characteristics, is a key question.

Does Profit Sharing Imply Lower Wages?

The driving force behind the share economy theory is that the perceived short-run cost of labor is lower for profit-sharing firms than for fixed-wage firms—in other words, profit sharing substitutes for a portion of fixed wages and benefits. If, however, the profit share is simply added to the fixed wages and benefits—i.e., it is simply "gravy"—no employment benefits would be predicted. This is complicated somewhat by higher pay which may result from higher company productivity, if the productivity theory applies. As will be discussed later, the profit share is only considered "gravy" if it is added to regular pay for the same level of employee performance; if however, employee performance is higher, then the profit share may substitute for regular pay in compensating the higher performance (so that the stability theory may still apply).

There are very few studies on the relative earnings of profit-sharing participants. Mitchell, Lewin, and Lawler (1990) use a 1974 compensation survey by the Bureau of Labor Statistics, and find that total compensation per hour and wage per hour are higher in firms with profit-sharing bonus payments.[7] In a 1988 survey, the U.S. Chamber of Commerce (1989) found similar results for nonmanufacturing firms, but not for manufacturing firms. For nonmanufacturing firms, compensation other than the profit share (adjusted for industry differences) averaged $14.06 for profit-sharing firms and $13.53 for non-profit-sharing firms. In contrast, excluding the profit share, manufacturing profit-sharing firms had average compensation of $14.89, compared to $15.08 for non-profit-sharing firms.[8] This would imply potentially stabilizing effects of profit sharing in manufacturing but not in nonmanufacturing.

Limited evidence on the substitution between profit sharing and other wages and benefits comes from union contracts. Mitchell, Lewin, and Lawler document the extent of profit sharing in concession bargaining: 36 percent of the U.S. union contracts with profit-sharing provisions in the 1981-88 period included first-year wage decreases, while only 14 percent of contracts without profit sharing involved first-year wage decreases.[9] Bell and Neumark (1993) found that, among manufacturing workers covered by negotiated contracts that included profit sharing in the 1979-88 period, over half of the workers also had wage concessions in 1982, 1983, and 1986, but not in other years.[10] Subsequent to adoption of contracts with profit sharing, they find that labor costs grew more slowly relative both to industry trends and preadoption firm trends. The association with concessions has clearly worsened the image of profit sharing in the eyes of unionists.[11] Finally, limited evidence from the United Kingdom and Germany goes against the idea of a trade-off between profit sharing and other pay. Average pay in British engineering and metalworking firms, excluding the profit share, was higher in profit-sharing firms for four of the five years between 1978 and 1982 (Estrin and Wilson 1989). Similarly, German evidence indicates that profit sharing is associated with higher individual wages (Hart and Hubler 1991; Hubler 1993) and higher average pay in manufacturing firms (Carstensen, Gerlach, and Hubler 1992).

The relative pay of profit-sharing companies is examined here in several different ways. To adjust for industry differences, each company's average compensation was divided by its industry average compensation.[12] Because fewer than half of the firms with public stock report their total labor expenses, the calculations of average compensation per worker are based on a substantially restricted sample. Due to the small sample size, for most of the comparisons in this section it is not possible to rule out random sampling error; the results are presented simply as indicative, without any strong claims about compensation patterns in profit-sharing firms.

Table 4.2 examines just those firms reporting both labor expenses and profit share in the 1975-90 period (number of firms = 30, with 254 observations). Including the profit share, total compensation was slightly higher than industry averages among all profit-sharing companies (indicated by both the mean and median values), while excluding the profit share leads to compensation slightly below the industry average.[13] Separate computations for the manufacturing and nonmanufacturing companies indicate that the average compensation levels (both with and without profit share) for profit-sharing firms are lower than industry averages for manufacturing firms, but higher for nonmanufacturing firms.

Yearly growth in average compensation (relative to the industry) is presented on the right side of table 4.2. There it can be seen that the growth levels of these companies were slightly lower than industry averages: within these profit-sharing companies, mean yearly growth of all compensation lagged 0.03 percent behind industry averages, while mean yearly growth of compensation excluding the profit share lagged 0.10 percent behind industry averages.

Table 4.2   Compensation in Profit-Sharing Companies, With and Without Profit Share, as Percent of Industry Average Compensation

Sample: 30 companies reporting both profit share and labor expenses within 1975-90. All figures are on per employee basis.

	Levels				Yearly growth			
	Median (%)	Mean (%)	(s.d.)	N	Median (%)	Mean (%)	(s.d.)	n
All compensation	102.7	103.8	(25.4)	254	-0.20	-0.03	(5.7)	216
Excluding profit share	97.3	97.6	(22.2)	254	-0.26	-0.10	(5.4)	216

NOTES: Compensation is calculated as a percentage of industry average compensation per employee, for each year, from the National Income and Product Accounts. The upper and lower 1 percent of the levels and growth variables have been trimmed.

A different approach is taken in table 4.3, which includes all firms reporting labor expenses in any year of the period (not just those reporting the profit share).[14] The levels and growth of compensation are reported for three groups: non-profit-sharing companies, "old" profit-sharing companies (in which profit sharing was adopted prior to 1975), and "new" profit-sharing companies (in which profit sharing was adopted in 1975 or later). For the new profit-sharing companies, figures are presented for preadoption, year before adoption, year of adoption, and postadoption (only for companies that report labor expenses both before and after adoption). This enables one to examine the possibility that high-compensation firms, or firms with faster growth in compensation, were more or less likely to adopt profit sharing.

A striking finding from table 4.3 is that the old profit-sharing (old PS) firms had higher levels of compensation than did either the non-profit-sharing (non-PS) or post-1975 adopter (new PS) firms. Mean compensation for the old PS firms was 108.2 percent of the industry average across the entire period (line 5), compared to 95.1 percent for the non-PS firms (line 4), and 98.7 percent for preadoption and 96.3 percent for postadoption for the new PS firms (lines 6 and 9). The difference between average preadoption and postadoption compensation is reported on line 10, where the mean of 0.9 percent and median of 1.9 percent indicates that total compensation (relative to industry averages) rose slightly after adoption.[15] Given that this slight rise in total

Table 4.3 Levels and Growth of Compensation as Percent of Industry Average

	Levels				Yearly growth			
	Mean	(s.d.)	Median	n	Mean	(s.d.)	Median	n
1991								
1. Non-PS	100.5	(22.0)	97.6	56	0.4	(4.7)	0.8	53
2. Pre-1975 adopters	109.2	(26.6)	104.5	18	-2.3	(6.2)	-1.6	18
3. Post-1975 adopters	100.9	(16.2)	100.4	23	0.3	(4.1)	0.4	21
Entire period								
4. Non-PS	95.1	(20.3)	92.8	2014	0.3	(5.2)	0.0	1817
5. Pre-1975 adopters	108.2	(29.5)	103.3	651	0.4	(6.2)	0.6	579
Post-1975 adopters								
6. Preadoption	98.7	(18.1)	98.8	397	0.4	(5.5)	0.4	354
7. Prior year	97.8	(17.0)	93.3	33	0.1	(6.3)	0.1	32
8. Adoption year	97.9	(17.1)	97.2	34	-0.1	(6.1)	0.2	33
9. Postadoption	96.3	(14.9)	95.7	213	0.4	(5.2)	0.5	204
10. Difference between average pre- and postadoption	0.9	(10.4)	1.9	42	0.2	(3.5)	0.2	35

NOTES: Compensation is calculated as a percentage of industry average compensation per employee, for each year, from the National Income and Product Accounts. The upper and lower 1 percent of the compensation levels and growth variables have been trimmed. PS = profit sharing.

compensation is less than the average value of profit sharing for this sample (the mean and median profit shares are approximately 3.5 percent of payroll), it appears that at least some of the profit share is coming at the expense of existing compensation for the post-1975 adopters. For the old PS firms, the much higher mean and median compensation levels makes it appear that profit sharing may simply be added on to existing compensation.

There appears to be very little difference in average compensation growth among the three groups of firms. The old PS firms had mean growth of compensation exceeding industry growth by 0.4 percent per year (line 5), compared to 0.3 percent per year for the non-PS firms (line 4). For the adopters, the preadoption and postadoption growth means were 0.4 percent per year (lines 6 and 9), although mean compensation growth in the adoption year and prior year was lower (lines 7 and 8), possibly indicating that profit sharing was adopted during times of financial stress.

Therefore there may be a fundamental difference between old and new PS firms: the old PS firms appear to pay better than industry averages, while the new PS firms do not.

Pay levels are obviously subject to many influences. Estimates were made of the relationship of profit sharing to 1991 compensation and to compensation growth over the full period, after controlling for the effects of unionization, defined benefit plans, and ESOPs.[16] A summary of key results is presented in table 4.4 (based on estimates presented in appendix table A4.1). The results are similar to those presented in table 4.3. Relative to non-profit-sharing companies, the presence of old profit sharing is associated with 11-14 percent higher compensation in 1991 (similar to table 4.3), while the presence of new profit sharing is associated with 7-9 percent lower compensation (unlike the pattern from table 4.3). Unionization of the workforce is associated with higher levels of compensation (consistent with the large literature surveyed by Lewis (1986), but this effect depends on whether a majority of union members are covered by profit sharing. If not, the union wage effect (for average union coverage) is 9.0 percent. However, if a majority of union members is covered by profit sharing, the union wage effect is only 2.0 percent. It is likely that this largely reflects the adoption of profit sharing in exchange for union wage and benefit concessions in the early and mid-1980s.[17]

Table 4.4 Summary Results on Compensation and Profit Sharing

Based on regressions presented in appendix table A4.1. Compensation is measured as the company's labor expenses per employee, which is divided by the industry's average compensation per employee (calculated from National Income and Product Accounts data). Controls in regressions include defined benefit plans and ESOPs.

1991 compensation levels

Estimated difference in 1991 compensation associated with	
Presence of pre-1975 PS[a]	11.3% to 13.8%
Presence of post-1975 PS[a]	-9.2% to -7.1%
Average proportion unionized	
If majority of union members are covered by PS[b]	2.0%
If majority of union members are not covered by PS[b]	9.0%
Estimated difference in 1991 nonpension compensation associated with	
Presence of cash/combination PS plan	2.5% to 6.1%
Presence of deferred PS plan[a]	-4.5& to -4.6%
Average proportion unionized	
If majority of union members are covered by PS[b]	-3.1%
If majority of union members are not covered by PS[b]	5.7%

Yearly compensation growth

Estimated difference in yearly compensation growth associated with	
Presence of pre-1975 PS[a]	-0.1%
Post-1975 PS plan[a]	-0.3%
Year of adoption	
Year after adoption	1.7%
Subsequent trend	0.8%
Average proportion unionized[b]	-0.1%
Estimated difference in yearly growth in nonpension compensation associated with	
Cash/combination plan[a]	
Year of adoption	-1.9%
Year following adoption	0.2%
Subsequent trend	0.5%
Deferred plan[a]	
Year of adoption	-1.5%
Year following adoption	-0.3%
Subsequent trend	-0.2%
Average proportion unionized[b]	0.0%

NOTES: The majority of these estimates are not significantly different from zero, due in part to the small number of firms reporting labor expenses. The estimates should therefore be seen only as indicative. PS = profit sharing.
a. Profit-sharing estimates are relative to nonprofit-sharing companies.
b. Union estimates based on difference between nonunion company (0 percent coverage) and average union coverage (35 percent).

The results of analyzing compensation growth across the entire period are summarized on the right side of table 4.4. There it can be seen that the presence of old PS had a slight negative effect (-0.1 percent per year), while the initial adoption of profit sharing was associated with a small decrease (-0.3 percent) in the adoption year, a 1.7 percent increase in the following year, and a 0.7 percent increase in subsequent years.[18] The increases after the adoption year may clearly be related to higher company productivity of adopters, as explored in chapter 3.[19]

On the bottom of table 4.4 are summaries of results that analyze non-pension compensation (as a proportion of industry average compensation), and divide profit-sharing plans into cash/combination plans vs. deferred plans to examine whether there are distinct effects of these plans on nonpension compensation. As can be seen, the presence of cash/combination plans is associated with slightly higher overall compensation, while the presence of deferred plans is associated with slightly lower compensation. When a majority of union members is not covered by profit sharing, the union effect on nonpension compensation is estimated at 5.7 percent (for average levels of coverage), while the effect is estimated as slightly negative (-3.1 percent) if a majority is covered (again reflecting the union wage concessions of the early 1980s). The adoptions of both cash/combination and deferred profit-sharing plans are accompanied by a slight decrease in overall compensation, and postadoption trends are positive for cash/combination plans but negative for deferred plans (again possibly reflecting larger productivity gains among companies adopting cash plans).

Does profit sharing imply lower wages or other benefits? The principal conclusion from the variety of evidence presented here is that there may be a substantial difference between old and new profit-sharing companies. The old profit-sharing companies had average compensation levels over the 1970-90 period that were higher when compared to the industry, new profit-sharing companies, and non-profit-sharing companies. This provides little evidence that profit sharing traded off against other wages and benefits for these companies—it may have been "gravy" for the employees (consistent with the analysis of 1974 data in Mitchell, Lewin, and Lawler 1990). Compensation growth kept up with industry averages for these companies.

For new profit-sharing companies, on the other hand, several pieces of evidence point to more of a trade-off between profit sharing and other compensation. Average compensation levels in these companies are lower than industry averages, as indicated by both simple comparisons and regressions. While the adoption of profit sharing in this sample is associated with an initial slight decline in compensation, the subsequent positive trend leads most of the adopters to have an increase in average compensation levels between pre- and postadoption periods (with a mean increase of 0.9 percent and a median of 1.9 percent). The overall increase in average compensation levels may reflect the sharing of benefits from higher productivity, as found in chapter 3. For the stability theory, the key element is whether base pay, excluding profit share, has increased or decreased. Since the average compensation increase is smaller than the typical profit share, it appears likely that regular fixed pay (relative to industry trends) may have slightly declined in a number of firms. The relationship of these compensation changes to the stability theory will be discussed and tested below. (Again, it should be cautioned that, due to the restricted sample of companies reporting compensation data, these results should be seen as indicative but not strong.)

Do Profit-Sharing Contributions Act Like Wages?

Proposition 1 of the stability theory is that profit-sharing payments are fundamentally different from straight wages in affecting employment. An increase in wage rates will increase the cost of the last labor hour employed (the marginal cost of labor), leading to lower employment levels. If profit-sharing payments are simply "disguised wages"—that is, the employer views them as a standard cost of employing labor—then such payments should act like wages in affecting employment. If, on the other hand, the employer views them not as a cost of employing labor, but as a "tax" on profits, then they should not affect employment levels in the same way as straight wages.[20] As displayed in table 4.1, this proposition has been addressed in eight studies, with mixed results.

The proposition that profit-sharing payments do not behave in the same way as other wages and benefits is tested using a standard labor demand function, relating employment levels to the cost of labor, augmented to separate profit sharing from other compensation. This enables one to compare the employment effects of base wages to profit-sharing payments.[21] The base compensation measure is defined as the (change in) average value of all compensation minus profit-sharing payments (including not just wage and salary payments, but all compensation other than profit-sharing payments).[22] The profit-sharing measure is defined as the change in the company's profit-sharing contribution as a percentage of participant payroll. Since the average compensation measure is defined across all employees, the profit-sharing measure is only meaningful when all or nearly all employees are participants. Therefore, profit-sharing companies with fewer than 90 percent of employees covered have been excluded. The profit-sharing portion of compensation, which is used as an explanatory variable, suffers from a serious bias due to the fact that good performance by the firm may increase both the profit share and the employment level, causing a spurious positive association between the two; this bias is corrected using the variables to predict profit-sharing adoption from chapter 2.[23] Finally, the estimates account for each company's change in output (measured as the change in sales adjusted for inventory changes) and time and industry effects.[24]

Results were calculated for five samples of firms. The first sample includes only those firms that reported both labor expenses and profit-sharing contribution in a given year. The remaining samples use predictions of labor expenses and profit-sharing contributions to impute values for these variables in four (progressively larger) samples: all firms reporting the profit-sharing contribution for a given year; all profit-sharing firms reporting labor expenses in a given year; all profit-sharing firms; and finally, all profit-sharing and non-profit-sharing firms.

The results (presented in appendix table A4.2) generally accord with theoretical expectations, with some exceptions. The company's output change is strongly positively related to employment changes, as expected. Increases in base compensation are negatively related to employment change in all but one estimate, with magnitudes generally in line with past studies (see Hamermesh 1993 for a survey and Kruse

1991b for a similar sample). The estimates are only significantly different from zero, though, in the two largest samples. The key variable of interest is the change in the profit-sharing contribution, which attracts a positive estimate in each column. Are the estimates equal between profit sharing and base compensation changes? A test for equality between the base compensation and profit-sharing estimates (reported on the last row of appendix table A4.2), shows that the hypothesis of no difference can be rejected at the 95 percent level for the largest two samples.

These results appear generally favorable for proposition 1 of the stability theory: profit-sharing payments do not appear to act like wages in affecting desired employment levels. Exploration of alternative methods for removing bias from the profit-sharing estimates, however, revealed that the results were quite sensitive.[25] While these results are generally favorable to the stability theory, no firm conclusion is drawn here regarding proposition 1.

Estimating the Stability Effects of Profit Sharing

Are profit-sharing firms more stable? The second proposition of Weitzman's stability theory of profit sharing is that profit sharing will increase the stability of employment. The theory predicts that, in the long run, an economy of profit-sharing firms will have compensation and employment levels equivalent to those in a fixed-wage economy. Starting from an equilibrium setting, the predicted response to positive demand shocks is equivalent for both economies; they both need to increase compensation to draw more workers into the labor force. The predicted response to negative demand shocks, however, is different: fixed-wage firms see the current compensation per worker as part of the cost of the last labor hour (the marginal cost of labor), and must lay off workers, while profit-sharing firms view only the (lower) base compensation as part of the cost of the last labor hour, and will be less likely to lay off workers (as illustrated in figure 4.1). In response to a subsequent positive shock that restores the previous level of demand and costs, the profit-sharing firms would also hire back fewer workers than would fixed-wage firms to return to the equilibrium position.

Simple comparisons of employment growth and stability are presented in table 4.5, with comparisons between non-profit-sharing and old and new profit-sharing firms, again using 1975 adoption as a cutoff between the two profit-sharing groups.[26] Average yearly employment growth was 0.9 percent for non-profit-sharing firms (line 1), and 2.9 percent for old profit-sharing (old PS) firms (line 2). For new profit-sharing (new PS) firms, average employment growth was 1.7 percent prior to adoption, -0.5 percent during the year of adoption, and 2.2 percent after adoption (lines 3 to 5). These comparisons are made for the paired differences in lines 6 to 9, and broken out for periods of rising and falling unemployment in lines 10 to 17. In both rising and falling unemployment, the old PS firms had higher average employment growth than did their non-profit-sharing pairs. This was also true for postadoption growth of new PS firms; however, prior to adoption and during the year of adoption, the new PS firms had inferior employment growth compared to their pairs when unemployment was rising.

This suggests that, prior to adoption, profit-sharing adopters may have been more sensitive to recessionary shocks than their pairs. The employment variability of firms is examined on the right side of table 4.5.[27] The variability of employment is slightly higher for non-profit-sharing companies (by comparing line 1 to lines 2 and 5), but the variability of adopters is equivalent between pre- and postadoption periods. The paired differences on lines 6 to 9 show that the old PS firms had, on average, lower variability of employment than did their same-industry pairs, while the profit-sharing adopters had a slight decline in relative variability between preadoption and postadoption periods.

The simple comparisons suggest that profit sharing is associated with higher employment growth, and that firms adopting profit sharing were less stable prior to adoption (both in overall variability and in responses to recessionary shocks). Employment behavior is here analyzed more intensively with regressions that control for growth trends, and separately examine positive and negative demand shocks using several measures of such shocks.

There are potentially important differences in compensation between old profit-sharing firms and new adopters—in particular, the profit share is more likely to be added onto regular compensation for old profit-sharing firms, and more likely to substitute for other compensation for new adopters (as revealed in tables 4.3 and 4.4). Since

Table 4.5 Simple Comparisons on Employment Growth and Variability

	Yearly percentage growth in employment		Std. dev. of change in ln(L), within company	
	Mean	N	Mean	N
Nonpaired values				
1. Non-profit-sharing	0.9	4807	0.141	247
2. Old (pre-1975) PS	2.9	1930	0.134	101
New (post-1975) PS				
3. Preadoption	1.7	1509	0.138	121
4. Year of adoption	-0.5	124		
5. Postadoption	2.2	784	0.138	106
Paired differences between PS and NPS				
6. Old (pre-1975) adopters	2.1 (3.30)	1505	-0.020 (1.45)	74
New (post-1975) adopters				
7. Preadoption	1.2 (1.99)	1210	0.019 (1.34)	99
8. Year of adoption	0.4 (0.13)	98		
9. Postadoption	1.2 (1.19)	648	0.008 (0.51)	78
Periods of rising unemployment				
10. Old (pre-1975) adopters	1.4 (1.29)	514		
New (post-1975) adopters				
11. Preadoption	-0.4 (0.39)	478		
12. Year of adoption	-6.9 (1.54)	23		
13. Postadoption	1.1 (0.73)	166		

Periods of falling unemployment

14. Old (pre-1975) adopters	2.5 (3.11)	911
New (post-1975) adopters		
15. Preadoption	2.1 (2.49)	676
16. Year of adoption	3.7 (1.13)	70
17. Postadoption	1.5 (1.21)	444

NOTES: Absolute values of *t*-statistics, testing whether paired difference equals zero, in parentheses. PS = profit sharing; NPS = nonprofit-sharing. Paired differences represent value for PS company minus the value for its same-industry NPS pair.

this distinction is crucial for the theory, the separate responses of old profit-sharing firms and new adopters are broken out in most of the estimates. This has the added advantage that the employment responses of new adopters can be compared before and after the adoption of profit sharing—giving an indication of whether the adopters were particularly stable or unstable beforehand. To obtain estimates on how firms responded to negative shocks prior to adoption, the adopters sample is restricted to firms that adopted after the 1973-75 recession. In addition (as with the estimates for proposition 1), the sample of profit-sharing firms is restricted to those that had all or nearly all (90 percent or more) of their employees participating in profit sharing, so that variations in overall company employment would be likely to affect profit-sharing participants.[28]

As with the productivity tests, estimates were made both from the entire sample (with industry variables to control for general industry growth and decline),[29] and then for the within-industry paired data. To allow for the possibility that defined benefit pension plans may have effects on employment changes, and to control for any potential bias created by their omission, the estimates include defined benefit plans interacted with the demand shocks. To control for differential employment growth, variables were included to capture growth trends of old profit-sharing firms and new adopters (with separate terms for pre- and postadoption periods). Several methods were used to control for potential selection bias,[30] and several extreme values of employment changes were trimmed.[31]

Demand shocks are measured with two economywide and one company-specific measure: (1) change in the national unemployment rate, (2) percentage change in Gross National Product, and (3) percentage change in the company's sales.[32] The values for the first two measures, and descriptive statistics for sales changes are given in appendix table A4.3.

Why not use just the company's sales changes, since these are most specific to the company? Ideally, the demand shocks will measure inward shifts of the demand curve for the company's product. Sales changes would appear to be the most specific to the company, but may suffer from the following problem. The stability theory predicts not only that employment will be more stable under profit sharing, but that output will be more stable. When faced with negative demand shocks, profit-sharing firms are predicted to be more likely to keep employment and output stable while cutting prices to sell the output. The problem with using sales changes as a demand measure is that it is impossible to distinguish changes in prices from changes in output. If sales changes primarily reflect output changes (as in a competitive market, or in an industry where price changes are highly correlated across firms and are picked up by industry terms), then under the stability theory, *even if* output and employment are more stable in the profit-sharing firm, there may be no estimated effect of profit sharing on employment stability (because the output-employment relationship is the same between the two types of firms).[33] If, in contrast, sales changes combine both output changes and company-specific price changes, then there should be an estimated effect of profit sharing on employment stability. This would be the case in an imperfectly competitive market where, based on several assumptions about the structure of costs and demand curves, it is estimated that the effect of sales changes on employment changes for profit-sharing firms would be approximately half the size of that for a non-profit-sharing firm.[34]

Since the stability theory predicts that both employment and output will be more stable under profit sharing, sales changes may or may not be an appropriate measure of demand shocks for the stability theory, which is why two economywide measures are also used (with the industry paired differences controlling for differential sensitivity to demand shocks by industry).

Finally, it is necessary to discuss the appropriate method of examining employment responses to demand shocks. As can be seen in figure 4.1, the relationship between profit sharing and demand shocks is not a simple linear one. According to the stability theory, the profit-sharing firm has a "cushion" of employees it will maintain in a demand shock (representing the difference between L_0 and L_1—the excess demand for labor); once this cushion is exhausted by a severe demand shock, it will lay off workers at a pace just as rapid as that of the non-profit-sharing firm. Therefore the relationship between profit sharing and employment changes is discontinuous and depends on the degree to which the profit share substitutes for regular compensation (i.e., the gap between c and w' in figure 4.1). If a subsequent positive shock restores the previous level of demand, the profit-sharing firm will hire back fewer people, since it laid off fewer to begin with. If starting from an initial equilibrium position, an increase in demand should cause the responses to be the same between the two types of firms, since labor would be available on the same conditions. However, the theory predicts that profit-sharing firms are generally more willing than fixed-wage firms to hire workers, so the employment response to a positive shock in a time of unemployment may be even stronger for a profit-sharing firm.

A full test of the stability theory therefore requires an estimate of the predicted nonlinear relationship between demand shocks and employment responses. A more complete discussion of the complicated relationship between profit sharing and demand shocks is given in appendix 4, where it is noted that the information required for a full test is not available (in particular, the degree to which profit sharing substitutes for fixed compensation, and an accurate measure of demand shocks which distinguishes whether they represent recovery from previous negative shocks). Some estimates will be reported which attempt to approximate the conditions for a full test of the theory. Most of the estimates presented, however, follows previous research by relying on a simpler test of whether profit-sharing firms respond differently from non-profit-sharing firms to positive and negative demand shocks. Because the stability theory's predictions about behavior under negative shocks are more straightforward, more attention will be paid to the employment responses to negative shocks.

Does Profit Sharing Increase Stability of Employment?

Summary results on several employment stability tests are presented in table 4.6 (based on estimates in appendix table A4.5). The employment sensitivity of non-profit-sharing firms is presented on line 1, where it can be seen that a 1 percent increase in GNP[35] is associated with a 1.3 percent increase in company employment (column 1), while a 1 percent decrease in GNP is associated with a 1.2 percent decrease in employment (column 3).[36] For old profit-sharing firms (that adopted profit sharing prior to 1975), line 2 shows a slightly lower sensitivity to GNP increases, and a slightly higher sensitivity to GNP decreases (nei-

Table 4.6 Summary Results on Employment Stability

Numbers represent estimated change in company employment for a 1 percent change in GNP, or in company sales.

| | GNP | | | | Company sales | | | | Table on which results are based |
| | 1 percent increase | | 1 percent decrease | | 1 percent increase | | 1 percent decrease | | |
	(1)	(2)	(3)	(4)	(5)	(6)	(7)	(8)	
Overall patterns									A4.5
1. Non-profit-sharing	1.3		-1.2		0.5	0.6	-0.6	-0.6	
2. Old PS	1.0	0.9	-1.5	-1.1	0.6	0.6	-0.5	-0.5	
New PS									
3. Preadoption	0.8	0.9	-2.2***	-1.9	0.4	0.5	-0.5	-0.6	
4. Postadoption	1.4	1.4	0.0	-1.2	0.5	0.7	-0.6	-0.5	
Unionization									A4.7
5. Nonunion, non-profit-sharing	1.3	1.3	-0.9	-0.9	0.5	0.6	-0.5	-0.6	
6. Average unionization,[a] non-profit-sharing	0.7	0.7	-1.2	-1.8	0.5	0.6	-0.5	-0.6	
Average unionization,[a] w/majority of union members in PS									
7. Old PS	0.3	0.6	-1.5	-2.1	0.5	0.5	-0.5	-0.5	
New PS									
8. Preadoption	0.6	0.6	-1.5	-1.6	0.5	0.5	-0.4	-0.5	
9. Postadoption	0.4	1.1	-1.0	-1.5	0.4	0.5	-0.4	-0.4	

NOTES: Columns 1, 3, 5, and 7 are based on regressions 3 and 5 of the indicated tables. Columns 2, 4, 6, and 8 are based on paired results in regressions 4 and 6 of indicated tables.

a. Assuming 37 percent of firm's workers are unionized (representing sample average for unionized firms).

***Difference between pre- and postadoption response is significant at p <.01.

ther of which were significantly different from the non-profit-sharing effects).[37]

Comparisons of employment stability before and after adoption of profit sharing are presented on lines 3 and 4. Compared to non-profit-sharing firms, under a positive shock the adopters were slightly less likely to increase employment prior to adoption (line 3), and slightly more likely after adoption (line 4). The notable difference appears for a 1 percent decline in GNP: prior to adoption the predicted employment decrease was 2.2 percent, and after adoption was very close to zero (column 3, lines 3 and 4). This change in sensitivity (unlike most of the other estimates to be reviewed), is significantly different from zero (at the 99 percent level). This same pattern is observed (but is no longer statistically significant) in the paired results in column 4, where the predicted employment decrease goes from a preadoption value of -1.9 percent to a postadoption value of -1.2 percent.[38]

These results may be more easily seen in figures 4.2 and 4.3, which give the predicted employment paths of non-profit-sharing firms, and old and new profit-sharing firms (under the assumption that the new profit-sharing firms adopted it in 1978). There are two things to note. First, the profit-sharing firms are faster-growing, with the new profit-sharing firms showing faster growth both before and after the adoption. Second, the sensitivity to negative shocks is seen by comparing the 1973-75 recession to the 1980-82 recession. In the earlier recession, all three types of firms show employment declines, but the new profit-sharing firms (prior to adoption) show the steepest decline.[39] In the 1980-82 period, after adoption, the new profit-sharing firms show no decline while the other two groups do show declines.

This appears to indicate that the new profit-sharing firms were particularly susceptible to negative shocks prior to adoption, and much less so afterwards. The results for the estimate on paired data are displayed in figure 4.3, which show a slightly different story.[40] The new profit-sharing firms are again seen to have a steeper employment decline than the old profit-sharing firms in the 1973-75 recession, but the two groups show equivalent declines in the 1980-82 recession.[41] Similarly, between the two periods the new profit-sharing firms show a slight improvement relative to the non-profit-sharing firms. The pattern makes it appear that the adopters were especially sensitive to negative shocks prior to adoption, and less so afterwards.

Figure 4.2
Predicted Employment
(regression 3, table A4.6)

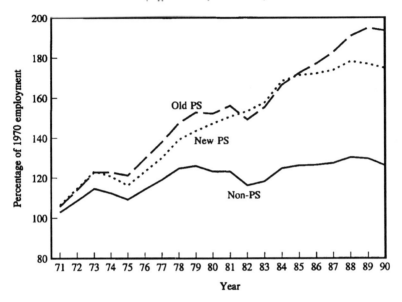

Figure 4.3
Predicted Employment
(regression 4, table A4.6)

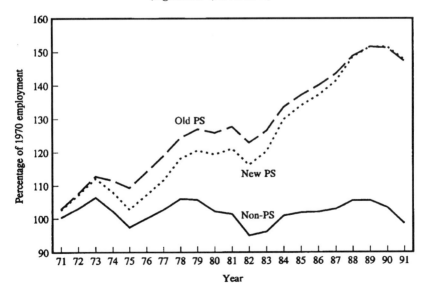

When demand shocks are measured by increases and decreases in company sales (summarized in columns 5 to 8 of table 4.6), there are no significant estimates indicating greater or less employment stability among profit-sharing firms, either compared to non-profit-sharing firms or to preadoption behavior. The decreased sensitivity to negative aggregate shocks but not to negative sales shocks implies that sales were more stable after adoption of profit sharing.

These estimates rely on a simple test of whether profit-sharing firms have different responses to demand shocks than do non-profit-sharing firms. As discussed in the preceding section and in appendix 4, the actual relationship predicted by the stability theory is a discontinuous nonlinear one, depending in part on whether or not the firm is recovering from a prior negative shock. A full test of the stability theory requires information on the degree to which the profit share substitutes for regular compensation, the relationship between wage levels and desired employment, and prior negative shocks. Using several pieces of data to make assumptions about these relationships, the results from an approximation of a full test are presented in appendix table A4.6.[42]

Three main conclusions may be drawn from these approximations of full tests. (1) Employment behavior of profit-sharing firms generally appears to be different from that of non-profit-sharing firms.[43] (2) Profit-sharing employment responses to demand shocks were favorable, compared to non-profit-sharing responses, when firms were not recovering from a prior negative shock.[44] Specifically, the profit-sharing firms had stronger employment responses to positive shocks, and smaller responses to negative shocks than did the non-profit-sharing firms, and the pattern was generally favorable for the stability theory.[45] (3) The situation was more mixed when firms were recovering from a prior negative shock, with profit-sharing firms having a favorable smaller response to further negative shocks and generally equal or larger responses to positive shocks, though this latter finding does not fit the theory since the theorized response should have been smaller.[46]

Unions, Profit Sharing, and Employment Stability

The proportion of a company's workforce that is unionized may have direct effects on employment stability, through union effects on labor costs and rules governing employment adjustments within the firm. While there have been a number of studies of union effects on turnover and temporary layoffs, only Leonard (1986) has directly examined the cyclical sensitivity of unionized vs. non-unionized firms. His findings were that blue-collar employment in unionized plants in California was less sensitive to changes in GNP than it was in non-union plants, and that there was little difference in termination and new-hire rates.

Results on the relationship of unionism to demand shocks, and the potential effects of having a majority of union members covered by profit sharing, are summarized in table 4.6 (based on full results in appendix table A4.7).[47] The estimated employment responses of non-profit-sharing firms are given on line 5 (for nonunion firms), and line 6 (for union firms with average unionization). With respect to changes in GNP, unionized firms have less favorable behavior: they have stronger employment cutbacks when GNP decreases, and smaller employment increases when GNP increases, than do nonunion firms. These differences, however, are not estimated as statistically significant, and there is no difference in sensitivity to company sales increases and decreases.

Does union participation in profit sharing make a difference in company employment responses? The results of table 4.4 indicate that average pay is lower when a majority of union members participate in profit sharing (essentially eliminating the union wage advantage), but this may be counterbalanced by greater employment stability for these union members. As summarized in table 4.6, there were no profit-sharing results that could be confidently established as significantly different from zero. For new profit-sharing firms, the pre- and postadoption estimates showed a favorable decrease in sensitivity to negative shocks (for example, prior to adoption the employment decline for a 1 percent GNP decline was 1.5 percent to 1.6 percent, and after adoption was 1.0 percent to 1.5 percent, for a firm with average unionization and a majority of employees covered by profit sharing). However, since this decline in sensitivity is never statistically significant, it is not a strong result.

Compensation Levels and Profit-Sharing Effects on Stability

A clear prediction of the stability theory is that profit sharing will have stabilizing effects only if the profit share substitutes (at least in part) for regular fixed pay. If it does not, there is no difference in employer views of the cost of maintaining profit-sharing and non-profit-sharing employees during business downturns.

Ideally one would have a measure of what total compensation levels would have been for each profit-sharing firm in the absence of profit sharing. Lacking this, there are two types of comparisons that can be made. First, for the profit-sharing adopters, a longitudinal comparison can be made between the preadoption and postadoption average compensation levels (adjusted for industry trends). Such a comparison in table 4.3 showed that the median increase in compensation was almost 2 percent. Second, for the old profit-sharing firms, the only comparison possible is a cross-sectional one with the non-profit-sharing firms. The simple comparisons in table 4.3 show that the mean and median compensation levels are higher than industry averages among the old profit-sharing firms.

Two methods are used here to examine the relationship of pay to stabilizing effects of profit sharing. First, an attempt is made to separate companies in which profit sharing appears to substitute for base pay from those in which it appears to add on to base pay. Second, to correct for the effect that increased productivity may have on worker pay (if the productivity theory applies), the potential stabilizing effects are examined in relation to whether unit labor costs (labor expenses/output) have increased or decreased. These calculations are necessarily restricted to the firms that reported labor expenses, and the resulting small sample sizes imply that the results can only be seen as indicative.

There is no neat method of determining whether profit sharing substitutes for other compensation, or is a pure add-on. The following method should be seen as a rough approximation. For new profit-sharing companies, where the mean and median increases in compensation per employee (relative to the industry) were close to 2.0 percent, profit sharing was designated as "substituting" for regular compensation if the increase was less than 2.0 percent (and otherwise "adding" to regular compensation). Since the median profit share as a percent of payroll was 3.65 percent, compensation rises of less than 2 percent are likely to represent a cut in other compensation, while rises of more than 2 percent represent little or no such cut.[48] Such before/after comparisons are not available for the old profit-sharing companies; therefore for these companies the compensation ratio was averaged across all years for which the company reported labor expenses, to create a measure of whether a company, on average, paid better or worse than its industry. If this figure indicated that a profit-sharing company exceeded industry averages by more than 2 percent, then the profit sharing was designated to be "substituting" for regular compensation (and otherwise "adding" to regular compensation).[49]

The results of using this approximation of whether profit sharing substitutes or adds on to regular pay are summarized in columns 1 and 2 of table 4.7.[50] Some support for the stability theory is provided by the results for new profit-sharing companies, though not for old profit-sharing companies. Focusing on the new profit-sharing companies, those in which profit sharing "substituted" for base pay had employment decreases of only 0.1 percent after adoption, compared to 0.4 percent before adoption, in response to a 1 percent sales decline (column 2, rows 3 and 4 of table 4.7). The postadoption response is significantly different from the non-profit-sharing employment response (0.7 percent decline), but the pre/post difference is not statistically significant. The corresponding figures for companies where the profit share was more likely to be an add-on are a 0.8 percent decline prior to adoption, and a 0.9 percent decline after adoption. The pattern for old profit-sharing firms is the opposite: in response to a 1 percent sales decline, those that paid less than 102 percent of the industry average pay had slightly stronger employment responses (0.8 percent decline) than the higher-paying profit-sharing firms (0.5 percent decline) (lines 2 and 5 of column 2). Neither of these responses, though, was significantly different from the non-profit-sharing response.

Some support for the stability theory is therefore provided by the pattern of responses to negative shocks for new profit-sharing firms, though not for old profit-sharing firms. A flaw in looking at pay levels

Table 4.7 Summary Results on Compensation Levels and Employment Changes

Numbers represent estimated change in company employment for a 1 percent change in company sales.

	By whether profit-sharing "substitutes" or is "added on" to regular pay per employee[a]		By whether profit sharing "substitutes" or is "added on" to regular pay in relation to output[b]	
	1 percent increase in sales (1)	1 percent decrease in sales (2)	1 percent increase in sales (3)	1 percent decrease in sales (4)
	(percent)		(percent)	
1. Non-profit sharing	0.5	-0.7	0.5	-0.7
Profit-sharing "substitutes" for regular pay				
2. Old profit sharing	0.9**	-0.8	0.9**	-0.6
New profit sharing				
3. Preadoption	0.3	-0.4	0.3	-0.9
4. Postadoption	0.3	-0.1**	0.4	-0.1**
Profit sharing "added on" to regular pay				
5. Old profit sharing	0.5	-0.5	0.7	-0.8
New profit sharing				
6. Preadoption	0.3	-0.8	0.4	-0.4
7. Postadoption	0.2**	-0.9	0.0**	-0.6

NOTES: **Significantly different from non-profit-sharing response at the 95 percent level.

a. Based on column 1 of appendix table A4.8. Profit sharing assumed to "substitute" for regular pay if average compensation in old PS firm is less than 102 percent of industry average, or if average compensation in new PS firm went up by less than 2 percent. Profit sharing assumed to "add on" to regular pay if these conditions do not hold. The ratio of company to industry compensation per employee is determined for each year, and the ratio is averaged across all years for old PS companies. For adopters, it is averaged across all preadoption, and then across postadoption years, to determine if average compensation increased.

b. Based on column 2 of appendix table A4.8. Profit sharing assumed to "substitute" for regular pay in relation to output if average unit labor costs in old PS firm are lower than industry average, or if average unit labor costs in new PS firm, relative to industry, declined. Profit sharing assumed to "add on" to regular pay if these conditions do not hold. The ratio of company to industry unit labor costs is determined for each year, and the ratio is averaged across all years for old PS companies. For adopters, it is averaged across all preadoption, and then across postadoption, year, to determine if average unit labor costs increased. Unit labor costs are measured as (labor expenses)/(sales+inventory change). See text for further discussion.

is that they are plausibly related to worker productivity—if there is a positive productivity effect of profit sharing (as explored in chapter 3), this should increase worker pay. An increase in worker pay after the adoption of profit sharing may not indicate that profit sharing is simply "gravy" on top of base pay; instead, it may reflect a return to increased effort and productivity by the workers. The appropriate measure is not necessarily pay per worker, but pay per unit of worker performance (either quantity or quality of work). Even if overall pay (base pay plus profit share) per worker has increased, the increased performance may mean that base pay relative to worker performance has declined. To use a simple illustration: if worker performance has increased by 10 percent, and has helped create a 10 percent profit-sharing bonus on top of base pay, the worker's base pay in relation to his or her performance has declined. Therefore the profit share is "substituting" for fixed pay in relation to the worker's performance. In this case, profit sharing may still have a stabilizing effect: the employer would have a strong incentive to maintain the workforce under a decline in product demand (provided the higher performance is maintained).

This means that the productivity and stability theories are not necessarily at odds with each other. If profit sharing does increase productivity and pay levels, the stability theory may still apply. In looking at whether profit sharing substitutes for base pay, how can one control for the effects of higher productivity on pay? One method is to calculate labor expenses as a proportion of the value of output (producing a measure of unit labor costs). Profit sharing may increase productivity (output per employee) as well as pay (compensation per employee), but unit labor costs (compensation/output) will only increase if the pay increase exceeds the productivity increase. Therefore the change in unit labor costs is a separate measure of whether profit sharing is substituting for, or adding onto, base pay.[51]

Support for the stability theory is stronger when pay substitution is measured in this way (table 4.7, columns 3 and 4). Where profit sharing appears to have substituted for base pay in relation to output, the employment response to negative shocks were much better after adoption than before. The preadoption response to a 1 percent sales decline was -0.9 percent (compared to -0.7 percent for non-profit-sharing firms), and after adoption was only -0.1 percent, with the change being statistically significant (lines 1, 3, and 4 of column 4). For the old profit-sharing firms, the response to negative shocks was insignificantly lower, but to positive shocks was significantly higher, compared to non-profit-sharing firms (line 2). In contrast, where profit sharing appears to have added on to regular pay in relation to output, there are no significant differences between profit-sharing and non-profit-sharing employment responses (except for a much lower postadoption response to positive shocks, as shown in line 7).

It definitely appears that compensation is an important variable in the stability effects of profit sharing. Both methods indicated that, when profit shares appear to partially substitute for base compensation, profit-sharing adopters had smaller employment cutbacks after adoption than before in response to negative demand shocks.[52] This was not true of companies where the profit share appeared to add on to regular compensation. While consistent with the stability theory, this result should only be seen as indicative due to the small number of firms reporting sufficient compensation data.

Stability Effects of Cash and Deferred Plans, Different Plan Formulas, and Occupational Participation

Several other features of profit sharing may make a difference in the stability effects, including the type of plan and the type of employees covered.

There may be differences in the stabilizing effects of profit sharing according to how the profit share is distributed. Since deferred profit sharing is a form of pension plan, employers may see contributions to such plans as more of a company obligation to ensure retirement security, so that they are less likely to be cut in business downturns.[53]

Profit-sharing plans were divided into those that have a cash component (including combination plans where a portion may be deferred), and those with totally deferred payments. The results (in appendix table A4.9) do not paint a clear picture of stabilizing effects for either type of plan. There is no consistent pattern for old cash or deferred plans of greater or less responsiveness to negative shocks. For new plans, adoption of deferred plans is associated with significant declines in responsiveness to negative aggregate shocks in two of the specifications (consistent with my results for deferred plans in Kruse 1991a), but there was no significant change in responsiveness associated with sales changes or with cash plans.

The formula that a profit-sharing company uses to determine the profit share may have a strong relation to the potential stability effects. The stability theory that Weitzman developed assumes that the profit share is based on a prespecified percent of company profits. It may also be argued to apply when the profit share is discretionary, since a discretionary contribution should not be seen by employers as part of the short-run marginal cost of labor (but may be seen by employers and employees as part of long-run expected compensation). The stability theory clearly does not apply when the profit share is a fixed percent of participants' pay, since in this case the profit share is viewed as part of the marginal cost of labor.

As for the productivity specifications, companies reporting plan formulas were divided into several groups: percent-of-profits, discretionary, percent-of-pay, and "other" formula. Results for the stabilizing effects of each type of plan are reported in appendix table A4.10,[54] and are weakly consistent with the stability theory. Only for percent-of-profits plans do the estimates consistently indicate smaller employment responses to negative shocks (line 4). The one estimate where sampling error may (weakly) be ruled out indicates that firms with such plans have a predicted employment cutback of only 0.4 percent, compared to 0.7 percent for non-profit-sharing firms, in response to a 1 percent decrease in sales (lines 2 and 4, column 6). For no other plan formulas are there significant estimates of profit-sharing effects on employment responses, or consistent patterns across the various estimates. The story with respect to positive shocks is similar: the estimates for percent-of-profits plans all indicate greater employment responses to positive shocks (but none where sampling error can be ruled out), while the estimates for other formulas show no consistent pattern of higher or lower responsiveness. Overall, the more favorable results for percent-of-profits plans is consistent with the stability theory, although the results are not strong.[55]

Finally, what is the relation between occupational composition and the stability effects of profit sharing? The survey asked companies to break their employees into three categories: clerical and technical (nonexempt), production and service (nonexempt), and professional and administrative (exempt). They were further asked for the proportion of employees covered by profit sharing within each group, and the overall numbers show that coverage was lowest among production and service workers (table 1.3).[56] The proportions of employees in each occupation group, and these proportions interacted with the proportion covered by profit sharing, were separately examined for their relationship to positive and negative shocks.[57] The results (in appendix table A4.11) show less sensitivity to decreases in GNP for each occupational group between the pre-and postadoption periods (where sampling error can be ruled out for the professional/administrative employees); also, they show less sensitivity to decreases in company sales for all but professional/administrative workers (but sampling error cannot be ruled out for any of the differences). Therefore there is no strong evidence that profit sharing is particularly good or bad for any occupational group.[58]

Summary and conclusions regarding these tests of the stability theory will be presented in the final chapter.

NOTES

1. For a discussion of wage flexibility in the United States, see Mitchell (1985).

2. For example, the Senate Finance Subcommittee report asserted that, "When wages remain rigid, the flexibility necessary to effect a balance between selling prices and consumer buying is missing and our economic system is stalemated" (U.S. Senate 1939: 63).

3. This simple model elides the complications introduced by firm-specific skills, firm insurance of risk-averse workers, and incomplete supervision.

4. Firms maximize profits by setting the MRP of labor equal to the marginal cost (MC) of labor. In graph 1 of figure 4.1, the MC of labor is simply the wage, so the firm maximizes profits at the point where the two curves intersect. In graph 2, the MC of labor lies between the w' and MRP lines (since workers share in the profits, or the difference between MRP and w'), and intersects those two lines at point B. Unlike in the fixed-wage firm, the MC curve slopes downward, reflecting the decreased labor cost per employee as more employees are hired and the profit share is split among a larger number.

5. For further discussion and theoretical treatment, see Burton (1986); Blinder (1986a, 1986b); Nuti (1987); Mitchell (1987); Cooper (1988); Fitzroy (1988); Fung (1989); John (1991); Bensaid and Gary-Bobo (1991); Eckalbar (1992); and LaCivita and Pirog (1992). For a practitioner's view see Parks (1990).

6. This review is based on all published studies that could be located in books or in economics, personnel, and business journals (using searches up through June 1993 of the Business Periodicals Index and the computerized databases ABI/INFORM, UNCOVER, ProQuest, and Business Dateline), and on unpublished studies made available by colleagues.

7. Each extra dollar of bonus was associated with higher compensation of $1.24 and $.39 per hour for nonoffice and office workers, respectively, and with higher straight-time wages of $.83 and $.27.

8. The profit share added $.43 to average compensation in manufacturing firms, and $.47 in nonmanufacturing firms.

9. There were 133 contracts with, and 1,666 contracts without, profit sharing. The prevalence of cost-of-living-adjustment freezes or eliminations were also higher among contracts with profit sharing (Mitchell, Lewin, and Lawler 1990: 25).

10. Wage concessions were defined as nominal wage freezes or declines in the first year of the contract. For further information on their data see table 1.1 and the accompanying text and notes in chapter 1. Also, Florkowski and Shastri (1992) find that among 45 announced union contracts with profit-sharing provisions over the 1979-88 period, 60 percent were accompanied by announced wage reductions.

11. One additional piece of evidence on the relationship of profit sharing to unionization comes from Cardinal and Helburn (1986), who find that a variety of fringe benefits are equally likely to be offered in unionized and nonunion profit-sharing firms.

12. Company average compensation was defined as (labor expenses)/(total employees), while industry average compensation was defined as (total compensation)/(total full-time and part-time employees) from the National Income and Product Accounts tables 6.4 and 6.6. Both include payroll taxes. Note that differences between company and industry average yearly pay may be due to differences in pay per hour, or to the proportion of part-time workers (e.g., a company paying only 80 percent of industry average yearly pay may simply be hiring a higher proportion of part-time workers.

13. The profit share in the industry average cannot be excluded, due to lack of data.

14. The upper and lower 1 percent of values, across the entire sample, have been excluded to eliminate the potential influence of outliers.

15. This slight rise in compensation would be expected if profit sharing is accompanied by higher productivity, as explored in chapter 3. This measure of the difference between average pre- and postadoption compensation levels gives equal weight to each of the 42 companies, while the numbers on lines 6-8 represent total observations, giving greater weight to companies that reported labor expenses more often.

16. The regressions used company labor expenses per employee divided by industry average compensation per employee as the dependent variable. To fully control for industry effects, the independent variables should also be adjusted for mean industry values. The limited number of observations, however, prevents this.

Regressions were also run using the occupational composition of the workforce to explain average compensation levels, using a smaller sample size due to nonresponse on occupational composition. One of these is presented in column 3 of appendix table A4.1. The results for the variables of interest were very similar.

17. See Katz and Meltz (1991) for comparison of auto workers' pay in the United States (where profit sharing was negotiated as part of wage concessions) and Canada (where it was not).

18. Due in large part to the small sample size, very few of the estimates are significantly different from zero at conventional levels. In the full results presented in appendix table A4.1, the only significant coefficient in regression 3 is a surprising negative coefficient on the adoption of a defined benefit plan (implying a 5 percent compensation cut), but this should be discounted because it is based on only four companies which adopted such plans in this period. For summaries of evidence on the relationship between pay and pensions, see Gustman and Mitchell (1992) and Gunderson, Hyatt, and Pesando (1992).

19. The estimated associations between productivity growth and profit-sharing adoption were similar between the full sample and this restricted subsample.

20. Just as it is possible that profit shares may act like fixed wages in affecting employment, wages may have an element of profit sharing by being affected by company profitability (as posited by rent-sharing theories in labor economics). For a review and some evidence, see Blanchflower, Oswald, and Sanfey (1992).

21. The labor demand function estimated here is:

$$\ln(L) = \beta_0 + \beta_1 * \ln(w) + \beta_2 * (b/w) + \beta_3 * Q + \beta_4 * X$$

where
L = employment level
w = base wage
b = size of profit-sharing bonus
Q = measure of company's output
X = other explanatory variables.

The coefficient β_1 measures the conventional wage elasticity of labor demand, while the coefficient β_2 measures the responsiveness of employment to bonus payments, holding wages constant. If β_2 is negative, and equal to or greater than β_1 in magnitude, then profit-sharing payments would appear to behave like wages in affecting labor demanded; whereas if β_2 is positive, or negative but smaller in magnitude than β_1, then profit-sharing payments would not appear to have the same negative effects as wages. The other explanatory variables would include the costs of other inputs, particularly the cost of capital. To be valid, this specification must account for the potential endogeneity of profit-sharing payments; such payments are likely to be influenced by factors that also affect labor demand. This study uses the above equation in first-difference form to exploit the panel data by removing any constant firm effects.

22. A complication is introduced by the fact that CompuStat reports only total labor expenses, so that this must be divided by total employment to arrive at an average compensation figure. However, any measurement error in employment will bias the coefficient, since the change in employment is the dependent variable. To correct for this, average compensation is instrumented on average industry compensation (from the National Income Product Accounts) for the current and two prior years (as in Kruse 1991b).

23. To correct for the endogeneity of the profit-sharing variable, it was instrumented on the variables from regression 5 of appendix table A2.2, excluding the profit margin and stock price variables (due to concerns about their exogeneity). As will be discussed, the results were sensitive to the choice of instruments.

24. Several experiments were made with cost-of-capital measures, following Kruse (1991b). As in the previous study, the coefficients on these measures were never significantly different from zero, and their inclusion made negligible difference in the parameters of interest. To maintain the highest sample size, these measures were omitted from the final results presented.

25. In Kruse (1991b), I used industry benefits as a percent of industry wages and salaries (current and two lagged values) as instruments for employer contributions to deferred profit-sharing plans; the results generally supported the stability theory. When the same instruments were used here they produced generally negative coefficients for the profit-sharing variable in this sample. Such instruments may not be applicable because cash profit-sharing payments are not included as part of the definition of benefits at the industry level; even so, the result makes a firm conclusion impossible. The sample here is too small to separate meaningfully profit sharing by type of plan; to maintain the highest response rate, firms were not asked to distinguish the size of cash vs. deferred contributions.

An additional instrument used in Kruse (1991b) was the percentage of company employees in deferred profit sharing in a given year, as reported on the Form 5500 for years 1980 86. Since year-to-year variation in percentage covered was not collected for this study, the variable was not used here to predict yearly changes in profit-sharing payments.

26. The 1975 cutoff has the advantage that preadoption employment behavior is analyzed both for years of expanding economic activity (1971-73) and contracting economic activity (1973-75). Experiments were made using other cutoffs in the 1970s and 1980 (in part, to account for misreporting of plan age, as discussed in chapter 3), but the results were not sensitive. Misreporting of plan age is not likely to be as large a problem here as for the productivity specifications, since the primary productivity estimates focused on immediate effects in adoption year, whereas the stability estimates do not.

27. Variability is defined as each company's standard deviation of yearly change in ln(employment), which may be interpreted as the dispersion of employment around a growth trend.

28. One alternative would be to include all firms and measure profit sharing as proportion of employees covered. This assumes, however, that if the stability theory is correct, a firm with 50 percent of employees covered would show twice the stability of a firm with 25 percent covered. Such an assumption is risky, since the variation among noncovered employees could easily be larger in the former firm. To avoid this, the sample was restricted to firms with all or nearly all employees in profit sharing. For 16 firms which did not report the percentage covered, the percentage was imputed from predictions based on age of plan, unionization, and industry membership; this added four firms to the 90 percent+ sample. Results excluding these firms were very similar.

29. The industry controls comprise 25 industry dummies and separate time trends.

30. As with the productivity specifications, several inverse Mill's ratios were tested and found to have insignificant coefficients and negligible effects on the coefficients of interest. The reported results include no selection terms.

31. Prior to trimming, the range of the yearly employment change variable (change in ln(employment)) was -4.77 to 4.64, implying, at the extremes, 100-fold changes in employment between years. The potentially stabilizing effects of profit sharing are likely to be swamped by the massive transformations which an organization is undergoing during such a time, and it is desirable to test the influence of profit sharing during more typical business fluctuations. Use of robust regression techniques on the basic specifications resulted in weights of zero or close to zero being given to the extreme values. For computational simplicity, two levels of trimming were tested for all specifications: eliminating five extreme values (restricting the dependent variable range to -2.04 to 1.87), and eliminating the upper 1 percent and lower 1 percent of employment changes (restricting the dependent variable range to -.53 to .53). There were no noteworthy differences in the results; results for the larger sample (with only five values trimmed) are presented here.

32. The GNP and sales figures were first deflated by the GNP deflator, and natural logarithms were taken so that changes would represent cumulative percentage changes. The ln(GNP) measure was regressed on a simple time trend, and the residual from this regression was used as the demand shock measure (with positive and negative residuals representing positive and negative shocks). The unemployment rate measure was specified as the change in ln(1 - civilian unemployment rate), with positive shocks representing decreases in unemployment (i.e., increases in this measure). Estimates were also made with nominal company sales, and with deflated company sales using the CPI for retail firms and industry inflation measures for manufacturing firms (at the 3-digit SIC level, from the NBER Trade and Immigration Dataset). There were no notable differences in results.

33. This distinguishes the stability theory from "labor hoarding" theories, in which firms may retain employees under negative shocks to maintain firm-specific skills and avoid turnover costs.

34. This is estimated as follows. The coefficient on ln(sales) in a labor demand equation is the elasticity of employment with respect to sales, or $\%\delta L/\%\delta$Sales which is $\%\delta L/(\%\delta P + \%\delta Q)$ (where δ is the difference operator, L = employment, P = price, and Q = physical output). Under the assumption of imperfect competition and constant elasticity of product demand, price is a fixed markup over marginal cost. Let the production function be $Q = A(L - f)$, where A is a technical coefficient and f is nonproduction labor. This has a constant marginal cost of output which is w/A, so that $p = (w/A)(\Phi/(\Phi - 1))$ where Φ = product demand elasticity, and w = compensation per worker.

Under these assumptions, an inward shift of the demand curve, provided it does not change the demand elasticity, will not affect P for a fixed-wage firm, and the entire $\%\delta$Sales will represent output changes. Under the production function $Q = A(L - f)$, the coefficient on ln(sales) will equal $\%\delta L/\%\delta Q = 1 - (f/L)$. As will be seen, empirical estimates of this coefficient are close to .5, which under the maintained assumptions implies that $f/L = .5$.

For a profit-sharing firm, the relevant marginal cost of labor after a negative demand shift is the base wage w' (assuming the demand shift is large enough to eliminate excess demand for labor). In this case the marginal cost of output is w'/A, the new price is $P' = (w'/A)(\Phi/\Phi-1))$, and the $\%\delta P = (w - c)/c$ (where c = total compensation per worker, following notation in figure 4.1). The coefficient on ln(sales), assuming as before that $\%\delta L/\%\delta Q = 1 - f/L$, will be $\%\delta L/\%\delta L/(1 - f/L) + (w' - c)/c)$. Assume (a) a profit share which substitutes for regular compensation and averages 3.6 percent of compensation (the median of profit shares from companies reporting profit share), (b) $f/L = .5$ (from above paragraph), and (c) a sales decrease of 6 percent (the median figure for sales decreases across all companies and years). Under these assumptions, the predicted change in employment for a non-profit-sharing firm would be -3.0 percent, and for a profit-sharing firm would be -1.2 percent (or only 40 percent of the non-profit-sharing cut in employment).

Therefore under these assumptions about product demand curves and cost structures with imperfect competition, the non-profit-sharing firms would respond to a typical sales decrease by maintaining prices and cutting employment, while the profit-sharing firms would respond by cutting prices and reducing employment by only roughly half as much. These calculations are obviously sensitive to the particular assumptions; without any direct measure of price changes in the firms, it is impossible to fully evaluate this model.

35. All references to increases and decreases in GNP refer to changes in constant-dollar GNP relative to a time trend over 1970-91.

36. The estimated effects on line 1 of table 4.6 represent the antilogs of the (coefficient * .01) on lines 1 and 2 of appendix table A4.5. The positive coefficients on negative shocks (line 2, table 4.13) indicate that employment moves in the same direction as the shock, so the estimated effects are given as negative in columns 3, 4, 7, and 8 of table 4.6.

37. These effects are estimated by adding the coefficients on lines 1 and 3 of appendix table A4.5, and then calculating the effect as described in previous footnote. The conclusion that the responses are not significantly different is based on the low t-statistics of the interaction coefficients (lines 3 and 4).

38. The paired results do not include an estimate for non-profit-sharing firms (line 1), since these are the base group for the paired differences. Since there is no base effect of demand shocks in the paired difference, the illustration of paired results in table 4.6 (columns 2, 4, 6, and 8) uses the non-profit-sharing effect from the preceding column as the base effect.

39. Reflecting the results from lines 1 to 3, column 3, table 4.6.

40. In using paired data, all comparisons are relative to the non-profit-sharing group, which is why there is no growth trend reflected for this group (i.e., it hovers around 100 percent). The

paired regression results do not show sensitivity to GNP changes for the baseline non-profit-sharing group, but only differential sensitivity compared to the profit-sharing pairs. For purposes of illustration, figure 4.3 borrows the coefficients on baseline sensitivity from regression 3 of appendix table A4.6.

41. Reflecting the numbers on lines 2, 3, and 4 of column 4, table 4.6.

42. As discussed there, these estimates are based only upon company sales changes as demand shock measures, because of the difficulty of distinguishing what would constitute a "large" and "small" shock for an individual firm from the aggregate measures.

43. The hypothesis that employment responses are equal between the two types of firms was rejected at the 95 percent level for regressions 2 and 4 (using F-tests), but not for the smaller samples in regressions 3 and 5.

44. Prior negative shock was defined as a decrease in (deflated) sales last year. These estimates are on lines 1 to 4 of appendix table A4.6.

45. In particular, the coefficients on line 3 were more positive for PS firms in three of the four regressions, indicating a larger cushion of employees who are retained under large negative shocks. Also, the coefficients on line 4 are smaller or more negative for the PS firms, indicating a smaller likelihood and magnitude of layoffs under small demand shocks. For a discussion of the theoretical expectations under the small and large shocks, see appendix 4.

46. This is seen in particular by comparing the PS and NPS coefficients on rows 7 and 8 with their theoretical expectation in column 1. In each case the PS firm had more hiring than the NPS firm. While this does not fit the theoretical expectation of behavior under a prior negative shock, it is nonetheless "favorable" behavior of greater willingness to hire by PS firms.

47. If unionization affects employment changes, obviously the proportion unionized will vary between years. If each year's proportion were used, this would introduce a substantial problem of simultaneity between employment changes and proportion unionized, biasing the coefficients. The use of 1991 proportion unionized as an "instrument" for proportion unionized across the time period will correct this bias (while introducing some measurement error since the proportion unionized may have changed since the beginning of the period).

48 The results were not sensitive to the use of other cutoff points, including a 0 percent cut-off (implying that the profit share must fully substitute for regular compensation). Even if profit sharing fully substitutes for regular compensation, the total compensation per employee may, on average, be higher because of a risk premium for the variability from profit-sharing compensation.

As noted previously, the limited information on labor expenses restricts the sample for these tests. These results are based on only 14 profit-sharing adopters that reported more than one year of labor expense data in both the pre- and postadoption periods, and had 90 percent or more of employees covered.

49. This cutoff was chosen for the same reason expressed above. Again, results were not sensitive to other cutoff points.

50. Since less than half of the companies reported labor expenses, there were too few observations for paired results within industry. Lacking within-industry comparisons of responses to aggregate demand shocks, only the company sales changes are used as demand shocks here.

51. This is clearly not an ideal measure for two reasons. First, changes in unit labor costs will reflect changes in productivity occurring from other sources, while the marginal cost of employing labor may have stayed constant. Second, total labor expenses as reported in CompuStat include the profit share—so that even if unit labor costs show a small increase, the profit share may still be partially substituting for regular fixed pay. For these reasons, the change in unit labor costs used here is not a clear indicator of whether the perceived cost of employing labor has changed following profit-sharing adoption; rather, an increase in unit labor cost is treated simply as indicating a greater likelihood of the profit share being an add-on.

Each firm's (labor expenses/sales) was calculated, the (2-digit) industry mean for that year was subtracted, and the within-company mean of the result (across years) was calculated. Old profit-sharing companies were divided according to whether this within-company mean was positive or negative (with a positive value representing a higher likelihood of profit sharing adding on to pay), while new profit-sharing companies were divided according to whether this mean increased or decreased after adoption (with an increase representing a higher likelihood of profit sharing adding on to pay). As with the previous estimates in table 4.7, the limited information on labor expenses restricts the sample size: only 14 profit-sharing adopters could be found that reported two or more years of labor expense data in both the pre- and postadoption periods (with six having a decrease in average unit labor costs).

52. The two measures of substitution did not classify the same adopters as "substituting" or "adding on" to base pay, with only six of the fourteen firms having the same status in both samples.

53. Results on motives for maintaining profit-sharing plans (from table 2.2) showed, not surprisingly, that providing for retirement security was a higher priority for firms maintaining only deferred plans.

54. The presented results do not divide old profit-sharing companies from new adopters; when this is done, the small number of observations in several categories produces very unreliable estimates. The pattern of results in the unreported regressions provided no clear indication of greater or lesser stability after adoption for any of the plan formulas.

55. The weak results may in part be due to the small sample size, since the question on formulas was on the mail portion of the survey and only half of profit-sharing companies responded.

56. Estimates of occupational composition by industry class showed roughly similar composition among the major classes, except for retail trade. Production and service workers constituted an average 41-53 percent of workers in all major industries except retail trade, where it was 80 percent. Similarly, professional/administrative workers constituted a mean of 22-37 percent of employees, and clerical/technical workers constituted a mean of 16-31 percent of employees across industries, except for retail trade (with means of 11 percent and 10 percent, respectively).

57. As with the estimate of union coverage, occupational composition was asked only as of the survey year (1991). This value was imputed back through the sample period to estimate the relationship of occupational composition to demand shocks. If each year's proportion were used, this would introduce a substantial problem of simultaneity between employment changes and occupational composition, biasing the coefficients. The use of 1991 proportions as "instruments" across the time period will correct this bias (while introducing some measurement error since the composition may have changed since the beginning of the period).

Including each occupation proportion with its demand shock interaction in a regression will lead to high multicollinearity and high standard errors, since the demand shocks are identical. The presented results were done separately for each occupation group.

58. The results in appendix table A4.11 are only for unpaired data, reflecting both between-industry and within-industry effects. The occupational composition tends to be very similar within an industry, so that paired within-industry differences were small and failed to produce reliable estimates of the relationship between occupation and demand shocks. Separate estimation of stability effects by industry class (using both 8-category and 25-category definitions) did not show greater or smaller stability effects in any industry.

5
Summary, Conclusions, and Policy Implications

Profit sharing with employees has existed since the earliest days of the United States. A major source of support has been ideological: profit sharing has been seen as a way to strengthen support for capitalism by tying worker rewards more explicitly to the health of the firms. There have been two main theories about the effects of profit sharing. One is tied to employee incentives: profit sharing has long been advocated on the grounds that it can improve business performance by encouraging worker effort, cooperation, and sharing of ideas and information (the "productivity theory"). A second, more recent, theory is tied to employer incentives: profit sharing has been theorized to change incentives to hire and retain employees, leading to greater employment and output stability for firms and the economy as a whole (the "stability theory").

Overview of Trends

Is there enough practice of profit sharing to make it even worthy of study? The disparate sources of evidence, summarized in chapter 1, indicate that roughly one-sixth to one-fourth of American businesses and employees participate in some form of profit sharing. The prevalence does not appear to vary greatly by occupational status or by firm size, but does appear to be more common among companies with public stock, and less common among unionized employees. This no doubt reflects a long history of suspicion of profit sharing by unions, although the incidence of profit sharing for unionized employees increased in the 1980s (often tied to wage concessions). Internationally, there has been substantial interest in profit sharing in Europe and elsewhere, but little data on actual incidence (Blanchflower 1991; Florkowski 1991; Uvalic 1990).

This study reports on a new database on profit sharing in U.S. companies with public stock. The survey found that 40.7 percent of such companies reported having a profit-sharing plan for employees other than top management, a figure very much in line with other data sources for U.S. public companies. Data were collected on profit-sharing coverage, types, and formulas, as well as on other personnel policies that may compete or interact with profit sharing in affecting firm behavior. A telephone survey was done of 500 public companies—half with profit sharing and half without, for purposes of comparison. To maximize comparability, an attempt was made to find for each firm a same-industry pair with the opposite profit-sharing status—for example, for each profit-sharing food processor, an attempt was made to find a non-profit-sharing food processor for comparison (resulting in pairs for 410 of the firms). To provide evidence on the productivity and stability theories of profit sharing, the survey data were matched with publicly available data from public companies on company characteristics and performance over the 1970-91 period.

Predicting Adoption of Profit Sharing

What factors influence the adoption of profit-sharing plans? Prior research has mostly relied on cross-sectional data to examine the correlates of company and industry variables with the presence of profit-sharing plans (11 studies summarized in table 2.1). While it has produced no clear consistent findings, some of the variables highlighted by this research as potentially important are: unionization, firm size, employee composition, firm growth, capital intensity, and industry variability.

In contrast to most previous research, the analysis presented here focused on what factors predict the *adoption* of profit sharing, relying mainly on changes in variables in the two years preceding the decision to adopt. Such analysis provides a better indication of the causality between company characteristics and the presence of profit sharing. It was difficult, however, to find strong predictors of adoption.

Improvements in profit margins and stock prices appear to increase the chance of profit-sharing adoption (consistent with British data from

Poole 1989). When profits, or expected profits, increase, a profit-sharing plan may be an attractive means of increasing compensation without obligating the company to a fixed amount each year. Growth in the profit margin over the two preceding years appears to be most important for predicting adoption of cash plans, while increases in the closing stock price appear to be most important for deferred plan adoption (as summarized in table 2.3).[1] The explanation offered here is that deferred plans represent a longer-term commitment (with higher start-up and shutdown costs), so that a longer-term increase in profitability (reflected in the stock price) favors deferred plans.

This finding, while interesting in itself, also serves to cast doubt on cross-sectional analyses of profit sharing, in which profit-sharing and non-profit-sharing companies are compared on measures of performance. If higher profits in fact help predict the adoption of profit sharing, then it is not surprising to find that profit-sharing companies score higher on profitability and other performance measures.[2]

The theory that increased variability of company sales or profits helps predict profit-sharing adoption receives some very weak support. The pattern of estimates indicates that this is primarily a between-industry, rather than within-industry, effect—that is, higher variability in one's industry during the past five years favors the adoption of profit sharing, while higher variability compared to industry competitors does not strongly favor this (although even here, the estimate signs support this story). Also, comparison of cash and deferred adoption indicates that increased variability may predict adoption of deferred plans, but does not predict adoption of cash plans.

The only other factor that may predict profit-sharing adoption is the presence of a union. Over the period of this study (1970-1990), union contracts were increasingly likely to include profit-sharing provisions (Bell and Neumark 1993). Union presence showed up in several estimates as a predictor of profit-sharing adoption, particularly for cash plans where it roughly doubled the chance of adoption in the sample period.

Just as noteworthy are the factors that do not predict adoption of profit-sharing plans. Deferred profit-sharing plans offer a potentially attractive source of capital for firms, since the assets of such plans may be heavily invested in employer securities. However, changes in two measures of the reliance on outside capital—debt/equity and interest payments—did not predict adoption of either type of plan. Changes in company and industry labor costs per employee did not predict adoption of profit sharing. The firm's expenditure on research and development was also hypothesized to be a potential predictor of profit sharing, since this is an area in which supervision costs and the value of cooperation may be higher. However, neither levels nor changes in R&D expenditures were significant predictors of profit-sharing adoption. Likewise, recent growth in sales and capital intensity did not predict adoption.

Finally, several company characteristics were addressed that predict participation by union employees and different occupational groups in profit sharing. Because such data were not easily available for the time at which profit sharing was adopted, this analysis relied on 1990 data in profit-sharing companies to examine the correlates of current coverage by union employees and occupational groups.

The age of profit sharing, and the share of professional/administrative employees within a company were significant predictors of employee coverage within profit-sharing plans. Higher union density predicts lower coverage in each of the three main occupational groups (professional/administrative, production/service, and clerical/technical), although a greater likelihood that a majority of union members participate. Overall, a 10 percentage point increase in unionization within a firm is associated with a 2.2 percentage point decline in employee coverage within a profit-sharing firm. Therefore, while unions have become more likely to participate in profit sharing in the past 20 years, their members are still less likely than nonunion employees to be covered.

The Productivity Theory

Does profit sharing improve company performance? For over a century there have been claims that it does, by encouraging workers to cooperate with each other and management, share ideas and information, and monitor co-workers. This theory has received new attention in the past two decades, given the slowdown in productivity growth in the United States (which averaged only 1.2 percent per year in the

1970s and 1980s, following growth of almost 3.0 percent per year between World War II and 1970) (*Economic Report of the President 1992*: table B-44).

The main argument against positive effects of profit sharing is the weak connection between individual effort and reward in group incentive systems; it is possible that this may be overcome by some form of cooperative agreement among employees, fostered by appropriate policies and climate in the firm. Other theoretical issues include employee self-selection into or out of profit-sharing companies, and the possibility of weaker incentives for managerial supervision and capital investment.

Research in the past 15 years supports the idea that profit sharing can improve corporate performance. Across 26 econometric studies summarized in table 3.1, a majority of estimated associations (57.4 percent) between profit sharing and productivity measures have been positive and strong enough that random sampling error can be ruled out as an explanation. The majority of these studies, though, have not compared companies before and after the adoption of profit sharing. This leaves open the question of causality: higher productivity may lead companies to adopt profit-sharing plans, rather than vice versa. This possibility is made more plausible by the finding in chapter 2 that increases in profitability help predict the adoption of profit-sharing plans.

A variety of methods and variables was employed in attempting to gauge the relationship between productivity and profit-sharing adoption and presence. As with most previous research, the estimates were based on a production function with capital and labor inputs. The availability of panel data made it possible to compare pre- and postadoption performance on the adopters, and remove the influence of any constant factors that make one firm more productive than another (such as market placement or managerial quality). Two productivity measures were used (value-added per employee and sales per employee). Estimates were made using all firms (controlling for broad industry and year effects), and using paired differences between firms in the same industry. The estimates also accounted for union presence and the adoption and presence of ESOPs and defined benefit pension plans.

The adoption of a profit-sharing plan within the sample period was associated with a 3.5 to 5 percent increase in productivity, with no consistent estimate of an upward or downward productivity trend after adoption (summarized in table 3.3, and illustrated in figure 3.1). Random sampling error could be ruled out for most of the adoption effects. When profit sharing is measured as proportion of employees covered rather than a simple dummy variable, the results are slightly weaker.[3] The estimated effect sizes are very much in line with those from other studies, where a meta-analysis indicated that the median productivity difference associated with profit sharing was 4.4 percent (Weitzman and Kruse 1990: 138-9). Simply adopting profit sharing, though, was not found to be automatically associated with productivity increases; across various estimates, between one-fourth and one-third of the adopters had no productivity increase beyond that predicted by other company characteristics (in fact, outcomes were just as dispersed for adopters as for nonadopters, but were on average shifted in a more positive direction for the adopters).

A variety of factors are commonly believed to influence the motivational value of profit sharing. First, cash plans are generally seen as better motivators than deferred plans, due to the immediacy of the reward. When broken down by plan type, the results are generally consistent with this belief; adoption of cash plans is associated with larger productivity increases in all estimates. Second, plans that explicitly tie contributions to profits—as opposed to a percentage of pay, a discretionary amount, or another method—are believed to be better motivators. The inferiority of percent-of-pay plans is generally confirmed by the estimates, although the results were more favorable for adoption of discretionary plans than for percent-of-profits plans. The estimated relationship between changes in profits and profit-sharing contributions is actually slightly higher for discretionary plans than for percent-of-profit plans (and much larger than for percent-of-pay plans). While discretionary plans are not generally viewed as good motivators, it was noted that such plans may be more effectively used to reward employee performance (subtracting out the "noise" from other influences on profits) in an atmosphere of high employee trust that better employee performance will be recognized and rewarded.

Company size is strongly expected to be a factor in the effect of profit sharing on performance, since individual incentives should grow weaker as the number of employees who share in profits grows larger. Analysis of profit-sharing effects in five size classes gives anomalous results (summarized in table 3.4). The productivity effects of profit-sharing adoption are in fact largest in the smallest size class (less than 775 employees). However, estimated productivity effects in the largest size class (more than 17,000 employees), while smaller in size, are also strong enough to rule out random sampling error. This is hard to reconcile with considerations of individual incentives, though it may indicate that the presence of profit sharing is as important as the size of the performance-pay link, and large companies may be able to develop a "corporate culture" in which profit sharing is most effective.

The size of the profit share in relation to employee compensation is also commonly believed to be an important factor in its motivational potential. The profit-sharing sample was split into "high-contribution" and "low-contribution" groups based on the average contribution as a percentage of payroll (to attempt a measure of company policy regarding contributions and minimize obvious problems of higher performance leading to higher contributions in any year). The estimates (table 3.4) indicated more positive effects for adoption and presence of high-contribution plans.

Finally, this study addressed the questions of whether profit sharing may simply be a proxy for other personnel policies, and whether profit sharing interacts with information-sharing and other policies designed to make better use of employee ideas and skills. When the adoption and presence of seven other personnel policies were accounted for, the profit-sharing estimates were virtually unchanged, indicating that profit sharing is unlikely to be a proxy for these other policies. When profit-sharing adoption and presence were interacted with three types of information-sharing, and with coverage of profit-sharing participants by the seven personnel policies, there were no clear indications that these policies enhance or detract from the effect of profit sharing. The one possible exception is for employee involvement programs covering profit-sharing participants, where the pattern of results was positive. To more fully explore this question, profit-sharing companies were also asked whether the adoption of profit sharing was accompanied by significant changes in other compensation or policies. One-sixth replied in the affirmative, and these companies had generally higher increases in productivity in the year of adoption (table 3.6). Examination of open-ended responses about the type of changes, though, gives no clear indication of what policies may interact with profit sharing: nearly half said that other incentive plans had been revised or dropped, and nearly half said there had been other changes in wages or benefits. Only one company reported a change in a personnel policy other than compensation (a new training program).

What is the verdict on whether profit sharing improves performance? Different conclusions may reasonably be drawn from the array of data presented here.

On the positive side, arguments in favor of profit sharing may be marshalled as follows: Adoption of profit sharing is statistically associated with significant productivity increases, with no negative postadoption trend (arguing against a simple "Hawthorne effect" from the novelty of an innovation). The productivity differentials are very much in line with results from previous studies. In line with expectations about the effect of profit sharing, these increases are found to be largest for cash plans, for small companies, and for plans with high average contributions, and nonexistent for percent-of-pay plans where the relationship to profits is the weakest. In addition, the positive results remain when accounting for other policies to solicit employee ideas, decisionmaking skills, and commitment; therefore prior positive results on profit sharing do not appear to be simply reflecting such policies. There was some weak evidence that profit sharing combines with employee involvement programs to positively affect productivity. A variety of techniques to control for statistical bias from company self-selection into profit sharing did not weaken the results.

On the negative side, skeptics of profit sharing may make the following arguments: It is difficult to believe that profit sharing causes a single immediate upward jump in productivity before employees have had a chance to become familiar with it. It takes time for people to learn how to work together cooperatively to improve performance, implying that the productivity effects should be more gradual. The great dispersion in outcomes is noteworthy, with a substantial number of adopters experiencing no productivity increase. The existence of significant upward jumps in productivity even in the largest size class is very suspicious: it strains credulity to think that 17,000 or more employees could be inspired to increase productivity when the individual incentive in such large companies is so weak. It is very possible that a profit-sharing plan is simply being used to share with employees some of the benefits from increased productivity (occurring for other reasons), without increasing fixed compensation levels. Discretionary plans should not be good motivators for employees, and the favorable results for them casts further doubt on the results. There is little clue as to what makes profit sharing "work": there was little evidence of patterns of interactions between profit sharing, information-sharing, and personnel policies. Finally, if profit sharing really caused upward jumps in productivity, it should be more widespread by now.

Much as it is tempting to offer a verdict on profit sharing and productivity, no definite one is possible. It is quite striking that, on average, companies adopting profit sharing have an upward jump in productivity relative to their peers, but it is not clear why this happens. This study has employed more detailed data surrounding the adoption and presence of profit sharing than have past studies, and has identified several features of plans that are associated with higher productivity, but it has not identified company characteristics that help profit sharing "work." The issue of causality has not been resolved. *If* profit sharing is in fact partly responsible for the productivity increases, it may be that the conditions that engender positive effects of profit sharing are highly specific to each workplace. "Corporate culture," trust in management, and history of employee relations are examples of situational factors that may determine how employees receive and respond to profit sharing (discussed further in the section on implications for companies).

The Stability Theory

Does profit sharing increase the stability of employment by changing the incentives of employers to hire and fire workers? This theory received much attention in the 1980s as a possible source of a cure for economic instability in capitalist economies. There have been 15 studies of profit sharing and employment stability (summarized in table 4.1). Most of the studies that directly measure stability have found some association between profit sharing and greater stability, though the studies on how the profit share is treated in employment decisions are more mixed.

One feature of the stability theory is that the profit share must substitute for other forms of regular fixed pay in order to alter employer views of the cost of hiring new workers and of maintaining workers during periods of decreased demand. If it does not, no stabilizing effects of profit sharing are expected. This question was approached in several ways in this study. For companies reporting labor expenses and profit-sharing contribution in a given year, the average compensation with and without the profit share was calculated as a percentage of industry average compensation. Results in this limited sample were consistent with a trade-off: mean and median values of these profit-sharing firms are slightly above industry averages for all compensation, but below industry averages for compensation excluding the profit share.

A second method to address the trade-off issue was to examine compensation levels and growth for all companies reporting labor expenses (table 4.3). This revealed a striking difference between companies that had adopted profit sharing prior to 1975 and those who adopted after that time. The "old" profit-sharing companies had mean compensation levels that were substantially higher than industry averages, while the "new" profit-sharing companies had mean compensation levels that were at or below industry averages. For the adopters with labor expense data both before and after adoption, the compensation levels showed small gains after adoption (with a mean of 0.9 percent, and median of 1.9 percent).

A third method was to predict compensation levels and growth using data on profit-sharing, unionization, defined benefit pensions, and ESOPs (summarized in table 4.4). The estimate sizes indicated that compensation levels for old profit-sharing companies were higher than for non-profit-sharing and new profit-sharing companies. The profit-sharing adopters were estimated to have slight initial decreases in compensation when profit sharing is adopted, followed by positive trends so that, on average, pay is higher after adoption than before.

Does profit sharing substitute for regular compensation? This appears to be unlikely for old profit-sharing firms, since they had compensation levels higher than industry averages and compensation growth at or above industry averages. Therefore the profit share is likely to be more of an "add-on" than a substitute for regular compensation among old profit-sharing firms (consistent with the 1974 finding of higher base pay among profit-sharing firms, in Mitchell, Lewin, and Lawler 1990). In contrast, the profit share appears more likely to substitute for fixed compensation among some of the new profit-sharing adopters, since the average increase in total compensation is smaller than the typical profit share.

A second feature of the stability theory is that employers do not treat profit-sharing payments and fixed wages in the same way when setting employment levels: unlike wages, profit-sharing payments should not be seen as part of the obligatory cost of a labor hour (the short-run marginal cost of labor). Rather, employers should essentially ignore the profit share when hiring and retaining employees. The estimated employment effects of wages and profit-sharing payments were generally consistent with this idea. The results were sensitive, though, to the choice of variables designed to remove bias from the effect of company performance upon the profit share, and no firm conclusion was drawn regarding this proposition.

A key prediction of the stability theory is that profit sharing should lead to employment stability. While this theory was developed at a macroeconomic level, it is based on firm-level incentives that in principle allow tests of the theory using firm-level data. This study compared the employment responses of profit-sharing firms under two types of economywide demand shocks (changes in the unemployment rate and in GNP, with the paired results accounting for industry differences), and under firm-specific demand shocks represented by sales changes. Sales changes were not used exclusively because the stability theory predicts greater stability in physical output as well as employment, and if sales changes are primarily reflecting physical output changes they would not provide an appropriate measure of a demand shock. The employment behavior of old profit-sharing companies was analyzed separately from that of new profit-sharing companies; this allowed comparison of the pre- and postadoption behavior of profit-sharing adopters, and separate analysis of the old profit-sharing adopters where profit sharing appears unlikely to substitute for regular pay.

The stability theory does not predict a simple and direct relationship between profit sharing and employment changes. Rather, it predicts a discontinuous relationship (discussed in appendix 4) that depends on the size of the demand shock, whether the shock is positive or negative, the extent to which the profit share substitutes for regular pay, the sensitivity of company employment to wage changes, and whether the demand shock follows upon a prior negative shock that may have eliminated the theorized excess demand for labor. A full test of the stability theory would require these data. An approximation to such a test was made with several assumptions about demand shocks and limited data on profit share sizes. The results indicated that: (1) The employment behavior of profit-sharing firms in response to demand shocks does appear to differ from that of non-profit-sharing firms; (2) The profit-sharing employment response to demand shocks was favorable (compared to non-profit-sharing firms), when firms were not recovering from a prior negative shock, and the pattern was generally favorable to the stability theory; and (3) The situation was more mixed when firms were recovering from prior negative shocks, with profit-sharing firms having a favorable smaller response to further negative shocks, and generally equal or larger responses to positive shocks, though this latter finding does not fit the theory since the theorized response should have been smaller (because the firm should have laid off fewer workers during the prior negative shock).

Following previous research, a simpler and more direct technique was used for the majority of tests of the employment behavior of profit-sharing firms (due to the difficulty of finding appropriate data for the full test). The employment responses of profit-sharing firms to positive and negative shocks were compared with those of non- and pre-profit-sharing firms, with emphasis on the negative shocks since the predictions are clearest with respect to employment cutbacks.

Did profit sharing lead to more employment stability in this period? The direct tests indicated that, comparing pre- and postadoption behavior, profit-sharing adopters had smaller cutbacks in response to GNP decreases after adoption (though sampling error could be ruled out only in the nonpaired data). The predicted employment paths in figures 4.2 and 4.3, showed higher growth for new adopters and old profit-sharing firms, relative to non-profit-sharing firms. For a firm that adopted profit sharing between the two recessions of the period (1973-75 and 1980-82), the employment cutback is relatively smaller during the later recession. However, there were no estimated differences in response to company sales decreases. The remainder of chapter 4 explored how different characteristics of profit sharing might relate to the theorized stability effects.

Does unionization make a difference? Higher unionization was generally associated with unfavorable employment behavior—smaller employment responses to positive shocks, and larger responses to negative shocks. Participation in profit sharing by a majority of union members was found to be associated with a slight decrease in responsiveness to negative shocks, but no estimates were found where sampling error could be ruled out.

Do compensation changes and levels make a difference? The theory is clear that profit sharing should only have a positive effect on stability if it substitutes, at least in part, for regular fixed pay. This does not mean that fixed pay levels must go down: as discussed in chapter 4, if the productivity theory is correct and workers put forth extra effort to raise productivity—thereby raising profit and pay—the stability theory may still apply if fixed pay is a smaller portion of worker output (and workers are being rewarded for their extra effort largely through the profit share). Two tests were made of whether the profit share substituted in part for regular fixed pay: one which looked at changes in average pay per employee, and a second which looked at changes in pay in relation to output. Both tests indicated that firms in which profit sharing appeared to substitute for regular pay had much lower responsiveness to negative shocks after adoption. Due to the small number of firms reporting sufficient labor expense data, these results should only be taken as indicative.

Finally, what is the relation of employment stability to cash and deferred profit sharing, different formulas, and participation by different occupations? Several estimates indicated that adoption of deferred plans was associated with lower responsiveness to negative aggregate shocks, but there were no consistent patterns for cash plans or for deferred plans under company sales shocks. Among plan formulas, the percent-of-profit plans had the only consistent estimates of lower responsiveness to negative shocks (consistent with the stability theory, though sampling error could be weakly ruled out only for one estimate) and of higher responsiveness to positive shocks. Looking at the profit-sharing participation of three occupational groups, adoption of profit sharing was associated with decreased responsiveness to GNP declines for all three groups, and decreased responsiveness to sales declines for clerical/technical and production/service workers, but not for professional/administrative employees (and sampling error could not be ruled out for most of these differences).

What is the verdict on the stability theory? The mix of evidence does not support a clear conclusion. The positive and negative arguments may be marshalled as follows.

On the positive side, the approximation of a full test of the stability theory found that the theorized patterns appeared to fit employment behavior when firms were not recovering from negative shocks. The generally higher responses to positive shocks by profit-sharing firms when they were recovering from negative shocks, which does not fit the theory, may simply illustrate that these firms are hungry for labor, as generally predicted by the stability theory. The simpler tests showed improvements in responsiveness to aggregate shocks after adoption. Adoption of profit-sharing plans in which a majority of union members participated showed a pattern of lower responsiveness to negative shocks. Both tests of the relation between the profit share and regular fixed pay were consistent with theory: the results were more favorable where profit sharing appeared to substitute for regular fixed pay. Finally, the results on plan formulas indicated that percent-of-profits plans, in line with theory, appear to be associated with the most favorable employment behavior. The tremendous variety of forms of profit sharing in the United States rarely match up with the pure form in the stability theory. Many employers may treat "profit-sharing" payments as regular wages. Given this, it is not surprising that the "grab bag" of what is called profit sharing in the United States does not produce strong results, and study of more relevant kinds of profit sharing is likely to be fruitful.

On the negative side, skeptics may note that there is no strong evidence for favorable effects of profit sharing on employment stability, and several pieces of the pattern are unfavorable (such as several estimates of profit-sharing companies, particularly old ones, having larger employment cutbacks in response to negative shocks). Several favorable results are based on distant aggregate shocks, or on small samples (in the case of the compensation results), and sampling error often cannot be ruled out. Even among percent-of-profits plans, where the theory should most directly apply, only one of the favorable results allows sampling error to be weakly ruled out. All in all, detractors may conclude, profit sharing has not been shown to produce any notable differences in employment behavior.

While no definite verdict is possible, the results indicate several ways in which profit sharing appears to affect employment behavior, and clearly leave the stability theory open for further research. This study has illustrated the complexity of the empirical issues in assessing the stability theory. As noted by Mitchell, empirical research in inconclusive on even such a basic issue of economic theory as the employment effects of the minimum wage, raising the question, "If we cannot settle that issue empirically, what hope is there for convincingly and definitively demonstrating (or refuting) the macro effects of particular pay systems?" (1993: 22). Recognizing that convincing and definitive empirical tests of the stability theory may be very unlikely, further research can nonetheless shed substantial light on the actual behavior of profit-sharing companies, and create a foundation for future policy debates and theoretical development.

The results from this study have several implications for future research. First, these results have highlighted the importance of examining compensation levels, and whether the profit share trades off against base compensation. Future research certainly needs to address this, to examine whether the perceived cost of hiring or retaining profit-sharing employees differs from that of non-profit-sharing employees (recognizing and taking into account the effects productivity may have on pay, requiring measures other than simple pay levels). Measurement of demand shocks also deserves more attention, both to take account of the theorized greater stability of physical output (which is a potentially serious limit on the applicability of sales measures), and to distinguish the point at which demand shocks should exhaust the theorized excess demand for labor (which requires measures of typical profit shares and the relationship of demand shocks to employment levels). Finally, while this study analyzed a broad spectrum of what is called "profit sharing" by U.S. companies, future research should focus more intensively on plans where profit shares are strongly linked to profitability.

Implications for Companies

What implications do these findings have for companies considering the use of profit sharing? The adoption of profit sharing was found to be associated with, on average, an increase in productivity, but the dispersion in outcomes was very large, and a number of adopters had decreases in productivity. This implies that, *if* profit sharing does in fact affect productivity, the effects are very likely to depend on a number of conditions and characteristics of a firm, its plan design, and its implementation. Such a conclusion is strongly echoed in the literature on case studies and the design of group incentive programs. Following is a brief review of the factors most often mentioned in the prescriptive literature on the design of group incentives, with several references to the results from this study.[4]

The prescriptive literature emphasizes, first, that a number of factors need to be assessed prior to installing a group incentive plan. These include (1) the hierarchical structure of decisionmaking in the firm (a centrally organized vs. decentralized "flat" structure); (2) current systems of accountability and performance measurement, and pay sensitivity to those measurements; (3) pay practices in the relevant industry or geographical area; (4) the presence of unions and history of union-management relations; (5) employee demographics that influence risk preferences, turnover probabilities, and training needs; (6) the ways in which the type of work, job responsibilities, and past management practice support an individual or team orientation; and (7) several interrelated elements that reflect the history of employment relations and company "culture," including the presence and structure of formal and informal employee involvement, communication and information-sharing, employee trust in and commitment to the company, and the pressure for performance. If employee involvement, trust, and commitment do not exist when a plan is installed, the prescriptive literature emphasizes that they will not automatically be created by a new plan.[5] Plan success in this case will depend on thoroughgoing efforts to create new management styles, communication, and processes for employee input to change the work structure and environment.

If a group incentive is deemed worthwhile, the literature recommends paying attention to the following elements of plan design and implementation: (1) which employee groups to include; (2) a formula that creates a "line of sight" from employee behavior to plan outcomes (possibly blending the plan with operational measures); (3) anticipated size of average contributions to ensure that the contribution is a significant portion of employee pay; (4) cash or deferred payouts; (5) employee involvement in plan design to meet employee needs and engender strong employee support; and (6) ensuring support at all levels of management to integrate the plan into management philosophy.

Results from this study are relevant to several of these points. There were larger productivity increases with the adoption of plans with high average contributions, and with the adoption of cash plans.[6] Somewhat surprisingly, the results also indicated the most positive effects for plans where the contribution is discretionary, with no set formula—it is possible that a discretionary plan may be used to more accurately reflect the contribution of employees to improved performance (subtracting much of the "noise" in profits which is due to other factors), but this would appear to require a high level of employee trust that the discretion will not be abused. The finding that productivity increases were largest in small firms is consistent with the prescription to keep the basis for payoff within the "line of sight" of employees. There was no strong support for the recommendation that profit sharing works best when combined with information-sharing and programs encouraging employee involvement. Given the strong prescription that these are very important for profit sharing to have motivational effects, this finding may either: (1) cast doubt on the conclusion that profit sharing is responsible for the average performance improvement observed here, or (2) cast doubt on the broad measures of information-sharing and employee involvement used here, suggesting that more detailed measures or company-specific analysis should be used.

What implications does the stability theory have for companies? The stability theory is oriented toward the economywide benefits of broad profit sharing rather than the benefits that one firm may reap by adopting profit sharing. While there are many ways in which firms may gain through employment stabilization strategies (e.g., by retaining employee skills in which the firm has invested, and by increasing employee commitment which can lead to a more motivated and flexible workforce),[7] the theory predicts that individual firms will not have sufficient incentive to adopt profit sharing since many of the theorized benefits from stability do not accrue directly to the firm. In fact, there may be some disincentives for individual firms to adopt profit sharing, such as employee aversion to fluctuating income. For firms that would like to pursue employment stabilization strategies, though, profit sharing may be a useful complement to such efforts. It may do this by adding flexibility to one element of labor costs: when the firm is hit with decreases in product demand, the profit share should be ignored by profit-maximizing managers as a cost of retaining employees (according to theory). Employee concerns about fluctuating income may be balanced by increased employment security, and by the prospect of higher income if company performance improves (whether or not due to higher employee productivity, as predicted by the productivity theory). Therefore profit sharing may prove useful in helping to stabilize employment at the firm level; once again, though, the major benefit in theory would be to the economy as a whole when profit sharing is widespread, with lower unemployment and a smaller or nonexistent business cycle. Whether such benefits are likely remains an important research question, given that there are several supportive findings but no strong support for the stability theory in the results presented here.

Implications for Unions

Unionized employees are less likely than nonunion employees to be participants in profit-sharing plans, though there has been an increase in profit-sharing provisions in union contracts in the 1980s (as described in chapter 1). While few unions have ever opposed profit sharing outright (Zalusky 1986: 177), the traditional union strategy has emphasized fixed wages and benefits,[8] and firms are less likely to maintain profit sharing after successful union drives (Freeman and Kleiner 1990; Czarnecki 1969).[9]

The distrust of profit sharing by unionists may be traced to three sources. First, profit sharing has been used by some employers as an antiunion tool (National Civic Federation 1920; Lindop 1989; Zalusky 1986). In this study, survey respondents indicated that "reducing likeli-

hood of unionization" was, on average, one of the least important reasons for maintaining profit sharing, yet it was still listed as "very
important" by a small percentage (see table 2.2).

Second, industrial unions have traditionally been committed to
establishing uniform fixed wages and benefits in an industry to "take
wages out of competition"—creating income stability, strengthening
worker solidarity, and forcing management to compete on "its ability
and innovation" (Zalusky 1986: 179). Profit sharing represents a challenge to this approach since it may increase variability of income,
wage dispersion among workers, and worker competition between
firms (Mitchell 1987). As shown by the experience of Ford and General Motors in the 1980s, differences in formulas and company performance can lead to very different worker payouts (Kruger 1986). Such
differences can provide lessons about the types of formulas and contract provisions that can most benefit workers; still, they also illustrate
the potential of profit sharing to increase wage dispersion and income
variability (balanced against greater job security, if the stability theory
is correct).

A third source of union concern is that, compared to fixed wages
and benefits, compliance with contract provisions regarding profit
sharing is more difficult to monitor. If a profit-sharing plan is part of a
union contract, labor law gives unions legal access to company records
to verify contract compliance. Such records may be easier to verify in
companies with public stock, where stockholders and the Securities
and Exchange Commission also monitor the information, than in private companies. One would expect the monitoring problem to lead
unions away from plans where the profit-sharing contribution is wholly
discretionary; in this context, it is noteworthy that discretionary plans,
while slightly less prevalent in unionized profit-sharing firms, nonetheless represent almost half of the plans in unionized firms (though it is
unclear whether these plans are negotiated in union contracts) (Cardinal and Helburn 1986: 169).

Can profit sharing be useful to unions? While not part of the traditional union strategy, profit sharing did figure into concession bargaining in the 1980s: "Profit sharing became part of a trade—an investment
of current wages for a promise of a share of future returns" (Zalusky
1986: 180). Over the 1981-88 period, 17.1 percent of the union contracts involving first-year wage cuts also included profit-sharing provi-

sions.[10] In this context, the concessions are designed to save jobs, while profit sharing provides potential for workers to automatically share in any recovery. The stability theory holds that this method of sharing in recovery—rather than through increases in fixed wages and benefits—will make future layoffs less likely. The evidence from this study on union participation in profit sharing (summarized in table 4.6) is mildly favorable to this idea—for a given demand shock, postadoption layoffs tend to be smaller than preadoption layoffs—but the variability in outcomes does not allow one to reject the possibility that there is no difference in behavior.[11]

Is the productivity theory applicable in unionized settings? It is clear that most instances of profit sharing in union contracts are not the result of efforts to improve productivity (Zalusky 1986, 1990). If it is applied in a unionized setting, there is no clear prediction on how unions will affect the results. As discussed by Cooke (1993), unions may enhance the effects of group-based pay incentives and employee participation through providing additional information channels, greater employment security, narrower pay and status differentials, and greater worker cohesion; they may instead detract from such effects through an adversarial stance against management, limiting efforts to reorganize work, and restricting employee monitoring and sanctions against those not cooperating in team-based activities. Unions clearly add to the complex interplay of factors that determine the performance of profit sharing in a particular setting. While there is potential for profit sharing to positively affect performance in a union setting, too little is known to make general conclusions.[12]

Both the stability and productivity theories imply advantages for workers and unions, through the potential for fewer layoffs under adverse conditions and the potential for higher pay from better performance. This study provides some limited support for both theories, but realizing these potentials (and whether they may be worth the costs of wage concessions when such a choice is presented) undoubtedly depends greatly on circumstances unique to each setting.[13]

Implications for Public Policy

Is there a role for public policy to play in the development of profit sharing? The issue has been a subject of policy debates, proposals, and legislation in a number of countries (Uvalic 1990; Florkowski 1991; D'Art 1992).[14] Current approaches by national governments, as noted by Florkowski (1991), can be divided into four categories: some form of mandatory profit sharing (in 13 countries, although enforcement is unclear), tax incentives (in four countries), advisory institutions (in one country—Denmark),[15] and nonintervention (in 29 countries). The United States has tax incentives only for deferred profit-sharing plans, but this incentive is not specific to profit sharing since it exists for other types of pensions. Great Britain, in contrast, established tax incentives in 1987 specifically targeted to cash profit sharing (motivated in large part by its potential to decrease high unemployment levels).[16]

Is there a role for public policy in the productivity theory? There is no obvious role. The gains from productivity improvement accrue to the company and the employees, so if profit sharing improves productivity, there should be sufficient private incentives for profit-sharing adoption. Tax incentives are likely inappropriate under this theory, since they are potentially costly and likely to encourage cosmetic schemes in workplaces where profit sharing is unlikely to have a positive impact.[17] The most appropriate government role under the productivity theory would be to gather and disseminate information on how profit sharing can be used to increase productivity. Such an approach recognizes that this information may have a "public good" nature, creating a potential role for government similar to its dissemination of information through the agricultural extension system and sponsorship of research on alternative energy sources.[18] As noted by Mitchell, the rationale for this approach is weakened when there is substantial information available from private sources, so that

> the argument for government dissemination of pay system information must be ...that the incentives for "reliable" information spreading are insufficient and that, because government is 'neutral,' its reports and conferences will be seen as more credible (better) than those of potentially- biased private disseminators (or possibly of fuzzy-headed academics left on their own). (1993: 10)

The approach that government should have a role in actively disseminating information is embodied in the recommendation by the Cuomo Commission on Competitiveness to create a "National Center for Employee Participation and Ownership." This would encourage a "new, more participatory type of American capitalism" by assisting companies considering or implementing participative systems such as profit sharing and employee ownership (Kaden and Smith 1992: 105). Florkowski recommends the creation of

> a national commission of government, business, and labor representatives. This body could act as a short-term catalyst by mobilizing expertise, serving as an information clearinghouse, and engaging in research—roles similar to those performed by the National Institute of Occupational Safety and Health. As Denmark's experience demonstrates, this policy choice will not by itself directly facilitate a share economy, but it will promote better quality information for decision making and solutions that are acceptable to all parties. (1991: 111)

He goes on to point out how, with or without such a commission, the U.S. federal government could redesign employer questionnaires "to gather data about the presence and structural features of profit-sharing plans and their outcomes," and could disseminate information through agencies such as the Federal Mediation and Conciliation Service or the (now defunct) Bureau of Labor Management Cooperation. Given the remarkable strength of associations between profit sharing and productivity, and given that productivity growth rates have been slow in the United States, such attention seems warranted.

Is there a role for public policy under the stability theory? Yes, because the gains to employment stability do not accrue only to the profit-sharing firm and employees, but to the entire economy (as worker purchasing power is maintained without unemployment insurance or government assistance).[19] The external benefits to government and the economy, if the stability theory is correct, would be justification for appropriate tax incentives (which was a large part of the rationale for Great Britain's adoption of tax incentives for cash profit sharing in 1987). The accumulated empirical evidence does not yet make a strong case for tax incentives, as may be true for many public policies and programs, but definitely makes a case for the attention of a commission as recommended above.

In line with several dozen studies over the past decade, this one has found higher productivity associated with profit sharing, and differences in employment behavior associated with certain kinds of profit sharing. Most fundamentally, there clearly are links between profit sharing, performance, pay, and employment that are remarkably intriguing and worthy of more analysis. A safe conclusion is the traditional call for further research—to determine if, and under what conditions, profit sharing aids productivity and employment stability—and such a call is made here.[20] Future studies can provide a more solid foundation for policy debates, informed decisions by companies and unions, and future theoretical development (even if, as is true in most areas of inquiry, the conclusions are disparate).

There are high stakes in exploring the potential of profit sharing, since the issues addressed by the profit-sharing theories—productivity, unemployment, and macroeconomic stability—are central to economic performance, security, and the standard of living.

NOTES

1. As discussed in the chapter, it cannot be ruled out that the stock price increase may have been due to the announcement of a profit-sharing plan.

2. This does not invalidate results of cross-sectional studies, particularly where researchers have made corrections for the endogeneity of profit sharing (e.g., Fitzroy and Kraft 1987), or where the effects are found to be labor-embodied (Shepard 1986).

3. If profit sharing is at all responsible for the productivity increases, the stronger results for the dummy variable may reflect the targeting of key employees in firms with less than 100 percent coverage.

4. Numerous journal, magazine, and newspaper articles describing successful and unsuccessful case studies, along with more general literature mentioning profit sharing, were obtained through searches of the ABI/INFORM, UNCOVER, ProQuest, and Business Dateline computerized databases, and the Business Periodicals Index up through June 1993. The following review is based on a small sample of the prescriptive literature on group incentives, drawing from the following books and articles: Belcher (1991); Cooper, Dyck; and Frohlich (1992); Gross (1989); Gross and Bacher (1993); Hubbartt (1991); May (1991); McAdams and Hawk (1992); Nickel (1990); Nichols (1989); Ost (1989); and Tomer (1987). Extended treatments are available in Belcher (1991) and Schuster and Zingheim (1992).

5. Employee trust in management of Fortune 500 firms appears to have declined in the 1980s (Denton 1991). Profit sharing may be a poor method of increasing trust, and may in fact have the opposite effect. In a survey of Michigan employers, a large majority viewed profit sharing by itself as having a negative effect on employee trust (Mishra and Morrissey 1990). A review of studies of employee attitudes under profit sharing, employee ownership, quality circles, and autonomous work groups also makes it clear that employee attitudes will not automatically improve with these workplace innovations (Kelly and Kelly 1991).

6. It remains possible, however, that deferred plans have some delayed advantage in reducing turnover.

7. See Dyer, Foltman, and Milkovich (1985); Osterman (1987); and Ichniowski (1992).

8. Exceptions include the "progress sharing" provision in the United Auto Workers-American Motors contract in 1961, and a number of negotiated profit-sharing plans in the 1980s (particularly in the automobile industry). See Zalusky (1986) for other examples and a discussion.

9. In the absence of formal contractual profit sharing, unions nonetheless affect firm profits, and in some sense may "share" in them by negotiating higher fixed wages and benefits in profitable companies. For evidence on the union-profit relationship, see Becker and Olson (1992).

10. Calculated from table 1 of Mitchell, Lewin, and Lawler. (1990: 25). Overall, 133 contracts included profit sharing, representing 7.4 percent of the contracts identified in this period. In contracts where cost-of-living allowances were frozen or eliminated, 17.6 percent and 12.3 percent (respectively) included profit sharing, again clearly suggesting a higher incidence of profit sharing in concession situations than in nonconcession situations.

11. The favorable but statistically insignificant results for union participation in profit sharing are comparable to those of Bell and Neumark (1993).

12. Limited existing evidence indicates that union participation can have positive effects. Cooke (1993) finds positive interactions of unions and profit/gainsharing on three performance measures in a sample of Michigan manufacturing firms (though the most positive interactions come from unions and employee participation). While the productivity effects of union participation in profit sharing were not a focus of the present study, a cursory examination of the profit-sharing adoptions in chapter 3 revealed positive but smaller and insignificant estimates on adoptions of plans in which a majority of union members participate (with a substantial dispersion in outcomes, indicating a number of positive and negative outcomes).

13. When profit-sharing plans are negotiated, Kruger emphasizes that: "[M]anagement and their unions must commit themselves to the plan if it is to be effective. For a plan to have credibility, it must have the complete support of management, unions, and employees. A key factor is the employees. They must be fully informed of the purposes and goals of the new plan. The features must be thoroughly explained, and they must be convinced or persuaded of its direct benefit" (1986: 153-4).

14. For a related discussion of policy options for employee ownership in the United States, see Blasi and Kruse (1993).

15. For a discussion of the history and debates in Denmark over public policy on profit sharing and employee stock ownership, see chapter 5 in D'Art (1992). Similar discussion for Sweden and Ireland are provided in chapters 4 and 6.

16. For a brief overview of the current status, see Singleton-Green (1992).

17. Tax incentives might, though, be used to encourage experimentation, as temporary incentives have sometimes been designed to encourage development and diffusion of new technologies. Also, it is possible that there are market failures acting against the combination of profit sharing with other participative arrangements, which may also justify tax incentives. See, e.g., Levine and D'Andrea Tyson (1990); and Levine (1992b).

18. If there are valuable lessons on productivity to be learned from company experiments in profit sharing, these "positive externalities" create a stronger case for active government encouragement of profit sharing.

19. This "macro rationale" for profit sharing is further discussed in Mitchell (1993). He also notes that public policy intervention can be based on a "social transformation rationale" (where the practice being encouraged is part of a desired social transformation, such as labor law or civil rights legislation) or on a "merit goods rationale" (where the government takes the lead in encour-

aging citizens to do what is in their long-term interest, such as encouraging retirement security by subsidizing private pension plans).

20. Whether government should sponsor such research, possibly through a commission as described above, is a question better left to those with less self-interest in the answer.

Appendix 1
Construction of Dataset and Analysis of Response

To test adequately the profit-sharing theories requires company performance and employment data over a number of years. The problem with picking companies with the most years of information is that they will be the oldest companies, and perhaps clustered in particular industries; this presents external validity problems in generalizing the results to younger and middle-aged companies and to other industries. The selection rule employed in constructing the sample frame was to identify those companies with at least eight years of employment data over the 1980s (1980-89), since employment data are crucial in testing both profit-sharing theories.

Past evidence indicates that fewer than 50 percent of U.S. companies have profit-sharing plans for employees other than top management. Profit-sharing firms were oversampled to increase their representation in the final dataset. Additionally, to increase the quality of industry controls, an attempt was made to find, for each company, a matched pair within the same (2-digit SIC) industry with the opposite profit-sharing status. For example, for each profit-sharing food processor, an attempt was made to find a non-profit-sharing food processor to act as a paired control.

The initial sample, drawn from the 1990 Standard and Poor's CompuStat at Rutgers University, included 1,085 companies. These were ordered by industry, and a systematic sample was drawn to ensure a representative distribution across industries. The Eagleton Institute at Rutgers, which conducted the survey, employed five interviewers to contact and complete interviews with 250 companies, asking for the Vice-President for Human Resources (if not, then "the person in the company who is most familiar with the employee benefits your company offers").[1] The interviews were completed between May and July of 1991 and took an average of 6.16 minutes. After the initial 250 successful contacts, the process of finding same-industry matched pairs began. For many firms the initial random sample produced matched pairs in the same industry, so that further systematic sampling could be done. Where a same-industry matched pair was needed, firms in that industry were contacted until one with the opposite profit-sharing status could be interviewed. The search for a matched pair was not successful in each industry, which led to the production of a larger sample frame. In those industries the standard was lowered to 7 out of 10 years of employment data in the 1980s, producing an additional 89 companies in the sample frame. Such choice-based sampling produces a final sample which is not representative of the population. This does not produce a bias in fixed-effects estimation (Heckman and Robb 1985: 219). For the sample selection terms and the few specifications that did not use fixed effects, variables were reweighted to reflect the choice-based sampling (Manski and Lerman 1977).[2]

Of the 1,174 companies in the final sample frame, at least one attempt was made to contact 906 of them. Of these, three had gone out of business at the time of the survey, and 36 could not be reached due to disconnected phone numbers, leaving 867 that were contacted. In the course of finding paired controls for the initial systematic sample, two profit-sharing and 53 non-profit-sharing firms were excluded because they could not serve as a paired control. Of the remaining 812 contacted firms, interviews were completed with 500, for a response rate among contacted firms of 61.6 percent. Unsuccessful contacts included 115 refusals and 197 cases where repeated attempts to locate and talk to the appropriate person were unsuccessful.

The information from non-profit-sharing firms was obtained entirely by phone. For profit-sharing firms, the respondents were asked at the end of the phone interview whether they would answer several further questions in a follow-up mail survey. The primary reason for doing so was that the desired information would generally require looking up records relevant to the plan. In particular, information was desired on what share of participants' pay was represented by profit sharing in each of the years 1975 to 1990. In addition, the questions on the profit-sharing formula, and whether profit-sharing adoption was accompanied by changes in management personnel, were reserved for the mail survey. Mail surveys were sent to the 253 profit-sharing participants, and after several call-backs to nonrespondents, were received completed by 124 respondents (a response rate of 49 percent on the mail portion).

The telephone and mail survey forms are reproduced in this appendix. At the beginning of the telephone survey, the confidentiality promise was made explicit for respondents who hesitated or inquired about the survey: "All your responses will be kept totally confidential—no one will know how you responded to any particular question. The results of the survey are presented in a statistical report and will not single out anyone in particular."

Appendix table A1.1 shows a comparison of the firms interviewed in the phone portion of the survey with the other firms that were contacted but not interviewed. As can be seen by comparisons of the mean values, the respondents on average had significantly lower sales, employment, and net assets in 1990 relative to the nonrespondents, but similar averages in profit margins and other financial measures. These measures were used in probit regressions predicting response. Regression 1 uses 1990 measures, and, to determine whether recent trends in these variables affect response, regression 2 uses both 1989 and 1990 measures. Few significant differences in size or financial measures appear in the regressions. In regression 1, at the 10 percent level of statistical significance, respondents appear to have higher capital intensity and lower debt/equity ratios. Recent changes in these variables appear not to matter, as indicated by the insignificance of these variables or their lags in regression 2—the only financial or size measure reaching significance at the 10 percent level is 1989 sales/invested capital. A variety of other measures was used with no greater success in predicting response. Selection corrections using inverse Mill's ratios were included with the subsequent regressions reported in chapters 2, 3, and 4.

NOTES

1. The distribution of respondents was as follows: 60 Vice-Presidents/Directors of Human Resources, 247 Directors/Managers of Employee Benefits, 33 other Vice-Presidents or Corporate Officers, with most of the remainder representing compensation or benefits analysts, or personnel/employee services staff.

2. The reweighting caused very minor changes in the results, largely due to the high incidence of profit sharing (40.7 percent) in the random sample, which did not vary greatly by broad industry.

Table A1.1 Self-Selection of Respondents

	Mean values respondents			Probit regressions (Dep. var. = 1 if respondent, 0 if not)	
	No		Yes	(1)	(2)
1990 values					
ln(sales)	6.237	**	6.782	0.049 (0.14)	0.116 (0.51)
ln(employees)	1.255	**	1.663	-0.161 (0.10)	0.310 (0.50)
ln(net assets)	5.196	**	5.728	0.180* (0.10)	-0.214 (0.43)
Debt/equity	0.383		0.352	-0.388* (0.23)	-0.683 (0.48)
Profit margin	0.166		0.156	-0.316 (0.58)	-0.615 (1.30)
Interest/assets	0.058		0.051	-0.147 (1.12)	0.590 (2.82)
Depreciation/assets	0.180		0.136	1.164 (0.80)	0.641 (1.53)
Sales/invested capital	1.842		1.843	0.009 (0.05)	-0.171 (0.11)
Stock price change	0.188		0.179	0.030 (0.09)	-0.023 (0.11)
Net assets (000,000s)	1236.823		1718.667		
Sales (000,000s)	2381.144	*	3623.414		
Employees (000s)	16.657		19.590		
1989 values					
ln(sales)	6.159	**	6.682		-0.042 (0.50)
ln(employees)	1.252	**	1.635		-0.509 (0.50)
ln(net assets)	5.070	**	5.651		0.413 (0.43)
Debt/equity	0.415		0.385		0.305 (0.45)
Profit margin	0.167		0.165		0.550 (1.40)
Interest/assets	0.062		0.119		-1.521 (3.03)

177

Depreciation/assets	0.178	0.134			0.603	(1.69)
Sales/invested capital	1.870	2.027			0.141*	(0.08)
Stock price change	0.330	0.159			-0.052	(0.07)
Net assets (000,000s)	1135.984	1596.169				
Sales (000,000s)	2129.009 **	3309.635				
Employees (000s)	15.814	19.328				
Industry	Number of companies					
Mining/construction	21	20	0.076	(0.35)	0.246	(0.39)
Nondurable manufacturing	83	153	0.616**	(0.27)	0.622**	(0.31)
Durable manufacturing	87	157	0.662**	(0.26)	0.779**	(0.30)
Communications	13	17	0.248	(0.35)	0.228	(0.37)
Utilities	43	74	0.396	(0.32)	0.365	(0.35)
Wholesale	9	18	0.920**	(0.42)	1.096**	(0.47)
Retail	17	25	0.647*	(0.33)	0.760**	(0.37)
FIRE	20	22	0.272	(0.41)	0.303	(0.46)
Service (omitted)	19	14				
Constant			-1.248	(0.50)	-1.418	(0.56)
N	312	500	711		662	
Log-likelihood			-451.985		-413.052	

NOTE: Standard errors in parentheses.
*For mean values, respondents and nonrespondents are significantly different at p <.10. For regressions, coefficient is significantly different from zero at p <.10 **p <.05.

PROFIT SHARING--TELEPHONE SURVEY

_____

<u>DK91</u>   _____   __1__   TIME BEGAN: _____
101-104   RESP ID   DECK
        105-107   108

_____

SCREENING QUESTIONS

<u>Introduction for Receptionist</u>:

Hello, I'd like to speak with the Vice President for Human Resources.

<u>Interviewer Note</u>:

<u>Other possible titles are</u>: Chief Operating Officer; Vice President for Industrial Relations or Personnel; Manager of Operations; Director of Employee Benefits.

<u>Description of Position</u>: I'd like to speak with the person in the company who is most familiar with the employee benefits your company offers.

<u>When appropriate person is on the telephone</u>:

Hello, my name is_____(first and last name). I'm on the staff of the Eagleton Institute at Rutgers University. We have randomly selected companies nationwide to conduct a survey on employee benefits. I'd like to ask you a few questions about your company.

1.   To begin, does your company have a profit sharing plan for employees <u>other than top management</u>?

109-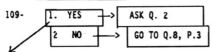

2.   Do you have one or more than one profit-sharing plan? (PROBE: IF MORE THAN 1 ASK: How many plans do you have?)

         110-   1. ONE PLAN
               2. TWO PLANS
               3. THREE PLANS
               4. FOUR PLANS
               5. MORE THAN FOUR PLANS
               9. DON'T KNOW

2A.   What is the name(s) of the plan(s)?

111-   PLAN 1: _____

112-   PLAN 2: _____

113-   PLAN 3: _____

114-   PLAN 4: _____

180

2

3. Could you please tell me what this (these) plan(s) is (are)?
    (INTERVIEWER CODE EACH PLAN NAMED UNDER A SPECIFIC PLAN)

	PLAN 1	PLAN 2	PLAN 3	PLAN 4
a. Cash plan (with payments directly to employees)	115- 1	116- 1	117- 1	118- 1
b. Pension plan (with payments to a pension trust)	2	2	2	2
c. Combination of cash and pension plan	3	3	3	3
d. Other (Specify:) _____	4	4	4	4
e. Other (Specify:) _____	5	5	5	5
F. Don't Know/Refused	9	9	9	9

4. Could you please tell me about how many years the plan (each of these plans)
    have been in existence?
    (INTERVIEWER: IF MORE THAN ONE PLAN, ASK FOR EACH PLAN NAMED IN Q.3)

119-120   PLAN 1: _____   (DON'T KNOW = 99)

121-122   PLAN 2: _____

123-124   PLAN 3: _____

125-126   PLAN 4: _____

5. When the (any) profit sharing plan(s) was (were) established, were any
    significant changes made in personnel policies or other compensation? (IF
    "YES," ASK: Please describe these changes.)

127-   1. YES /___/___/___ _____
                  128 129

       2. NO _____

       9. DON'T KNOW/REFUSED

6. Approximately, what percentage of your company employees, excluding top
    management, is covered by the profit sharing plan(s)?

    _____ %
    130 - 132

7. About what percentage of all (name each type of employee) at the company are
    covered by the plan(s)?
                                                    (999=DON'T KNOW/REFUSED)

133-135 a. Production/service employees (non-exempt)   _____ %

136-138 b. Clerical/technical employees (non-exempt)   _____ %

139-141 c. Professional/administrative employees (exempt) _____ %

3

ASK EVERYONE

Now just some general questions about your company.

8.   About what percentage of your company's employees, excluding top management, falls into each of the following categories?

(99=DON'T KNOW/REFUSED)

142-143	Production/service (non-exempt)	_____ %
144-145	Clerical/technical (non-exempt)	_____ %
146-147	Professional/administrative (exempt)	_____ %

(INTERVIEWER NOTE: THIS SHOULD ADD TO 100%)

9.   Are any of your employees covered under a union contract?

.48-

| 1. YES | ―> | ASK Q. 10 |

| 2. NO |
| 9. DON'T KNOW | ―> | GO TO Q. 12 |

(IF "YES" TO Q. 9, ASK:)

10.   What is the approximate percentage of all employees covered by a union contract?

_____ %   (DON'T KNOW/REFUSED = 999)
149 - 151

(ASK ONLY IF HAVE PROFIT SHARING)

11.   Do a majority of union employees participate in the profit-sharing plan(s)?

152-   1. YES, MAJORITY PARTICIPATES
        2. NO, MAJORITY DOES NOT PARTICIPATE
        9. DON'T KNOW

12.   About how many corporation employees, excluding top management, are routinely provided with (READ ITEM BELOW)--none, some, about half, most, or all?

			None 0%	Some 1-40%	About Half 41-60%	Most 61-99%	All 100%	Don't Know
a.	Information about the company's overall operating results	153-	1	2	3	4	5	9
b.	Information on business plans and goals	154-	1	2	3	4	5	9
c.	Information on competitors' relative performance	155-	1	2	3	4	5	9

182

13. Now I'm going to read a list of programs or policies. For each, just tell me how many years your company has had that program or policy. If your company does not have it, just say so. First, how about (START AT DESIGNATED POINT) ...

Number of Years Had Program	Do Not Have This Program				None 0%	Some (1-40%)	About Half (41-60%)	Most (61-79%)	All (100%)	Don't Know
	98	( )	a.	Attitude Survey Feedback						
156-157				--Corporate employees	209- 1	2	3	4	5	9
				--Union employees	210- 1	2	3	4	5	9
				--Members of the profit-sharing plan	211- 1	2	3	4	5	9
	98	( )	b.	Suggestion System						
158-159				--Corporate employees	212- 1	2	3	4	5	9
				--Union employees	213- 1	2	3	4	5	9
				--Members of the profit-sharing plan	214- 1	2	3	4	5	9
	98	( )	c.	Job Enrichment or Redesign						
160-161				--Corporate employees	215- 1	2	3	4	5	9
				--Union employees	216- 1	2	3	4	5	9
				--Members of the profit-sharing plan	217- 1	2	3	4	5	9
	98	( )	d.	Employee Involvement groups, such as, Quality Circles or other formal committees						
162-163				--Corporate employees	218- 1	2	3	4	5	9
				--Union employees	219- 1	2	3	4	5	9
				--Members of the profit-sharing plan	220- 1	2	3	4	5	9
	98	( )	e.	Self-Managed work teams						
164-165				--Corporate employees	221- 1	2	3	4	5	9
				--Union employees	222- 1	2	3	4	5	9
				--Members of the profit-sharing plan	223- 1	2	3	4	5	9
	98	( )	f.	Employment Security						
166-167				--Corporate employees	224- 1	2	3	4	5	9
				--Union employees	225- 1	2	3	4	5	9
				--Members of the profit-sharing plan	226- 1	2	3	4	5	9
	98	( )	g.	Productivity-Related Group Bonuses						
168-169				--Corporate employees	227- 1	2	3	4	5	9
				--Union employees	228- 1	2	3	4	5	9
				--Members of the profit-sharing plan	229- 1	2	3	4	5	9

DUP
301-307 208

READ THIS QUESTION FOR EACH PROGRAM/POLICY THE COMPANY HAS:

14. Now, thinking about your company's (START AT DESIGNATED POINT), about how many (TY OF EMPLOYEE) participate in this plan--none, some, about half, most or all.

NOTE: ONLY ASK ABOUT "MEMBERS OF PROFIT-SHARING PLAN" IF COMPANY HAS PROFIT SHARING

FOR COMPANIES WITH PROFIT SHARING:

Thank you very much for your cooperation.

For this study Rutgers University is particularly interested in companies that have profit-sharing. There are some additional questions we would like you to answer on a short 3 page questionnaire. Could I please have your name, address and position to ser you this follow-up questionnaire in the mail?

NAME: _____

ADDRESS: _____

_____

POSITION: _____
230-231

FOR COMPANIES WITHOUT PROFIT SHARING:

Could I please have your name, address and position.

NAME: _____

ADDRESS: _____

_____

POSITION: _____

_____

AREA CODE: /___/___/___/
232 233 234

DATE: /___/___/___/
235 235 167

FILE NUMBER: /___/___/___/___/
238 239 240 241

INTERVIEW LENGTH: /___/___/
242 243

SIC CODE: /___/___/___/___/
244 245 246 247

SEX: 248- 1. MALE   2. FEMALE

STATE: /___/___/
249 250

TIC: /___/___/___/___/___/
251 252 253 254 255

IDN: /___/___/___/___/___/___/___/___/___/
256 257 258 259 260 261 262 263 264

TYPE:

265- 1. PRIMARY
     2. MATCHED

IF MATCHED:

MATCHED FILE NUMBER:

/___/___/___/___/
266 267 268 269

INTERVIEWER: /___/___/
270 271

184

91-08—51491

PROFIT SHARING SURVEY

<u>SUMMARY OF RESPONSES TO TELEPHONE SURVEY</u>

According to the telephone interview we had with you, the following are the profit sharing plans you offer to employees (other than top management):

TYPE OF PLAN	YEARS PLAN HAS BEEN IN EXISTENCE
PLAN 1 _____	_____
PLAN 2 _____	_____
PLAN 3 _____	_____
PLAN 4 _____	_____

As we described on the telephone, there is some additional information we would like to have about these plans.

I. For each plan you have, circle the number "1" next to the option(s) that describes what your company's contribution to the plan is based upon?

Company Contribution Options	Plan 1	Plan 2	Plan 3	Plan 4
1. Specific percentage of profits	110- 1	122- 1	134- 1	146- 1
(Please write in what percent:)	___% 111-113	___% 123-125	___% 135-137	___% 147-149
2. Specific percentage of profits in excess of amount reserved for dividends or retained earnings	114- 1	126- 1	138- 1	150- 1
(Please write in what percent:)	___% 115-117	___% 127-129	___% 139-141	___% 151-153
3. Fully discretionary	118- 1	130- 1	142- 1	154- 1
4. Specific percentage of profits plus discretionary amount	119 1	131- 1	143- 1	155- 1
5. Specific percentage of participants' pay	120- 1	132- 1	144- 1	156- 1
Other (please describe: _____	121- 1	133- 1	145- 1	157- 1

_____

Was the profit-sharing plan adopted following a change in management personnel?

58- 1. YES

2. NO

IF YES, ON THE LINES BELOW, BREIFLY DESCRIBE THE CHANGES:

59-160 _____

_____

What was the company's contribution to the profit-sharing plan(s) as a percent of the total payroll for participants in each of the following years?

(NOTE: THIS DOES NOT INCLUDE PLANS FOR TOP MANAGEMENT)

(If fiscal year basis, indicate beginning month: _____)
181-182

1975 _____ %   1979 _____ %   1983 _____ %   1987 _____ %
163-165   210-212   222-224   234-236

1976 _____ %   1980 _____ %   1984 _____ %   1988 _____ %
166-168   213-215   225-227   237-239

1977 _____ %   1981 _____ %   1985 _____ %   1989 _____ %
169-171   216-218   228-230   240-242

1978 _____ %   1982 _____ %   1986 _____ %   1990 _____ %
172-174   219-221   231-233   243-245

KIP: 175-180

DUP   2
01-208 209

186

1. Each of the following are reasons for <u>maintaining</u> the profit-sharing plan(s). Please use the five point scale to indicate how important each is for maintaining the profit-sharing plan(s) in your company.

		Not Important				Very Important
16-	a. Providing a source of retirement income	1	2	3	4	5
17-	b. Recruiting and retaining personnel	1	2	3	4	5
18-	c. Motivating existing employees	1	2	3	4	5
19-	d. Reducing likelihood of unionization	1	2	3	4	5
20-	e. Reducing the probability or size of layoffs	1	2	3	4	5
21-	f. Stabilizing corporate cash flow	1	2	3	4	5

Please list any other reasons for maintaining the profit-sharing plan(s) on the lines below and indicate the importance of each:

			Not Important				Very Important
2-	_____	256-	1	2	3	4	5
3-	_____	257-	1	2	3	4	5
4-	_____	258-	1	2	3	4	5
5-	_____	259-	1	2	3	4	5

se the lines below for any comments you have about why your company maintains the profit-sharing plan(s).

2-261 _____

2-263 _____

_____

.EASE RETURN IN THE ENCLOSED PASTAGE PAID ENVELOPE TO:

Center for Public Interest Polling
Eagleton Institute of Politics
Rutgers University
Wood Lawn - Neilson Campus
90 Clifton Avenue
New Brunswick, NJ 08901-1568

Appendix 2
Econometric Specification of Prediction Equations

The prediction of profit-sharing adoption was done with both linear probability and binomial logit models. The linear probability model was specified as:

(1) $\quad PS_{it} = \alpha_i + \beta 1 * X_{i, t-1} + \beta 2 * X_{i, t-2} + e_{it}$

where

PS	= dummy for existence of profit sharing in firm i, year t
α_i	= firm-specific intercept term
$\beta 1$ and $\beta 2$	= coefficient vectors
$X_{i, t-1}$	= vector of explanatory variables in firm i, year t - 1
$X_{i, t-2}$	= vector of explanatory variables in firm i, year t - 2
e_{it}	= error term.

The firm-specific intercept α_i was removed through using deviations from firm-specific means for all variables, and an AR(1) correction was done to adjust for autocorrelation. The binomial logit model was based on first-differenced data, with the dependent variable PS_{it} - $PS_{i, t-1}$ and independent variables $X_{i, t-1}$ - $X_{i, t-2}$. For both models, lagged independent variables were chosen to avoid simultaneity problems. The logit specification was chosen since this transformation will produce consistent estimates of the parameters of interest (unlike probits, where there is not a consistent estimator with panel data) (Hsiao 1986: 163). Because the firm intercept is removed by both procedures, the value of the dependent variable varies only when profit sharing is adopted—therefore these regressions involve prediction of profit-sharing *adoption* rather than the presence of profit sharing.

For both of these procedures, the regressions were done with the full sample, and then using only the paired sample, with the difference between each pair representing a single observation.

Results are presented in appendix tables A2.2 and A2.3, with descriptive statistics and variable definitions in appendix table A2.1.

Table A2.1 Descriptive Statistics and Definitions for Appendix Tables A2.2 and A2.3

	Linear Prob.		First differences[a]		Definition
	Mean	(s.d.)	Mean	(s.d.)	
PS	0.314	(0.46)	0.024	(0.15)	Presence of profit-sharing plan in year t[a]
Cash			0.010	(0.10)	Adoption of plan with cash elements in year t
Deferred			0.008	(0.09)	Adoption of deferred-only plan in year t
Salesvar	0.025	(0.06)	0.000	(0.05)	Variance of change in ln(sales) over $t - 5$ to $t - 1$
PMvar	0.127	(0.51)	0.004	(0.23)	Variance of change in ln(profit margin) over $t - 5$ to $t - 1$
PM (-1)	0.162	(0.10)	-0.001	(0.03)	Profit margin in $t - 1$
PM (-2)	0.162	(0.11)			Profit margin in $t - 2$
Sales (-1)	6.323	(1.65)	0.085	(0.16)	Ln(total sales) in $t - 1$
Sales (-2)	6.228	(1.66)			Ln(total sales) in $t - 2$
Price (-1)	18.234	(20.00)	0.183	(0.39)	Closing stock price in $t - 1$
Price (-2)	16.840	(18.13)			Closing stock price in $t - 2$ (first-differenced value is percentage change in price)
KL (-1)	3.592	(1.46)	0.077	(0.18)	Ln(net assets/employees) in $t - 1$
KL (-2)	3.514	(1.47)			Ln(net assets/employees) in $t - 2$
Debt/eq. (-1)	0.326	(0.24)	-0.010	(0.71)	Debt/equity ratio in $t - 1$
Debt/eq. (-2)	0.333	(0.68)			Debt/equity ratio in $t - 2$

Interest (-1)	0.035	(0.05)	0.000	(0.02)	Interest payments as percent of sales in $t - 1$
Interest (-2)	0.035	(0.04)			Interest payments as percent of sales in $t - 2$
Union trend	61.713	(36.11)	0.782	(0.41)	Time trend for unionized companies

NOTES: For the paired differences in appendix tables A2.2 and A2.3, the value of each variable in a nonprofit-sharing company was subtracted from the value for its paired profit-sharing company. Each observation represents a matched pair.
a. For first-differenced PS (including cash and deferred), variable value is profit-sharing dummy in t minus value in $t - 1$. For other first-differenced data, variable equals $t - 1$ minus $t - 2$ value (except for price change, which is percentage change in price from $t - 2$ to $t - 1$).

Table A2.2 Prediction of Profit-Sharing Adoption

Independent variable	Firm-intercepts, linear probability dummy for presence of profit sharing in year t		Paired differences		Independent variables	First-differences, logits dummy for adoption of profit sharing in year t^a		Paired differences	
	(1)	(2)	(3)	(4)		(5)	(6)	(7)	(8)
					Change from $t-2$ to $t-1$ in:				
Salesvar	0.074* (0.04)		0.118 (0.09)		Salesvar	0.655 (1.95)		0.572 (2.20)	
PMvar		0.015** (0.01)		0.013 (0.01)	PMvar		0.626* (0.33)		0.133 (0.23)
PM (-1)	0.090* (0.05)	0.087* (0.05)	0.225** (0.10)	0.268** (0.11)	PM	1.983 (3.05)	1.140 (3.16)	5.753* (3.37)	7.134** (3.60)
PM (-2)	0.031 (0.05)	0.011 (0.05)	0.011 (0.11)	0.049 (0.12)					
Sales (-1)	0.021* (0.01)	0.017 (0.01)	0.058** (0.02)	0.059** (0.02)	Sales	0.935 (0.62)	0.763 (0.66)	0.143 (0.78)	0.255 (0.83)
Sales (-2)	-0.010 (0.01)	-0.014 (0.01)	-0.006 (0.02)	-0.027 (0.02)					
Price (-1)	2E - 04 (0.0002)	3E - 04 (0.0002)	1E - 04 (0.0004)	1E - 04 (0.0004)	Price	0.827** (0.20)	0.924** (0.21)	0.457* (0.26)	0.422 (0.27)
Price (-2)	4E - 04* (0.0002)	-2E - 04 (0.0002)	-1E - 04 (0.0005)	0E + 00 (0.0005)					
KL (-1)	-0.009 (0.01)	-0.015 (0.01)	-0.004 (0.02)	-0.004 (0.02)	KL	-0.462 (0.48)	-0.361 (0.50)	0.399 (0.68)	0.236 (0.72)

	(1)	(2)	(3)	(4)
KL (-2)	-0.004 (0.01)	-0.010 (0.01)	-0.007 (0.02)	-0.006 (0.02)
Debt/eq. (-1)	-0.001 (0.01)	0.004 (0.02)	0.001 (0.02)	-0.004 (0.04)
Debt/eq. (-2)	-0.001 (0.00)	-0.003 (0.02)	-0.001 (0.00)	0.048 (0.04)
Interest (-1)	-0.051 (0.11)	-0.002 (0.12)	-0.146 (0.23)	-0.251 (0.24)
Interest (-2)	-0.074 (0.11)	0.000 (0.13)	-0.180 (0.23)	-0.180 (0.25)
Union trend	0.005** (0.00)	0.006** (0.00)	0.000 (0.00)	0.001 (0.00)
Year squared	0.001** (0.00)	0.000** (0.00)		
Year	-0.070** (0.03)	-0.055** (0.03)		
AR (1) correction	Yes	Yes	Yes	Yes
N	6276	6056	2093	1969
R-squared	0.930	0.930	0.816	0.814

	(1)	(2)	(3)	(4)
Debt/eq.	0.252 (0.48)	0.801 (0.86)	-1.393 (1.40)	-1.359 (1.54)
Interest	0.198 (6.23)	-0.800 (6.36)	-3.679 (11.97)	-5.118 (12.01)
Union trend	0.336* (0.28)	0.277 (0.29)	-0.158 (0.26)	-0.279 (0.27)
Year squared	0.045** (0.01)	0.041** (0.01)		
Constant	-11.335 (2.11)	-10.621 (2.20)	-2.153 (0.13)	-2.178 (0.14)
N	4084	3912	619	519
Log-likelihood	-449.310	-419.147	-222.045	-205.947

NOTES: Standard errors in parentheses. See appendix table A2.1 for definitions and descriptive statistics.
a. Logit sample restricted to firms which did not have profit sharing in t - 1.
*Significantly different from zero at p <10   **p <.05.

Table A2.3 Prediction of Cash and Deferred Plan Adoption

Independent variable	Cash plans		Paired differences		Deferred plans		Paired differences	
	(1)	(2)	(3)	(4)	(5)	(6)	(7)	(8)
Change from $t-2$ to $t-1$ in:								
Salesvar	-2.190		-3.217		3.598		2.157	
	(1.82)		(2.90)		(2.83)		(2.34)	
PMvar		0.181		-0.191		0.523**		0.178
		(0.55)		(0.58)		(0.25)		(0.25)
PM	0.478	2.601	7.552*	8.957**	-2.931	-3.980	2.636	3.230
	(4.49)	(4.44)	(4.24)	(4.35)	(4.40)	(4.50)	(3.98)	(4.19)
Sales	-0.211	-0.131	-0.349	-0.587	0.356	0.404	-0.313	-0.206
	(0.95)	(0.95)	(1.00)	(1.08)	(0.76)	(0.89)	(0.84)	(0.90)
Price	0.793***	0.873**	0.162	0.012	0.836***	0.956**	0.714***	0.867***
	(0.29)	(0.35)	(0.38)	(0.45)	(0.25)	(0.28)	(0.27)	(0.31)
KL	-0.257	-0.401	0.441	0.483	-0.961*	-1.000	-1.067	-1.056
	(0.84)	(0.79)	(0.92)	(0.97)	(0.54)	(0.56)	(0.70)	(0.77)
Debt/eq.	0.180	0.395	-0.130	0.158	0.123	0.374	-0.098	-1.207
	(0.72)	(1.23)	(1.26)	(1.61)	(0.81)	(1.57)	(0.39)	(1.41)
Interest	5.857	3.397	-9.708	-11.449	-0.832	-2.227	0.365	2.844
	(9.24)	(9.91)	(11.48)	(11.90)	(8.13)	(7.86)	(6.53)	(5.19)
Union trend	0.996**	0.826**	0.621*	0.482	0.302	0.314	-0.228	-0.241
	(0.49)	(0.49)	(0.36)	(0.38)	(0.37)	(0.37)	(0.30)	(0.32)
Year squared	-0.559***	0.082***			0.010	0.013		
	(0.84)	(0.02)			(0.02)	(0.02)		

Constant	-19.253	-18.890	-4.123	-4.108	-6.269	-6.634	-3.637	-3.682
	(3.41)	(3.59)	(0.20)	(0.20)	(2.89)	(2.92)	(0.18)	(0._9)
N	5443	5203	1742	1640	5199	4961	1420	1318
Log-likelihood	-254.170	-230.626	-150.160	-141.265	-265.215	-261.653	-183.139	-167.679

NOTES: See appendix table A2.1 for variable definitions and descriptive statistics.
*Statistically significant at p <.10   **p <.05   ***p <.01.

Table A2.4 Participation in Profit Sharing by Union and Occupational Status

Independent variable	Probit: Dummy for majority of union members participating (1)	Means (s.d.) for col. 1 (2)	OLS: Percentage of clerical/ technical workers participating (3)	OLS: Percentage of professional/ admin. workers participating (4)	OLS: Percentage of production/ service workers participating (5)	OLS: Percentage of all employees participating (6)	Means (s.d.) for cols. 3-5 (7)	Brief definition
Prof./admin. share	0.014 (0.01)	25.952 (14.09)	0.311 (0.30)	0.636** (0.28)	1.049** (0.41)	0.439** (0.21)	25.440 (13.56)	Percent of employees in professional or administrative (exempt) jobs
Prod./service share	0.000 (0.01)	52.424 (19.33)	0.402** (0.20)	0.563** (0.19)	0.492* (0.27)	0.082 (0.15)	48.060 (22.22)	Percent of employees in production or service (nonexempt) jobs
KL	0.288 (0.26)	4.107 (1.21)	1.505 (4.42)	-0.369 (4.13)	1.569 (5.95)	0.064 (3.54)	3.953 (1.27)	Ln(net assets/employees), 1990
Ln(employment)	0.098 (0.10)	1.634 (1.77)	0.646 (1.79)	0.490 (1.68)	-0.179 (2.42)	-1.535 (1.43)	1.311 (1.73)	Ln(employment), 1990
Profit margin	-1.705 (2.41)	0.138 (0.10)	31.071 (41.93)	31.072 (39.23)	7.547 (56.53)	-4.068 (33.60)	0.141 (0.12)	Profit margin, 1990
Percent in union	0.016** (0.01)	37.894 (24.52)	-0.148 (0.12)	-0.194* (0.11)	-0.376** (0.16)	-0.221** (0.09)	24.870 (26.87)	Percent of employees in union
PS age	-0.006 (0.01)	13.518 (11.58)	0.156 (0.27)	0.465* (0.26)	0.300 (0.37)	0.421** (0.18)	15.930 (12.15)	Age of oldest profit-sharing plan
Seven industry dummies	Yes		Yes	Yes	Yes	Yes		
Constant	-1.562 (1.55)		3.498 (31.81)	-3.342 (29.75)	-14.377 (42.87)	51.575 (21.34)		

N	85	100	100	100	124
Log-likelihood	-48.71				
R-squared		0.222	0.227	0.226	0.216
Dependent var. mean	0.435	85.410	71.010	87.320	80.355
	(0.50)	(28.55)	(38.58)	(26.80)	(25.96)

NOTES: The sample in column 1 is restricted to profit-sharing firms with unions, while the samples in columns 3 to 6 are restricted to profit-sharing firms. Standard errors in parentheses for coefficients, and standard deviations in parentheses for means.

*Significantly different from zero at p <.10   * p <.05.

Appendix 3
Econometric Specification and Selection Corrections

The estimating equation is based upon the first terms of a translogarithmic production function (Christensen, Jorgensen, and Lau 1975):

$$\ln(Q) = \beta_1{}^*\ln(L) + \beta_k{}^*\ln(K) + \beta_{11}{}^*\ln(L)^*\ln(L) +$$

$$\beta_{kk}{}^*\ln(K)^*\ln(K) + \beta_{k1}{}^*\ln(L)^*\ln(K)$$

where

Q = output, alternatively measured as sales and as value-added
L = total employees
K = capital stock
$\beta_1, \beta_k, \beta_{11}, \beta_{kk}, \beta_{k1}$ = coefficients representing the relationship of these factors to output.

In the analysis presented here, this function is augmented to include: profit sharing, defined benefit plan, and ESOP variables alone and interacted with time trends, year dummies, and industry time trends. In addition, a union trend variable has been included due to the possibility that union presence affected productivity growth over this time period (Hirsch 1991). Ln(L) was subtracted from both sides to make the dependent variable the natural logarithm of output per worker (identical to the measure used in the simple comparisons of table 3.2). (While measurement error in ln(L) will bias coefficients on the independent variables using ln(L), the results for profit sharing were found to be nearly identical when $\ln(L)$ is not subtracted from both sides.) The resulting specification, where the subscript i indicates company and t indicates year, is:

$$
\begin{aligned}
\ln(Q_{it}/L_{it}) = {} & (\beta_1-1)*\ln(L_{it}) + \beta_k*\ln(K_{it}) + \\
& \beta_{11}*\ln(L_{it})*\ln(L_{it}) + \\
& \beta_{kk}*\ln(K_{it})*\ln(K_{it}) + \beta_{k1}*\ln(L_{it})*\ln(K_{it}) + \\
& \beta_p*PS_{it} + \beta_{pt}*(\text{Age of PS}) + \\
& \beta_d*DB_{it} + \beta_{dt}*(\text{Age of DB}) + \\
& \beta_e*ESOP_{it} + \beta_{et}*(\text{Age of ESOP}) + \\
& \beta_u*(\text{Union}*\text{time}) + (\text{industry time trends}) \\
& + (\text{year dummies}) + \alpha_i + e_{it}
\end{aligned}
$$

where

      PS   = profit-sharing plan
      DB   = defined benefit pension plan
  ESOP = Employee Stock Ownership Plan
  Union = union presence
     α_i = firm-specific fixed effect
     e_{it} = error term.

To remove the effects of any unobserved variables that may be in the firm-specific fixed effect (α_i), this equation is first-differenced so that all measured values represent the difference between t and $t - 1$.[1] This results in the estimated equation, where δ is the first-difference operator and the i subscripts have been suppressed:

$$
\begin{aligned}
(1) \quad \delta\ln(Q/L) = {} & (\beta_1-1)*\delta\ln(L) + \beta_k*\delta\ln(K) + \\
& \beta_{11}*\delta[\ln(L)*\ln(L)] + \\
& \beta_{kk}*\delta[\ln(K)*\ln(K)] + \beta_{k1}*\delta[\ln(L)*\ln(K)] + \\
& \beta_p*\delta PS + \beta_{pt}*PS_t + \beta_d*\delta DB + \beta_{dt}*DB_t + \\
& \beta_e*\delta ESOP + \beta_{et}*ESOP_t + \beta_u*\text{Union} + \\
& (\text{industry dummies}) + (\text{year dummies}) + e.
\end{aligned}
$$

The key parameters of interest for this study are β_p and β_{pt}. These can be interpreted in two equivalent ways: as measures of profit-sharing presence and trend effects on productivity levels, or as measures of profit-sharing *adoption* and profit-sharing *presence* on productivity *growth*. The same interpretations can be applied to the coefficients on defined benefit (β_d and β_{dt}), ESOP (β_e and β_{et}) and union (β_u) variables.[2]

A variety of experiments with alternative lag structures for the production function terms made little difference in the estimated effects of profit sharing, so only the first-differenced results are presented here.

The reported results have had the upper 1 percent and lower 1 percent of productivity changes trimmed to remove any undue influence these outliers may have upon the results. Prior to trimming, the minimum (maximum) value of $\delta\ln(Q/L)$ was -5.71 (4.35) when Q was measured as sales per employee, and -4.60 (4.47) when Q was measured as value-added per employee. These extremes imply productivity changes on the order of 100-fold, and it is considered unlikely that profit sharing will be a key influence in such extreme circumstances. After trimming the upper and lower 1 percent, the minimum (maximum) value of $\delta\ln(Q/L)$ was -.40 (.56) when Q was measured as sales per employee, and -.40 (.51) when Q was measured as value-added per employee, implying productivity changes of no more than -33 percent to 75 percent. The basic results in appendix table A3.2 are not substantially affected by inclusion of the outliers, or by use of a robust regression technique (as packaged in the Stata statistical package) that gives smaller weight to outliers (Rousseeuw and Leroy 1987).[3] The productivity specifications were also run with the upper 1 percent and lower 1 percent of $\delta\ln(L)$ and $\delta\ln(K)$ trimmed (restricting the range of $\delta\ln(L)$ to -.536 to .526, and the range of $\delta\ln(K)$ to -.489 to .746), with very similar results for the profit-sharing coefficients.

Adoption of profit sharing may be accompanied by accounting changes and/or company mergers or acquisitions, either of which could impart a bias to the estimated profit-sharing effects. Both events were less common in adoption years than in the sample as a whole: for the sample used in regression 1 of table A3.2, an accounting change was reported in 2.4 percent of the adoption years compared to 2.5 percent of all observations, while a merger or acquisition was reported in 6.1 percent of adoption years compared to 12.4 percent of all observations. Tests were made alternatively excluding these observations, and including them with variables representing the events, and the results were nearly identical to those reported in table A3.2.

As discussed in chapter 3, the above framework may be tainted by selection bias (see, e.g., Maddala 1983; Heckman and Robb 1985; Heckman and

Hotz 1989). There may be factors that predict profit-sharing status and, through correlation between profit-sharing status and the distribution of the error term, violate standard assumptions about the error term in equation (1).

While self-selection may create a bias, it does not necessarily do so. Heckman and Robb (1985: 216-223) review several models using panel data in which a bias does not exist under certain decision rules and error processes.

In the presence of selection bias, there are two standard procedures for removing the correlation between the variable of interest and the error term: instrumental variables to predict profit-sharing variables that are uncorrelated with the error term, and the addition of a selection term to correct for the distribution of the error. Both techniques were tested for the correction of selection bias caused by systematic choice of adoption and maintenance of profit-sharing plans. The results employing a selection term (inverse Mill's ratio) are presented here since extensive use of instrumental variable techniques failed to produce credible estimates. A sampling of those estimates will be briefly described here.

Instrumental variable estimates were attempted using both linear probability and probit techniques to predict both profit-sharing adoption and profit-sharing maintenance. When adoption and maintenance are separately predicted using exogenous variables and the lagged variables represented in table 2.3, and the predicted δPS and PS_t are inserted in equation (1), the estimated β_p and β_{pt} are 2.226 and .209 when the dependent variable is $\delta\ln$(sales/employees), and 3.367 and .217 when the dependent variable is $\delta\ln$(value-added/employees). These coefficients, which are all highly statistically significant (at $p < .01$), imply productivity increases of more than eightfold when profit sharing is adopted, and more than 20 percent each year it is in place. When probits are used to predict δPS and PS_t, the estimated coefficients for β_p and β_{pt} are .329 and .468 when $\ln$(sales/employees) is used, and .785 and .534 when $\ln$(value-added/employees) is used. These are again highly statistically significant and imply adoption effects of 40-120 percent and trend effects of 60-70 percent per year. A variety of other instrumental variable techniques produced results that were similarly not credible; such results argue for the use of other techniques for the correction of selection bias.

The bias created by self-selection into a program may be corrected by the inclusion of a selection correction term in the estimated equation. Construction of a term relies on prediction of profit-sharing status (with variables Z_i and coefficients τ), then creation of a normal density function $f(\tau Z_i)$ and cumulative density function $F(\tau Z_i)$ using those estimates. One method to correct for the distribution of the error term under sample selection, based on Heckman (1979), is to create a variable $f(\tau Z_i)/F(\tau Z_i)$ where the profit-sharing status equals one, and $-f(\tau Z_i)/(1 - F(\tau Z_i))$ where it equals zero. A second method allowing different coefficients between the profit-sharing and non-profit-sharing samples uses, in addition to the common explanatory variables, the values of these variables multiplied by $F'(\tau Z_i)$, as well as $f(\tau Z_i)$ as an independent regressor (Maddala 1983: 227). A third method tested here is to predict what the expected outcome would be if the non-profit-sharing firms decided to adopt profit sharing, by using the coefficients on the non-profit-sharing sample with the additional selection term $f(\tau Z_i)/F(\tau Z_i)$, and comparing the predicted productivity change with the actual productivity change for the profit-sharing firms (Maddala 1983: 261).

In addition, two alternative methods, developed to assess the effect of training programs on worker earnings, were tested to correct for selection bias. The first is based on a control function developed by Heckman and Robb (1985: 224-5) that removes the correlation between the error term and program participation. This control function relies on prediction of program participation using preprogram error terms. For this study, the prediction was done using an unrestricted process for the four error terms prior to profit-sharing adoption. A second method employed is based on Bassi (1984), who uses a transformation of the equation designed to purge the correlation between program participation and the error terms.

Two variables that predicted profit-sharing adoption and raised a strong possibility of selection bias were the change in the stock price, and change in the profit margin, from $t - 2$ to $t - 1$. To examine the influence of these variables, the profit-sharing adopters were divided into two groups—those that had positive and negative values on these variables (relative to industry means for that year)—and separate productivity effects were calculated for comparison with columns 1 to 4 of appendix table A3.2. The coefficients on profit-sharing adoption were of similar magnitude between the two groups, and neither group had consistently larger or smaller coefficients.

The tests on these alternative sample selection correction techniques did not produce noteworthy differences in the results. For example, looking at the profit-sharing adoption coefficient in the full sample with ln(sales/employee) as the dependent variable (comparable to column 1 of appendix table A3.2) gave the following results. Estimation of the model assuming different coefficients between profit-sharing and non-profit-sharing firms (Maddala 1983: 227) gives a coefficient of .040 ($t = 3.58$). Estimation of the model which predicts the outcome if non-profit-sharing firms were to adopt profit sharing (Maddala 1983: 261) produces a coefficient of .042 ($t = 3.29$). Use of the control function based on preprogram error terms (Heckman and Robb 1985: 224-5) produces a coefficient of .045 ($t = 3.49$) when all firms are included, and .066 ($t = 3.42$) when only adopters are included. Finally, use of Bassi's technique produces an average coefficient of .044 over the first three postadoption years.

Since these techniques did not produce noteworthy differences, only the results from the first method are presented here (with common production parameters across the sample). Specifically, because the productivity regressions primarily indicate a profit-sharing adoption effect, and the selection bias is likely to be strongest among adopters, the selection term used the specification from regression 5 of appendix table A2.1 to predict profit-sharing adoption (excluding the change in stock price, due to concerns about its exogeneity). Once the adoption had been made, the adopters maintained the selection term from the time of adoption. Old profit-sharing companies that had no preadoption values were simply assigned the mean postadoption selection term from the adopters. Separate selection terms were created for cash and deferred plans (appendix table A3.3), type of formula (appendix table A3.4), and size of employer contribution (appendix table A3.6). The coefficients on the selection terms are not presented here since they were never distinguishable from zero and had no pattern of positive and negative coefficients. Experiments with a number of other specifications of the selection term (including prediction of profit-sharing presence as well as adoption) failed to produce any consistent patterns or substantial effects on the results. This indicates that sample selection is unlikely to be an important factor in the productivity effects.

A separate form of selection bias may be present with missing observations on incomplete panel data (see, e.g., Hausman and Wise 1979; Ridder 1990; Verbeek 1990). The selection rule on when observations are reported may be related to the variable of interest. There was, however, no discernible relationship between the pattern of profit-sharing adoption and missing observations in the panel. The possibility of bias was checked and discounted with the variable addition test and comparison of random effects estimators from the balanced and unbalanced panels (Verbeek and Nijman 1992).

NOTES

1. A random effects model, in which α_i is treated as a random variable, was also estimated (Hsiao 1986: 32-47). Consistency of results depends on orthogonality between the random effects and other regressors, which was strongly rejected by the data. When using random effects specifications, the results indicated much larger effects of profit-sharing adoption (e.g., using sales per employee as the dependent variable on the full sample, the coefficient on profit-sharing adoption was .112 with a t-statistic of 6.29).

2. The survey collected data on union presence and proportion unionized as of the survey date, but not over the entire sample period. For this reason, equation (1) does not attempt to measure the effects of *changes* in union presence or proportion unionized in the period. While proportion unionized may have varied across this period, the assumption made here is that union presence is unlikely to have varied, and any variations are unlikely to have been correlated with profit-sharing status. The same regressions were run without the union variable and showed equivalent results.

3. When all observations are included in the specifications reported in columns 1 to 4 of appendix table A3.2, the estimated effects of profit-sharing adoption with equally weighted observations are slightly larger (between .034 and .055), and with robust regressions are slightly smaller (between .032 and .037), and all are statistically significant at the 95 percent or 99 percent levels.

Table A3.1 Definitions and Descriptive Statistics for Productivity Regressions

Means (s.d.) for variables in appendix table A3.2

Regressions	(1)	(2)	(3)	(4)	(5)	(6)	(7)	(8)	Definitions
δln(sales/L)	0.067 (0.116)	-0.007 (0.150)			0.067 (0.117)	-0.007 (0.150)			Change in ln(sales/employees) from $t-1$ to t
δln(value-added/L)			0.064 (0.111)	-0.005 (0.145)			0.064 (0.111)	-0.005 (0.145)	Change in ln(value-added/employees) from $t-1$ to t[a]
PS adoption	0.015 (0.120)	0.033 (0.179)	0.014 (0.118)	0.029 (0.168)	0.010 (0.091)	0.024 (0.142)	0.009 (0.088)	0.021 (0.130)	Change in presence of profit-sharing plan from $t-1$ to t (measured as dummy in cols. 1-4, proportion covered in 5-8)
PS trend	0.310 (0.462)	0.719 (0.449)	0.341 (0.474)	0.748 (0.434)	0.235 (0.391)	0.553 (0.434)	0.258 (0.402)	0.582 (0.427)	Presence of profit sharing in t (measured as dummy in cols. 1-4, proportion covered in 5-8)
DB adoption	0.004 (0.066)	-0.001 (0.088)	0.005 (0.070)	-0.002 (0.100)	0.001 (0.028)	-0.001 (0.032)	0.002 (0.029)	-0.002 (0.043)	Change in presence of defined benefit plan from $t-1$ to t (measured as dummy in cols. 1-4, proportion covered in 5-8)
DB trend	0.752 (0.432)	-0.020 (0.632)	0.742 (0.437)	-0.025 (0.632)	0.329 (0.321)	-0.015 (0.426)	0.277 (0.279)	-0.010 (0.387)	Presence of defined benefit plan in t (measured as dummy in cols. 1-4, proportion covered in 5-8)
ESOP adoption	0.016 (0.127)	0.003 (0.181)	0.017 (0.130)	0.006 (0.184)	0.005 (0.056)	0.002 (0.081)	0.005 (0.052)	0.004 (0.078)	Change in presence of ESOP from $t-1$ to t (measured as dummy in cols. 1-4, proportion covered in 5-8)
ESOP trend	0.426 (0.495)	0.069 (0.696)	0.386 (0.487)	0.100 (0.705)	0.142 (0.278)	0.036 (0.324)	0.084 (0.192)	0.045 (0.264)	Presence of ESOP in t (measured as dummy in cols. 1-4, proportion covered in 5-8)
Union trend	0.753 (0.431)	-0.068 (0.537)	0.723 (0.448)	-0.066 (0.546)	0.756 (0.430)	-0.057 (0.523)	0.726 (0.446)	-0.054 (0.530)	Union presence in t

	(1)	(2)	(3)	(4)	(5)	(6)	(7)	(8)	Description
δln(L)	0.008	0.011	0.008	0.014	0.007	0.010	0.007	0.012	Change in ln(employees) from $t-1$ to t
	(0.142)	(0.192)	(0.150)	(0.197)	(0.084)	(0.192)	(0.150)	(0.196)	
δln(K)	0.085	0.011	0.089	0.015	0.084	0.010	0.087	0.012	Change in ln(net assets) from $t-1$ to t
	(0.177)	(0.239)	(0.195)	(0.264)	(0.176)	(0.237)	(0.195)	(0.258)	
δln(L)ln(L)	0.022	0.003	0.022	0.012	0.018	-0.002	0.016	0.003	Change in square of ln(employees) from $t-1$ to t
	(0.573)	(0.760)	(0.627)	(0.838)	(0.570)	(0.750)	(0.625)	(0.824)	
δln(K)ln(K)	0.898	0.001	0.899	0.037	0.882	-0.017	0.880	0.005	Change in square of ln(net assets) from $t-1$ to t
	(1.802)	(2.474)	(1.939)	(2.656)	(1.796)	(2.398)	(1.934)	(2.552)	
δln(L)ln(K)	0.188	0.014	0.197	0.032	0.178	0.003	0.185	0.014	Change in (ln(net assets) times ln(employees)) from $t-1$ to t
	(0.976)	(1.288)	(1.033)	(1.361)	(0.970)	(1.257)	(1.027)	(1.316)	
N	5652	1807	4673	1510	5499	1725	4533	1428	

NOTE: Labor expense was instrumented as described in text.
a. Value-added was calculated from CompuStat as (sales - (cost of goods sold - labor expenses - rental expense)).

Table A3.2 Productivity Growth and Profit-Sharing Adoption and Presence

	δln(Sales/L)		δln(Value-added/L)		δln(Sales/L)		δln(Value-added/L)	
	Dummies		Dummies		Proportion covered		Proportion covered	
Dependent variable	Unpaired (1)	Paired (2)	Unpaired (3)	Paired (4)	Unpaired (5)	Paired (6)	Unpaired (7)	Paired (8)
PS adoption	0.043*** (0.014)	0.042** (0.018)	0.049*** (0.014)	0.034* (0.020)	0.035** (0.017)	0.035 (0.026)	0.046*** (0.017)	0.064** (0.029)
PS trend	0.002 (0.010)	0.008 (0.019)	0.010 (0.010)	0.019 (0.021)	-0.005 (0.008)	-0.012 (0.013)	-0.004 (0.008)	0.006 (0.013)
DB adoption	0.011 (0.021)	0.023 (0.037)	0.009 (0.020)	0.026 (0.034)	0.025 (0.050)	0.018 (0.103)	0.035 (0.050)	0.088 (0.082)
DB trend	-0.001 (0.003)	-0.004 (0.005)	-0.006 (0.004)	-0.009 (0.006)	-0.004 (0.005)	-0.007 (0.008)	-0.010 (0.005)	-0.017* (0.009)
ESOP adoption	0.014 (0.011)	0.003 (0.018)	0.008 (0.011)	0.011 (0.019)	0.023 (0.025)	-0.011 (0.042)	-0.006 (0.029)	0.004 (0.046)
ESOP trend	-0.001 (0.003)	0.001 (0.005)	0.000 (0.003)	-0.001 (0.005)	0.001 (0.006)	0.006 (0.011)	0.005 (0.008)	0.005 (0.014)
Union trend	-0.004 (0.004)	-0.008 (0.006)	0.001 (0.004)	-0.001 (0.006)	-0.004 (0.004)	-0.010 (0.007)	0.001 (0.004)	-0.001 (0.007)
δln(L)	-0.387*** (0.027)	-0.394*** (0.048)	-0.395*** (0.027)	-0.334*** (0.048)	-0.387*** (0.028)	-0.382*** (0.048)	-0.391*** (0.027)	-0.319*** (0.049)
δln(K)	0.058** (0.024)	0.098*** (0.043)	0.026 (0.024)	0.005 (0.043)	0.060** (0.025)	0.120*** (0.044)	0.024 (0.025)	0.010 (0.045)
δln(L) ln(L)	-0.019*** (0.005)	-0.031*** (0.009)	-0.009 (0.006)	-0.004 (0.010)	-0.020*** (0.005)	-0.032*** (0.009)	-0.010* (0.006)	-0.007 (0.011)

δln(K) ln(K)	0.006**	0.000	0.010***	0.016**	0.006*	-0.003	0.011***	0.014**
	(0.003)	(0.006)	(0.003)	(0.006)	(0.003)	(0.006)	(0.003)	(0.006)
δln(L) ln(K)	0.008	0.019	0.002	-0.013	0.008	0.017	0.001	-0.014
	(0.007)	(0.012)	(0.008)	(0.014)	(0.007)	(0.013)	(0.008)	(0.015)
Year dummies	Yes		Yes		Yes		Yes	
25 industry dummies	Yes		Yes		Yes		Yes	
R-squared	0.245	0.178	0.259	0.211	0.246	0.178	0.259	0.218
N	5652	1807	4673	1510	5499	1725	4533	1428

NOTE: See appendix table A3.1 for variable definitions and descriptive statistics.
*Statistically significant at p <.10   ** p <.05   ***p <.01.

Table A3.3 Cash and Deferred Profit Sharing and Productivity Growth

	Regression coefficients (s.e.)				Descriptive statistics			
	δln(Sales/L)		δln(Value-added/L)		Means (s.d.)			
Dependent variable	Unpaired (1)	Paired (2)	Unpaired (3)	Paired (4)	(1a)	(2a)	(3a)	(4a)
Cash PS adoption	0.034**	0.063**	0.035**	0.042	0.008	0.020	0.008	0.019
	(0.016)	(0.029)	(0.017)	(0.032)	(0.089)	(0.140)	(0.089)	(0.136)
Cash PS presence	0.005	0.008	-0.003	0.008	0.116	0.281	0.132	0.316
	(0.008)	(0.017)	(0.008)	(0.018)	(0.320)	(0.450)	(0.338)	(0.465)
Deferred PS adoption	0.018	0.009	0.014	-0.011	0.006	0.021	0.006	0.019
	(0.018)	(0.030)	(0.020)	(0.035)	(0.078)	(0.145)	(0.075)	(0.136)
Deferred PS presence	0.002	0.025	0.035***	0.027	0.173	0.269	0.184	0.248
	(0.011)	(0.015)	(0.011)	(0.019)	(0.378)	(0.443)	(0.388)	(0.432)
DB adoption	-0.009	0.054	-0.011	0.024	0.004	-0.002	0.005	-0.003
	(0.020)	(0.041)	(0.020)	(0.040)	(0.067)	(0.087)	(0.070)	(0.097)
DB presence	0.000	0.001	-0.005	-0.001	0.759	-0.021	0.749	-0.028
	(0.003)	(0.006)	(0.004)	(0.007)	(0.428)	(0.635)	(0.433)	(0.632)
ESOP adoption	0.010	0.009	0.011	0.019	0.017	0.004	0.017	0.009
	(0.011)	(0.019)	(0.011)	(0.021)	(0.128)	(0.186)	(0.131)	(0.190)
ESOP presence	-0.002	-0.001	0.001	-0.004	0.434	0.035	0.394	0.069
	(0.003)	(0.006)	(0.003)	(0.006)	(0.496)	(0.702)	(0.489)	(0.712)
Union presence	-0.006	0.002	0.000	0.010	0.769	-0.078	0.742	-0.079
	(0.004)	(0.007)	(0.004)	(0.008)	(0.421)	(0.526)	(0.438)	(0.532)
Translog terms	Yes	Yes	Yes	Yes				
Year dummies	Yes	Yes	Yes	Yes				

209

25 industry dummies	Yes		Yes					
Dependent variable					0.069	-0.007	0.065	-0.003
					(0.115)	(0.151)	(0.111)	(0.-49)
R-squared	0.247	0.214	0.257	0.216				
N	5608	1443	4638	1160	5608	1443	4638	1160

NOTES: See appendix table A3.1 for variable definitions. Cash PS represents those with any cash element, while deferred PS represents those which are only deferred.

*Statistically significant at p <.10 **p <.05 ***p <.01.

Table A3.4 Profit-Sharing Formulas and Productivity Growth

| | Regression coefficients (s.e.) | | | | Descriptive statistics | | | |
| | $\delta\ln$(Sales/L) | | $\delta\ln$(Value-added/L) | | Means (s.d.) | | | |
Dependent variable	Unpaired (1)	Paired (2)	Unpaired (3)	Paired (4)	(1a)	(2a)	(3a)	(4a)
Percent-of-profits formula								
Plan adoption	0.047	0.022	0.076**	0.014	0.003	0.009	0.003	0.009
	(0.030)	(0.046)	(0.035)	(0.047)	(0.051)	(0.096)	(0.052)	(0.094)
Subsequent trend	-0.002	0.036	-0.025	0.005	0.047	0.136	0.054	0.145
	(0.012)	(0.057)	(0.023)	(0.060)	(0.211)	(0.343)	(0.225)	(0.352)
Discretionary								
Plan adoption	0.074**	0.037	0.088**	0.100**	0.002	0.007	0.002	0.008
	(0.037)	(0.051)	(0.038)	(0.050)	(0.042)	(0.086)	(0.043)	(0.088)
Subseqent trend	-0.004	0.034	0.021	0.049*	0.036	0.096	0.041	0.102
	(0.012)	(0.026)	(0.012)	(0.026)	(0.186)	(0.294)	(0.198)	(0.302)
Percent-of-pay formula								
Plan adoption	0.022	0.032	-0.016	0.043	0.002	0.007	0.002	0.006
	(0.033)	(0.051)	(0.037)	(0.058)	(0.047)	(0.086)	(0.043)	(0.075)
Subsequent trend	-0.017	0.024	-0.028	-0.052*	0.044	0.154	0.046	0.151
	(0.017)	(0.026)	(0.018)	(0.030)	(0.206)	(0.361)	(0.210)	(0.358)
Other formula								
Plan adoption	0.016	0.029	0.007	0.016	0.005	0.017	0.005	0.016
	(0.023)	(0.034)	(0.023)	(0.035)	(0.068)	(0.128)	(0.069)	(0.124)
Subsequent trend	-0.001	-0.009	-0.004	-0.012	0.087	0.258	0.099	0.275
	(0.018)	(0.021)	(0.020)	(0.022)	(0.282)	(0.438)	(0.299)	(0.447)

Dependent variable							
				0.068	-0.004	0.064	-0.007
				(0.115)	(0.150)	(0.112)	(0.146)
R-squared	0.247	0.173	0.278	0.334			
N	4565	1077	3711	959	4587	1077	3711	896

NOTES: Variable definitions: Percent-of-profits plan: company contribution based on fixed percent of profits (may include discretionary element in addition). Discretionary plan: company contribution wholly discretionary. Percent-of-pay plan: company contribution based on fixed percent of participants' pay. Other: company contribution based on formula other than above three. All regressions include variables listed in appendix table A3.2 (except for PS adoption and presence), plus separate inverse Mill's selection terms for each of the four classes of formula. See appendix table A3.1 for other variable definitions and descriptive statistics.

*Statistically significant at p <.10   **p <.05   ***p <.01.

Table A3.5 Profit Sharing and Productivity by Employment Size Class

Analysis of profit-sharing effects by five size classes, representing the smallest 10 percent, 10-25 percent, 25-50 percent, 50-75 percent, and 75-100 percent classes of employment size at time profit sharing was adopted.

Size class	$\delta\ln(Sales/L)$ (1)	$\delta\ln(Value\text{-}added/L)$ (2)	Mean (s.d.) (1a)	Mean (s.d.) (2a)
Empl. <775				
PS adoption	0.105***	0.159***	0.001	0.001
	(0.037)	(0.040)	(0.038)	(0.036)
PS trend	-0.007	0.001	0.027	0.029
	(0.014)	(0.014)	(0.161)	(0.167)
775 <= Empl. <1681				
PS adoption	-0.015	0.060	0.002	0.001
	(0.029)	(0.037)	(0.048)	(0.039)
PS trend	-0.003	0.011	0.043	0.047
	(0.013)	(0.013)	(0.202)	(0.211)
1681 <= Empl. <4599				
PS adoption	0.041*	-0.034	0.004	0.003
	(0.024)	(0.026)	(0.059)	(0.057)
PS trend	0.002	0.022*	0.071	0.077
	(0.011)	(0.011)	(0.257)	(0.267)
4599 <= Empl. <17,000				
PS adoption	0.022	0.029	0.003	0.003
	(0.024)	(0.025)	(0.058)	(0.058)
PS trend	0.001	0.012	0.090	0.095
	(0.011)	(0.011)	(0.286)	(0.294)

Empl. >= 17,000

PS adoption	0.067***	0.056***	0.004	0.005
	(0.022)	(0.021)	(0.062)	(0.069)
PS trend	0.001	0.008	0.094	0.108
	(0.011)	(0.011)	(0.292)	(0.310)
R-squared	0.251	0.269		
N	5652	4672	5652	4672

NOTES: The regressions include variables from regressions 1 and 3 of appendix table A3.2 (translog terms, year dummies, 25 industry dummies, and DB, ESOP, and union terms). Translog production terms have been fully interacted with the five size classes.

*Statistically significant at p <.10   **p <.05   ***p <.01.

Table A3.6 Productivity Growth and Size of Employer Contribution

For those reporting profit-sharing contribution as a percentage of participant payroll (n=71), the mean figure for each company was calculated. The median of these figures was 3.62 percent. A mean contribution less (greater) than 3.62 percent was designated as a "low" ("high") mean employer contribution.

Dependent variable	δln(Sales/L) Unpaired (1)	Paired (2)	δln(Value-added/L) Unpaired (3)	Paired (4)	Means (s.d.) (1a)	(2a)	(3a)	(4a)
PS plans with low mean employer contributions								
Adoption	0.014 (0.038)	-0.019 (0.048)	0.021 (0.047)	-0.019 (0.060)	0.002 (0.047)	0.023 (0.151)	0.002 (0.042)	0.018 (0.134)
Presence	0.008 (0.013)	-0.014 (0.028)	0.008 (0.015)	-0.033 (0.033)	0.047 (0.213)	0.304 (0.461)	0.046 (0.210)	0.257 (0.438)
PS plans with high mean employer contributions								
Adoption	0.123*** (0.037)	0.102* (0.053)	0.070* (0.041)	0.095 (0.069)	0.002 (0.047)	0.020 (0.141)	0.002 (0.046)	0.014 (0.120)
Presence	0.043** (0.018)	-0.003 (0.029)	0.029 (0.018)	-0.011* (0.035)	0.065 (0.247)	0.499 (0.501)	0.076 (0.265)	0.547 (0.499)
Translog terms	Yes	Yes	Yes	Yes				
Year dummies	Yes		Yes					
25 industry dummies	Yes		Yes					
Dependent var. mean	0.068 (0.116)					-0.008 (0.146)	0.065 (0.114)`	-0.005 (0.154)

R-squared	0.265	0.305	0.287	0.399			
N	3598	345	2861	276	3598	345	2861	276

NOTES: All regressions include variables from regressions reported in appendix table A3.2, plus separate inverse Mill's terms for the high- and low-contribution plans.

*Statistically significant at $p < .10$ **$p < .05$ ***$p < .01$.

216

Table A3.7 Definitions and Descriptive Statistics for Personnel Policy Variables in Appendix Table A3.8

	(1)	(2)	(3)	(4)	(5)	(6)	(7)	(8)	Definitions
Survey adoption	0.012 (0.107)	0.001 (0.152)	0.011 (0.103)	0.000 (0.146)	0.007 (0.074)	0.001 (0.114)	0.006 (0.068)	0.001 (0.105)	Change in presence of attitude survey feedback from $t-1$ to t (measured as dummy in cols. 1-4, proportion covered in 5-8)
Survey trend	0.128 (0.334)	0.026 (0.475)	0.119 (0.324)	0.036 (0.469)	0.082 (0.252)	0.023 (0.339)	0.070 (0.232)	0.040 (0.308)	Presence of attitude survey feedback in t (measured as dummy in cols. 1-4, proportion covered in 5-8)
Job enrichment adoption	0.008 (0.087)	0.003 (0.127)	0.008 (0.089)	0.002 (0.134)	0.002 (0.037)	0.002 (0.053)	0.003 (0.041)	0.002 (0.059)	Change in presence of job enrichment or redesign from $t-1$ to t (measured as dummy in cols. 1-4, proportion covered in 5-8)
Job enrichment trend	0.147 (0.354)	0.066 (0.432)	0.152 (0.359)	0.040 (0.435)	0.055 (0.198)	0.067 (0.269)	0.052 (0.192)	0.064 (0.278)	Presence of job enrichment or redesign in t (measured as dummy in cols. 1-4, proportion covered in 5-8)
Autonomous workteam adoption	0.008 (0.087)	0.002 (0.097)	0.008 (0.090)	0.003 (0.106)	0.003 (0.042)	0.001 (0.034)	0.003 (0.044)	0.002 (0.038)	Change in presence of autonomous workteams from $t-1$ to t (measured as dummy in cols. 1-4, proportion covered in 5-8)
Autonomous workteam trend	0.100 (0.300)	0.052 (0.329)	0.096 (0.295)	0.055 (0.350)	0.032 (0.147)	0.019 (0.212)	0.034 (0.151)	0.012 (0.217)	Presence of autonomous workteams in t (measured as dummy in cols. 1-4, proportion covered in 5-8)
Employee involvement adoption	0.019 (0.138)	-0.002 (0.185)	0.019 (0.137)	0.001 (0.187)	0.009 (0.076)	0.000 (0.091)	0.008 (0.073)	0.001 (0.086)	Change in presence of employee involvement from $t-1$ to t (measured as dummy in cols. 1-4, proportion covered in 5-9)
Employee involvement trend	0.063 (0.243)	0.051 (0.480)	0.070 (0.254)	0.047 (0.484)	0.058 (0.194)	0.028 (0.256)	0.056 (0.187)	0.021 (0.239)	Presence of employee involvement in t (measured as dummy in cols. 1-4, proportion covered in 5-8)

									Description
Employment security adoption	0.002 (0.050)	-0.001 (0.058)	0.002 (0.044)	-0.001 (0.051)	0.002 (0.042)	-0.001 (0.054)	0.002 (0.040)	-0.001 (0.051)	Change in presence of employment security policy from $t-1$ to t (measured as dummy in cols. 1-4, proportion covered in 5-8)
Employment security trend	0.069 (0.253)	0.040 (0.355)	0.058 (0.233)	0.051 (0.327)	0.052 (0.215)	0.052 (0.329)	0.040 (0.193)	0.060 (0.309)	Presence of employment security policy in t (measured as dummy in cols. 1-4, proportion covered in 5-8)
Suggestion system adoption	0.011 (0.102)	0.001 (0.133)	0.010 (0.098)	-0.002 (0.129)	0.003 (0.038)	0.001 (0.033)	0.003 (0.035)	0.001 (0.035)	Change in presence of suggestion system from $t-1$ to t (measured as dummy in cols. 1-4, proportion covered in 5-8)
Suggestion system trend	0.235 (0.424)	-0.015 (0.625)	0.217 (0.412)	-0.048 (0.618)	0.088 (0.224)	-0.010 (0.300)	0.075 (0.207)	-0.018 (0.287)	Presence of suggestion system in t (measured as dummy in cols. 1-4, proportion covered in 5-8)
Gainsharing adoption	0.010 (0.100)	0.001 (0.137)	0.010 (0.100)	0.001 (0.139)	0.005 (0.066)	0.000 (0.098)	0.005 (0.062)	0.001 (0.089)	Change in presence of gainsharing from $t-1$ to t (measured as dummy in cols. 1-4, proportion covered in 5-8)
Gainsharing trend	0.138 (0.345)	0.018 (0.477)	0.159 (0.365)	0.021 (0.500)	0.061 (0.200)	0.028 (0.311)	0.069 (0.210)	0.043 (0.321)	Presence of gainsharing in t (measured as dummy in cols. 1-4, proportion covered in 5-8)
N	5652	1807	4673	1510	4621	1262	3776	1024	

NOTES: Definitions and descriptive statistics for other regression variables are in appendix table A3.1. Personnel policies are defined in table 3.5. See table 1.3 for comparisons of personnel policies between profit-sharing and non-profit-sharing companies.

Table A3.8 Productivity Growth and Personnel Policies

Dependent variable	δln(Sales/L) Dummies		δln(Value-added/L) Dummies		δln(Sales/L) Proportion covered		δln(Value-added/L) Proportion covered	
	Unpaired (1)	Paired (2)	Unpaired (3)	Paired (4)	Unpaired (5)	Paired (6)	Unpaired (7)	Paired (8)
PS adoption	0.043***	0.041**	0.050***	0.033*	0.033*	0.020	0.034*	0.049
	(0.014)	(0.018)	(0.014)	(0.020)	(0.018)	(0.031)	(0.019)	(0.036)
PS trend	0.003	0.009	0.011	0.019	-0.004	-0.011	0.002	0.015
	(0.010)	(0.019)	(0.010)	(0.022)	(0.009)	(0.016)	(0.009)	(0.017)
Personnel policies								
Survey adoption	-0.012	-0.001	-0.016	-0.013	-0.020	-0.061	-0.042*	-0.084
	(0.013)	(0.022)	(0.014)	(0.024)	(0.021)	(0.038)	(0.025)	(0.043)
Survey trend	0.004	0.003	0.004	0.007	0.007	0.010	0.007	0.021
	(0.005)	(0.008)	(0.005)	(0.008)	(0.007)	(0.014)	(0.008)	(0.016)
Job enrichment adoption	-0.018	-0.026	-0.032	-0.039**	-0.030	-0.050	-0.069*	-0.113
	(0.017)	(0.027)	(0.017)	(0.027)	(0.042)	(0.078)	(0.041)	(0.074)
Job enrichment trend	0.000	-0.004	0.000	-0.002	0.000	-0.013	0.000	-0.009
	(0.005)	(0.009)	(0.006)	(0.010)	(0.008)	(0.017)	(0.009)	(0.016)
Autonomous workteam adoption	0.018	0.022	0.013	-0.056	-0.001	0.021	0.024	-0.146
	(0.017)	(0.036)	(0.017)	(0.035)	(0.040)	(0.121)	(0.041)	(0.117)
Autonomous workteam trend	0.002	0.014	0.004	0.009	0.001	0.014	0.012	-0.013
	(0.006)	(0.012)	(0.006)	(0.012)	(0.012)	(0.023)	(0.012)	(0.026)
Employee involvement adoption	0.012	0.010	0.005	-0.001	-0.012	0.055	0.000	0.075
	(0.011)	(0.019)	(0.011)	(0.019)	(0.023)	(0.048)	(0.025)	(0.054)
Employee involvement trend	0.001	0.011	0.002	0.012	0.002	0.018	-0.001	0.013
	(0.005)	(0.008)	(0.005)	(0.008)	(0.009)	(0.019)	(0.010)	(0.022)

Employment security adoption	0.012	0.042	0.011	0.039	-0.009	-0.032	-0.008	-0.025
	(0.028)	(0.057)	(0.033)	(0.066)	(0.037)	(0.075)	(0.041)	(0.083)
Employment security trend	-0.004	-0.006	-0.002	0.003	-0.008	-0.012	-0.001	0.012
	(0.006)	(0.010)	(0.007)	(0.012)	(0.008)	(0.014)	(0.009)	(0.017)
Suggestion system adoption	-0.017	-0.001	-0.002	0.010	-0.008	0.060	0.007	0.145
	(0.014)	(0.025)	(0.015)	(0.027)	(0.040)	(0.123)	(0.047)	(0.125)
Suggestion system trend	-0.003	-0.001	-0.002	0.001	-0.007	-0.002	0.001	0.008
	(0.004)	(0.006)	(0.004)	(0.006)	(0.008)	(0.015)	(0.009)	(0.017)
Gainsharing adoption	0.014	0.000	0.018	0.024	-0.008	-0.031	0.033	-0.038
	(0.014)	(0.025)	(0.015)	(0.025)	(0.024)	(0.045)	(0.027)	(0.052)
Gainsharing trend	0.001	-0.006	0.001	-0.008	0.000	-0.001	0.005	0.002
	(0.004)	(0.008)	(0.004)	(0.008)	(0.009)	(0.015)	(0.009)	(0.015)
R-squared	0.247	0.183	0.261	0.219	0.260	0.194	0.268	0.218
N	5652	1807	4672	1510	4620	1261	3776	1024

NOTES: All regressions include variables from appendix table A3.2, and variables representing personnel policies of uncertain age (see text). See tables 3.5, appendix table A3.1, and appendix table A3.7 for variable definitions and descriptive statistics.
*Statistically significant at p <.10 **p <.05 ***p <.01.

Table A3.9 Profit Sharing and Information Sharing

Dependent variable	δln(Sales/L)		δln(Value-added/L)		Means (s.d.)			
	Unpaired (1)	Paired (2)	Unpaired (3)	Paired (4)	(1a)	(2a)	(3a)	(4a)
PS adoption	0.060*	0.049	0.016	0.032	0.014	0.035	0.014	0.031
	(0.033)	(0.038)	(0.033)	(0.037)	(0.119)	(0.183)	(0.118)	(0.173)
PS presence	0.003	0.002	0.006	-0.006	0.313	0.679	0.348	0.706
	(0.014)	(0.024)	(0.014)	(0.026)	(0.464)	(0.467)	(0.476)	(0.456)
Info-sharing on company results interacted with								
PS adoption	0.006	-0.017	0.023	-0.021	0.012	0.025	0.011	0.019
	(0.049)	(0.054)	(0.048)	(0.055)	(0.104)	(0.155)	(0.101)	(0.138)
PS presence	0.004	-0.010	0.008	-0.005	0.282	0.485	0.310	0.477
	(0.011)	(0.012)	(0.011)	(0.013)	(0.434)	(0.500)	(0.444)	(0.500)
Info-sharing on business plans interacted with								
PS adoption	-0.062	-0.060	0.010	-0.014	0.009	0.015	0.008	0.010
	(0.043)	(0.051)	(0.045)	(0.060)	(0.086)	(0.120)	(0.081)	(0.098)
PS presence	-0.005	0.012	0.002	0.019	0.200	0.278	0.219	0.288
	(0.008)	(0.012)	(0.008)	(0.013)	(0.360)	(0.448)	(0.372)	(0.453)
Info-sharing on competitors' performance interacted with								
PS adoption	0.080*	0.200**	0.014	0.090	0.004	0.002	0.003	0.002
	(0.045)	(0.088)	(0.052)	(0.104)	(0.045)	(0.047)	(0.043)	(0.042)
PS presence	0.002	-0.018	0.000	-0.030	0.090	0.074	0.097	0.073
	(0.010)	(0.015)	(0.010)	(0.016)	(0.217)	(0.262)	(0.219)	(0.260)

Dependent variable			
0.068 (0.116)	-0.009 (0.152)	0.064 (0.112)	-0.007 (0.148)
4970	1377	4073	1129

R-squared	0.245	0.189	0.264	0.233
N	4970	1377	4073	1129

NOTES: All regressions include variables from appendix table A3.2 (with definitions and descriptive statistics in appendix table A3.1). PS adoption and presence are measured as dummy variables. Definitions of information-sharing variables: Respondents were asked: "About how many corporation employees, excluding top management, are routinely provided with:

  a. Information about the company's overall operating results?

  b. Information on business plans and goals?

  c. Information on competitors' relative performance?"

The proportion of employees provided with such information was interacted with PS adoption and presence. PS=profit sharing.

*Statistically significant at p <.10 **p <.05 ***p <.01.

Table A3.10 Productivity Growth and Interaction of Profit Sharing with Personnel Policies

Dependent variable	δln(Sales/L)		δln(Value-added/L)		Means (s.d.)			
	Unpaired (1)	Paired (2)	Unpaired (3)	Paired (4)	(1a)	(2a)	(3a)	(4a)
PS adoption	0.042***	0.033	0.053***	0.041*	0.015	0.033	0.014	0.029
	(0.016)	(0.022)	(0.016)	(0.023)	(0.120)	(0.179)	(0.118)	(0.168)
PS trend	0.000	0.008	0.009	0.018	0.310	0.719	0.341	0.748
	(0.010)	(0.020)	(0.010)	(0.022)	(0.462)	(0.449)	(0.474)	(0.434)
Personnel policy interactions:								
Survey • PS								
adoption	0.014	0.006	0.001	-0.013	0.004	0.010	0.004	0.008
	(0.025)	(0.039)	(0.027)	(0.043)	(0.060)	(0.091)	(0.059)	(0.084)
trend	0.000	-0.005	0.003	0.007	0.036	0.092	0.039	0.097
	(0.010)	(0.015)	(0.010)	(0.016)	(0.170)	(0.263)	(0.178)	(0.271)
Job enrichment • PS								
adoption	0.009	0.022	-0.011	0.003	0.002	0.005	0.002	0.005
	(0.040)	(0.062)	(0.040)	(0.063)	(0.037)	(0.057)	(0.039)	(0.060)
trend	0.003	0.001	-0.008	-0.017	0.032	0.060	0.025	0.058
	(0.013)	(0.020)	(0.013)	(0.020)	(0.134)	(0.191)	(0.129)	(0.189)
Autonomous workteam • PS								
adoption	0.056	0.000	0.046	-0.092	0.002	0.002	0.002	0.003
	(0.047)	(0.108)	(0.046)	(0.102)	(0.032)	(0.031)	(0.035)	(0.034)
trend	0.009	0.007	-0.007	-0.010	0.028	0.045	0.021	0.046
	(0.014)	(0.021)	(0.012)	(0.022)	(0.132)	(0.180)	(0.123)	(0.181)

Employee involvement • PS								
adoption	0.042	0.092*	0.016	0.066	0.004	0.008	0.004	0.008
	(0.031)	(0.052)	(0.032)	(0.053)	(0.051)	(0.068)	(0.051)	(0.059)
trend	0.001	0.006	0.008	0.015	0.024	0.064	0.031	0.057
	(0.012)	(0.019)	(0.013)	(0.020)	(0.126)	(0.191)	(0.134)	(0.191)
Employment security • PS								
adoption	-0.103**	-0.080	-0.113**	-0.099	0.001	0.003	0.001	0.002
	(0.044)	(0.066)	(0.049)	(0.078)	(0.034)	(0.055)	(0.031)	(0.048)
trend	0.003	0.000	0.003	0.013	0.019	0.052	0.024	0.057
	(0.011)	(0.018)	(0.011)	(0.018)	(0.119)	(0.208)	(0.145)	(0.219)
Suggestion • PS								
adoption	-0.012	0.064	-0.017	0.025	0.003	0.007	0.003	0.005
	(0.036)	(0.062)	(0.036)	(0.066)	(0.043)	(0.059)	(0.044)	(0.056)
trend	-0.005	0.015	-0.007	-0.008	0.021	0.065	0.035	0.066
	(0.012)	(0.021)	(0.012)	(0.021)	(0.136)	(0.181)	(0.143)	(0.186)
Gainsharing • PS								
adoption	0.015	-0.032	0.027	-0.023	0.003	0.007	0.003	0.007
	(0.031)	(0.048)	(0.032)	(0.052)	(0.048)	(0.072)	(0.048)	(0.070)
trend	-0.001	0.007	0.002	0.011	0.033	0.068	0.038	0.076
	(0.010)	(0.017)	(0.010)	(0.016)	(0.152)	(0.221)	(0.162)	(0.231)
R-squared	0.246	0.183	0.259	0.218				
N	5652	1807	4673	1510	5652	1807	4673	1510

NOTES: All regressions include variables from appendix table A3.2. See table 3.5 and appendix table A3.1 for personnel policy definitions.
*Statistically significant at p <.10 **p <.05 ***p <.01.

Table A3.11 Change in Other Policies When Profit Sharing is Adopted

Profit-sharing companies were asked, "When the profit-sharing plan was established, were any significant changes made in personnel policies or other compensation?" "Yes" and "no" answers are interacted with PS adoption and presence.

| | Regression coefficients (s.e.) | | | | Means (s.d.) | | | |
| | δln(Sales/L) | | δln(Value-added/L) | | | | | |
Dependent variable	Unpaired (1)	Paired (2)	Unpaired (3)	Paired (4)	(1a)	(2a)	(3a)	(4a)
Other changes made:								
PS adoption	0.059**	0.072**	0.070***	0.072*	0.004	0.011	0.004	0.011
	(0.024)	(0.036)	(0.024)	(0.038)	(0.063)	(0.103)	(0.066)	(0.106)
PS trend	0.007	0.063*	0.010*	0.067*	0.047	0.127	0.057	0.150
	(0.018)	(0.038)	(0.018)	(0.038)	(0.212)	(0.333)	(0.232)	(0.358)
Other changes not made:								
PS adoption	0.036**	0.022	0.034**	0.008	0.011	0.029	0.011	0.024
	(0.014)	(0.021)	(0.015)	(0.026)	(0.105)	(0.169)	(0.102)	(0.152)
PS trend	0.019	0.025	0.037	0.031	0.198	0.527	0.213	0.538
	(0.022)	(0.025)	(0.024)	(0.028)	(0.398)	(0.499)	(0.410)	(0.499)
Dependent variable					0.068	-0.006	0.064	-0.006
					(0.116)	(0.148)	(0.112)	(0.148)
R-squared	0.246	0.204	0.264	0.222				
N	5008	1390	4077	1137	5008	1390	4077	1137

NOTES: All regressions include variables from regressions presented in appendix table A3.2, with descriptive statistics in appendix table A3.1. PS = profit sharing.
*Statistically significant at p <.10   **p <.05   ***p <.01.

Appendix 4
Stability Theory and Econometric Specifications

Theory

The basics of the stability theory of profit sharing can be illustrated as follows. If profit shares are equally distributed among workers, each worker's compensation is

$$c = w' + s[(R(L) - w'L)/L] = w'(1 - s) + sR(L)/L$$

where

$R(L)$ = one-input revenue function of the firm
  s = share of profits going to workers collectively, set by firms in advance
  L = number of workers
  w' = base wage.

The firm's problem is to maximize profits, defined as revenue minus labor costs:

$$\text{Maximize } R(L) - Lc = R(L) - L[w'(1 - s) + sR(L)/L] = (1 - s)[R(L) - w'L].$$

With s fixed in the short-run, maximizing with respect to L leads to the first-order condition that

$$R'(L) = w'$$

where $R'(L)$ is the marginal revenue product (MRP) of labor (the first derivative of revenue with respect to labor). In other words, the firm would hire workers up to the point where the MRP of labor equals the base wage. The profit share is essentially ignored—it acts as a form of "tax" on profits that is irrelevant in the firm's calculations of maximizing revenues minus fixed obligations.

Firms in the long run will adjust their compensation parameters (s and w') so that the expected c will equal $R'(L)$ (Weitzman 1983). If $c < R'(L)$, firms will find it profitable to attract more workers by raising the values of the compensation parameters (s and/or w') to increase c. When $c = R'(L)$, firms will not find it profitable to change the compensation parameters. Since $w' < c$, the firm's short-run first-order condition $R'(L) = w'$ cannot hold in long-run equilibrium; consequently $R'(L) > w'$, implying an excess demand for labor by the firm. This excess demand is manifested in the firm's eagerness to hire workers at the current compensation parameters and willingness to retain workers when business conditions slump. A higher share component s, and lower base wage w', will lower both the probability and extent of layoffs in a profit-sharing firm.

What employment changes are predicted by the stability theory? The theory does not predict a simple linear relationship between demand shocks and amount of profit sharing. The prediction is that the profit-sharing firm will have a "cushion" of employees, representing the theorized excess demand for labor, who will be retained in a negative demand shock (as long as $R'(L) > w'$). Once the excess demand for labor is exhausted by a negative shock, the profit-sharing firm will lay off workers just as readily as the non-profit-sharing firm. When hiring workers under a positive demand shock, the firms will behave similarly if the positive shock does not represent recovery from a previous negative shock, but the profit-sharing firm will hire back fewer workers if it does represent such a recovery (since the profit-sharing firm laid off fewer to begin with). The complex, nonlinear relationship between employment and profit sharing may be mapped out as follows.[1] Theorized relationships between profit sharing and demand shocks, *ceteris paribus*:

Definitions

δL = change in employment

Dpos = positive demand shock (continuous)

Dneg = negative demand shock (continuous)

EDL = excess demand for labor by a profit-sharing firm (always positive; determined by labor demand elasticity and the degree to which profit share substitutes for fixed compensation)

Θ_{d+} and Θ_{d-} = coefficients on positive and negative demand shocks

For a non-profit-sharing firm:

(1) $\delta L = \Theta_{d+}*(\text{Dpos})$ if demand shock is positive

  $= \Theta_{d-}*(\text{Dneg})$ if demand shock is negative.

For a profit-sharing firm:

If negative demand shock does not exhaust EDL,

(2) $\delta L = 0*(\text{Dneg}) = 0$.

If negative demand shock does exhaust EDL,

(3) $\delta L = \Theta_{d-}*(Dneg) + EDL$.

If negative demand shock follows upon a prior negative shock that exhausted EDL,

(4) $\delta L = \Theta_{d-}*(Dneg)$.

If firm has a positive demand shock starting from an equilibrium position (i.e., not recovering from a prior negative shock),

(5) $\delta L = \Theta_{d+}*(Dpos)$.

If firm is recovering from a prior negative shock that did not exhaust its EDL (relationship 2),

(6) $\delta L = 0*(Dpos) = 0$.

If firm is recovering from a prior negative shock that exhausted its EDL (relationship 3),

(7) $\delta \ln(L) = \Theta_{d+}*(Dpos) - EDL$.

These seven relationships can be explained as follows. If profit-sharing firms have an incentive to hire labor to the point where $R'(L) = w'$, as described above (i.e., to the point of L_1 in figure 4.1), the difference between the desired and actual employment level (between L_0 and L_1) can be estimated in percentage terms as the labor demand elasticity (the percentage change in desired employment for a 1 percent change in wages) multiplied by the gap between w' and c. If, for example, the labor demand elasticity is 0.5 and the gap between w' and c is 3.6 percent of the wage (representing the median profit-sharing contribution as a percent of wages, making the assumption that it fully substitutes for base pay), the gap between desired and actual employment is 1.8 percent. This 1.8 percent becomes, in effect, a cushion for negative demand shocks. As illustrated in the bottom of figure 4.1, a small negative shock that causes a non-profit-sharing firm to lay off 1.8 percent of workers (relationship 1 above) should lead the profit-sharing firm to lay off none (relationship 2 above), while a large negative shock will cause both firms to lay off workers, but the profit-sharing firm will lay off fewer workers (the amount represented by EDL) (relationships 1 and 3 above).

What are the theorized responses to positive demand shocks? If starting from an initial equilibrium position, the responses should be the same between the two types of firms, since labor would be available on the same conditions (relationships 1 and 5 above). If the positive demand shock represents a recovery from a previous negative shock, however, the profit-sharing firm will hire back fewer workers since it laid off fewer to begin with. If recovering from a small shock, in which it laid off no workers (relationship 2), it will hire back no workers (relationship 6). If recovering from a large negative shock, in which the profit-sharing firm laid off 1.8 percent fewer workers (relationship 3), the profit-sharing firm will hire back fewer workers (relationship 7).

Complete empirical estimation of the stability theory therefore requires several types of information: (1) the degree to which profit sharing substitutes for fixed compensation ($c - w'$); (2) accurate measures of demand shocks, allowing the calculation of the point at which a negative demand shock exhausts the theorized excess demand for labor of the profit-sharing firm; (3) a measure of demand shocks that distinguishes whether they follow upon a previous negative shock that may have eliminated the theorized excess demand for labor; and (4) the labor demand elasticity. Information on the first and third of these types of information is particularly difficult to obtain, and the results are likely to be sensitive to assumptions about their magnitudes. Attempts to specify this full model, and the reliance on a simpler model, will be described in the following discussion of econometric techniques.

Econometric Estimation of Stability Effects

Estimates of stability effects are based on the following first-difference variant of a labor demand equation:

$$(8) \quad \delta\ln(L) = \Theta_0 + \Theta_w * \delta\ln(w) + \Theta_d * \delta D + \Theta_{psd} * PS * \delta D + \Theta_{ps} * PS + \Theta_{pst} * PS * t + \Theta_x * X$$

where

    L = employment level
    w = base wage
    D = measure of demand for firm's products
    PS = dummy indicating presence of profit-sharing plan
    X = other explanatory variables (cost of capital, cost of other production inputs)
    t = time trend
    δ = first-difference operator (from $t - 1$ to t)
    Θ = coefficients.

In this specification Θ_w measures the wage elasticity of labor demand, Θ_d measures the employment response to changes in demand for the firm's products, Θ_{psd} measures any differential in employment response for firms that have profit-sharing plans in effect, and Θ_{ps} and Θ_{pst} measure any general difference in growth rates (apart from demand shocks) associated with profit sharing.

As described above, the stability theory predicts that the employment response of profit-sharing firms will depend on the degree to which the profit share substitutes for fixed compensation, the size of negative and positive demand shocks, and whether the demand shocks were preceded by shocks that eliminated the excess demand for labor. A specification that incorporates relationships (1) to (7) above is the following:

$$(9) \quad \delta\ln(L) = \Theta_0 + \Theta_w * \Theta\ln(w) + \Theta_{d+} * (\text{Dpos}_{nps}) + \Theta_{d-} * (\text{Dneg}_{nps}) +$$

$$\Theta_{ns} * (\text{Dneg}_{small}) * PS +$$

$$\Theta_{d-} * (\text{Dneg}_{large}) * PS + EDL_{large} * PS +$$

$$\Theta_{d-} * (\text{Dneg}_{exhaust}) * PS +$$

$$\Theta_{d+} * (\text{Dpos}_{new}) * PS + \Theta_{rs} * (\text{Dpos}_{small(-1)}) * PS +$$

$$\Theta_{d+} * (\text{Dpos}_{large(-1)}) * PS - EDL_{large(-1)} * PS +$$

$$\Theta_{ps} * PS + \Theta_{pst} * PS * t + \Theta_x * X$$

where

Dneg_{nps} = change in demand for NPS firm's products, if the change is negative, and 0 otherwise

Dneg_{small} = change in demand for PS firm's products, if the change is negative and small (i.e., does not exhaust EDL), and 0 otherwise

Dneg_{large} = change in demand for PS firm's products, if the change is negative and large (i.e., does exhaust EDL), and 0 otherwise

$\text{Dneg}_{exhaust}$ = change in demand for PS firm's products, if the change is negative and a prior negative shock exhausted the EDL, and 0 otherwise

Dpos_{new} = change in demand for PS firm's products, if change is positive and firm is not recovering from prior negative shock

$Dpos_{nps}$ = change in demand for NPS firm's products, if the change is positive, and 0 otherwise

$Dpos_{small(-1)}$ = change in demand for PS firm's products, if the change is positive and the firm is recovering from a prior negative shock that was small (i.e., did not exhaust the EDL), and 0 otherwise

$Dpos_{large(-1)}$ = change in demand for PS firm's products, if the change is positive and the firm is recovering from a prior negative shock that was large (i.e., did exhaust the EDL), and 0 otherwise

EDL_{large} = excess demand for labor for PS firm, if firm was subject to demand shock large enough to exhaust EDL

$EDL_{large(-1)}$ = excess demand for labor for PS firm, if prior negative demand shock was large enough to exhaust EDL

Other variables defined above.

The Θ_{d+} and Θ_{d-} coefficients should be strongly positive, since employment is expected to move in the same direction as the demand shock. The Θ_{ns} and Θ_{rs} coefficients are expected to be close to zero, since they measure employment adjustments within the profit-sharing firm's excess demand for labor. Several experiments were made with cost-of-capital measures, but as these had inconsistent signs and magnitudes and made no difference in the profit-sharing variables (as in Kruse 1991b), they were dropped from the final runs.

Equation (9) was estimated on the full sample, and on a restricted sample comprising PS firms which reported at least three years of profit-sharing contribution data, with NPS firms from the same industries (with unpaired and paired results for both samples). For this test, it was necessary to determine the size of the demand shock that would be expected to exhaust the theorized excess demand for labor. This was estimated as follows. In the restricted sample, for profit-sharing firms which reported profit-sharing contributions as a percentage of participant payroll, the mean value was calculated within the company. It was alternatively assumed that this fully substituted for fixed pay (representing $c - w'$), and that only half of it substituted for fixed pay. The excess demand for labor was estimated by multiplying this mean value (or half of the mean value) by an estimated labor demand elasticity of 0.5 for fixed pay (obtained from estimates on non-profit-sharing firms). This was multiplied by the coefficient on the estimated output elasticity of labor for decreases in product demand (which equaled .642),[2] to determine the size of a negative demand shock that would be expected to eliminate this excess demand for labor. The result is the estimated decrease in sales which is necessary to eliminate the EDL (and the corresponding increase in sales which is necessary to restore the EDL), which divides the demand shocks according to whether they were "small" or "large." (The median of this measure was .030, with a mean of .036 and a standard deviation of .025.)

It may be that non-profit-sharing firms will have different responses to large and small demand shocks. Therefore, to compare the employment responses of profit-sharing and non-profit-sharing firms, sales shocks for NPS firms were divided into "large" and "small" according to whether they exceeded, or failed to exceed, the above mean estimate for PS companies (.036) of the demand shock sufficient to eliminate the EDL. Also, separate coefficients were estimated for each situation facing the firms (i.e., the Θ_{d+} and Θ_{d-} coefficients in equation (9) were not constrained to be equal across the terms in which they appear). To take account of the terms including EDL, dummy variables were specified to take a value of one for a large negative shock (and zero otherwise), with the coefficient presumably reflecting the size of the EDL (or more generally, any fixed employment response to a large negative shock that does not vary with the size of the shock). The sample of PS companies which reported sufficient contribution data were combined with NPS firms in the same industries for the restricted sample estimates, reported in columns 4 and 5 of appendix table A4.6.

For the full sample of PS and NPS firms, with results reported in columns 2 and 3, the EDL was assumed to be 1.8 percent for all PS firms (representing the median profit share as a percent of payroll, multiplied by a labor demand elasticity of 0.5). This was used to create measures of "small" and "large" demand shocks for both PS and NPS firms, again by dividing this figure of .018 by the coefficient on sales decreases (estimated as described above) in order to determine the size of a demand shock which would be sufficient to exhaust the EDL. In the full sample, unlike the restricted sample, the cutoff between large and small was identical for all firms.

The results using discontinuous measures rely only upon sales changes as demand shock measures. This is due to the great difficulty in trying to determine for a firm what constitutes a large and small shock, and recovery from a prior negative shock, from aggregate measures. The period saw two recessions, in 1973-75 and 1980-82, but there was no means of separating these into large and small shocks, which is necessary for the tests being developed here.

The changes in sales were deflated by the GNP deflator prior to estimation, and "negative" shocks were defined as those in which the change in ln(deflated sales) was negative. Tests were also made using nominal data (since declines in nominal sales represent obvious negative shocks), and deflated data using more detailed inflation measures (comprising 3-digit industry inflation measures for manufacturing firms from the NBER Trade and Immigration

Dataset, the CPI for retail firms, and the GNP deflator for all others); the methods produced similar findings.

The results, presented in appendix table A4.6, do not show a clear pattern with respect to the stability theory. Presented results assume the profit share fully substituted for fixed compensation; results assuming that only half substituted were very similar. When not recovering from a negative demand shock, the employment responses of PS firms are larger than that of NPS firms for sales increases (line 1), and are smaller than that of NPS firms for sales decreases (lines 2 to 3, where positive values on line 3 can be interpreted as companies retaining more employees during a big negative shock, and the negative values on line 4 can be interpreted as slight increases in employment when negative shocks occur). When recovering from a prior negative shock, the PS firms continue to have smaller responses to further negative shocks (line 5), have mixed results in response to big positive shocks (lines 6 and 7), and have more positive responses to small positive shocks (line 8). The stability theory would predict that, because the PS firms laid off fewer employees to begin with under the prior negative shock, the response to a subsequent positive shock should not be as positive—a prediction which does not fit neatly with these results, though it may indicate that PS firms are simply hungrier for labor under most circumstances. As described in the main text, these results give some support to the view that employment behavior differs between PS and NPS firms. When not recovering from negative shocks, the behavior of PS firms is favorable (lower responses to negative shocks, and higher responses to positive shocks), and generally fits the stability theory. When recovering from negative shocks, the behavior of PS firms is likewise favorable in that there is less response to negative shocks and a more positive response to small positive shocks, though this latter result does not fit the theory, and the mixed results with respect to large positive shocks provide no clear guide.

As noted, these estimates make strong assumptions about the size of the excess demand for labor, and whether a firm is experiencing or recovering from a large or small negative demand shock. On top of this, the stability theory predicts that profit-sharing firms should be generally more willing than fixed-wage firms to hire workers, so that the employment response to a positive shock in a time of unemployment may even be stronger for a profit-sharing firm. Determining what conditions apply to the hiring decision—whether the profit-sharing firm has an "excess demand for labor" at that point—is fraught with conceptual and empirical problems.

A simpler approach, as used in most previous research, is employed for the other regression results presented in this chapter: comparing the overall employment responses to positive and negative demand shocks between non-profit sharing and profit-sharing firms. This uses the following specification:

(10) $\delta\ln(L) = \Theta_0 + \Theta_w * \delta\ln(w) + \Theta_{d+} * (Dpos) + \Theta_{d-} * (Dneg) +$

$\Theta_{ps+} * (Dpos) * PS + \Theta_{ps-} * (Dneg) * PS +$

$\Theta_{ps} * PS + \Theta_{pst} * PS * t + \Theta_x * X$

Dpos = change in demand for firm's products, if the change is positive, and
        0 otherwise
Dneg = change in demand for firm's products, if the change is negative, and
        0 otherwise
Other variables and coefficients as defined above.

The estimated responses of NPS firms to positive and negative demand shocks are, respectively, Θ_{d+} and Θ_{d-} (both estimated as positive, since employment is expected to move in the same direction as the demand shock), while the estimated responses of PS firms include the interaction coefficients ($\Theta_{d+} + \Theta_{ps+}$ for positive shocks, and $\Theta_{d-} + \Theta_{ps-}$ for negative ones). Profit-sharing firms are theorized to have generally smaller employment responses to negative demand shocks (implying that the interaction coefficient Θ_{ps-} is negative), and to have roughly similar responses to positive demand shocks (with smaller responses if recovering from a previous negative shock, but stronger responses if unemployment exists and workers are available, so that the sign of Θ_{ps+} is ambiguous). Since the prediction is clearer with respect to negative shocks, more attention is paid to negative shocks.

As described in the main text, there are potentially important differences between old profit-sharing firms and new adopters in whether the profit share is substituting for, or adding onto, fixed compensation. Therefore separate Θ_{ps+} and Θ_{ps-} coefficients are estimated for the old profit-sharing firms and for the adopters both pre- and postadoption, which has the advantage that pre- and postadoption responses can be compared.

NOTES

1. The seven relationships should be interpreted not as full equations of labor demand, but as the relationship between demand shocks and employment changes, *ceteris paribus*.

2. Estimated with change in ln(employment) as the dependent variable, separate coefficients on change in ln(sales) for increases and decreases, instrumented change in average pay, year dummies, and 25 industry dummies and time trends as independent variables.

Table A4.1 Compensation Levels and Growth Regressions

	Company compensation/industry average compensation						
Dependent variable	1991 levels (1)	1991 levels (2)	1991 levels (3)	First-differences, full period (4)	Means (s.d.) for (1) & (2)	Means (s.d.) for (3)	Means (s.d.) for (4)
Presence of pre-1975 PS	0.107 (0.071)	0.129 (0.074)	0.026 (0.092)	-0.001 (0.003)	0.133 (0.341)	0.164 (0.373)	0.146 (0.353)
Presence of post-1975 PS	-0.097 (0.122)	-0.074 (0.126)	-0.156 (0.176)	0.007 (0.007)	0.253 (0.437)	0.236 (0.429)	0.108 (0.310)
PS adoption				-0.003 (0.011)			0.015 (0.123)
Year following PS adoption				0.017 (0.012)			0.014 (0.119)
DB plan presence	-0.021 (0.067)	-0.013 (0.067)	-0.121 (0.095)	0.001 (0.003)	0.843 (0.366)	0.855 (0.358)	0.805 (0.396)
DB plan adoption				-0.051* (0.026)			0.002 (0.045)
ESOP presence	0.031 (0.050)	0.029 (0.050)	0.017 (0.066)	-0.001 (0.002)	0.566 (0.499)	0.582 (0.498)	0.551 (0.498)
ESOP adoption				-0.014 (0.007)			0.026 (0.159)
Union proportion	0.216** (0.094)	0.235** (0.097)	0.174 (0.132)	-0.003 (0.005)	0.365 (0.281)	0.379 (0.275)	0.350 (0.282)
Majority of union members in PS (dummy)		-0.066* (0.083)			0.120 (0.328)		

Professional/admin. share			0.057 (0.365)	0.276 (0.122)
Production/service share			0.007 (0.213)	0.502 (0.203)
Intercept	1.530*** (0.150)	1.187*** (0.120)	1.731*** (0.245)	0.011* (0.006)
Dependent variable mean		1.018 (0.220)	1.037 (0.234)	0.003 (0.052)
R-squared	0.207	0.119	0.271	0.007
N	83	83	55	1960

	Company nonpension compensation/ industry average compensation				
	1991 levels (5)	1991 levels (6)	First-differences full period (7)	Means (s.d.) for (5) & (6)	Means (s.d.) for (7)
Cash/combo plan presence	0.025 (0.057)	0.059 (0.067)	0.005 (0.004)	0.241 (0.430)	0.109 (0.311)
Cash/combo plan adoption			-0.019 (0.013)		0.009 (0.095)
Year following cash adoption			0.002 (0.012)		0.009 (0.095)
Deferred plan presence	-0.046 (0.073)	0.047 (0.073)	-0.002 (0.004)	0.133 (0.341)	0.126 (0.332)
Deferred plan adoption			-0.015 (0.019)		0.004 (0.064)

	(1)	(2)	(3)	(4)	(5)
Year following deferred adoption			-0.003 (0.020)		0.004 (0.060)
DB plan presence	-0.020 (0.064)	-0.011 (0.065)	0.002 (0.003)	0.843 (0.366)	0.804 (0.397)
DB plan adoption			-0.045* (0.025)		0.004 (0.064)
ESOP presence	0.024 (0.049)	0.020 (0.049)	-0.001 (0.002)	0.566 (0.499)	0.550 (0.498)
ESOP adoption			-0.015 (0.007)		0.026 (0.159)
Union proportion	0.132 (0.087)	0.153 (0.090)	-0.001 (0.004)	0.365 (0.281)	0.350 (0.282)
Majority of union members in PS (dummy)	-0.087 (0.087)			0.120 (0.328)	
Intercept	1.493*** (0.137)	1.473*** (0.138)	0.011 (0.006)		
Dependent variable mean			0.008	0.995 (0.212)	0.005 (0.050)
R-squared	0.192	0.203			
N	83	83	1963	83	1963

NOTES: tandard errors in parentheses in regression columns.
PS = profit sharing; DB = defined benefit; ESOP = Employee Stock Ownership Plan.
Dependent variable for regressions 1 to 3 is the company's average compensation (total labor expenses/employees) divided by the industry average compensation per employee (calculated from National Income and Product Accounts data). Dependent variable in regression 4 is the difference in this ratio between the current and preceding year. The dependent variables in regressions 5 to 7 are based on the same denominator, but the numerator is based on (total labor expenses minus total pension expenses)/employees.
*Statistically significant at p <.10   **p <.05   ***p <.01.

Table A4.2 Labor Demand Elasticities

Dependent variable	Sample definition					Means (s.d.)				
	Reported comp. & PS cont. (1)	All reporting PS cont. (2)	PS firms reporting comp. (3)	All PS firms (4)	All firms (5)	(1a)	(2a)	(3a)	(4a)	(5a)
Base compensation change	-0.478 (0.742)	0.236 (0.470)	-0.319 (0.256)	-0.620*** (0.190)	-0.720*** (0.137)	0.070 (0.022)	0.066 (0.023)	0.071 (0.024)	0.068 (0.023)	0.068 (0.023)
PS contribution change	1.485 (2.299)	1.796 (1.736)	0.229 (0.817)	0.875 (0.776)	0.529 (0.560)	4.3E-04 (0.005)	2.0E-04 (0.004)	1.2E-03 (0.004)	4.2E-04 (0.000)	4.2E-04 (0.004)
Output change	0.502*** (0.082)	0.592*** (0.047)	0.505*** (0.024)	0.532*** (0.015)	0.520*** (0.011)	0.083 (0.105)	0.097 (0.113)	0.088 (0.126)	0.091 (0.146)	0.088 (0.145)
Time trend	-0.001 (0.004)	0.002 (0.003)	-0.002 (0.001)	-0.002 (0.001)	-0.002 (0.001)					
8 industry dummies	Yes	Yes	Yes	Yes	Yes					
R-squared	0.474	0.503	0.510	0.422	0.394					
N	79	190	522	1880	3838					
Dependent variable						0.013 (0.086)	0.026 (0.097)	0.009 (0.092)	0.020 (0.122)	0.015 (0.121)
P-value for equality of base compensation and PS coefficients	0.316	0.340	0.436	0.034	0.014					

NOTES: Numbers in parentheses are standard errors in columns 1-5 and standard deviations in 1a to 5a.
Sample definitions: Column 1: Only firms which reported both compensation and PS contribution in a given year; Column 2: Only firms which reported PS contribution in a given year; Column 3: Only PS firms which reported compensation in a given year; Column 4: All PS firms; Column 5: All firms.
In columnns 2 to 5, compensation and PS contribution were imputed from instruments.
Variable definitions: Base compensation change: change in ln(total compensation per employee, minus profit share), from t - 1 to t.
PS contribution change: change in profit-sharing contribution as percentage of compensation from t - 1 to t.
Output change: change in ln(sales + inventory) from t - 1 to t.
Change in base compensation and PS contribution were instrumented as described in text.
PS = profit sharing; Cont. = contribution; Comp. = compensation.
*Statistically significant at $p < .10$ **$p < .05$ ***$p < .01$.

Table A4.3 Demand Shock Measures and Descriptive Statistics for Employment Change Regressions

Unemployment rate = change in ln(1 - civilian unemployment rate) from t - 1 to t (positive value represents decrease in unemployment)
GNP = change in ln(deflated Gross National Product) relative to time trend, from t - 1 to t
Company sales = change in ln(deflated company sales) from t - 1 to t (deflated by GNP deflator)
"Positive shock" is defined as decrease in unemployment rate, increase in GNP, and increase in sales

Year	Unemployment rate (1)	GNP (2)	Company sales[a] (3)		N[a]
Across all years	-0.0008	-0.0005	0.0324	(0.133)	
Negative shocks	-0.013	-0.027	-0.099	(0.098)	
Positive shocks	0.006	0.015	0.103	(0.087)	
1971	-0.011	0.002	0.024	(0.108)	320
1972	0.003	0.022	0.078	(0.099)	329
1973	0.007	0.025	0.096	(0.111)	330
1974	-0.007	-0.032	0.097	(0.138)	328
1975	-0.030	-0.039	-0.024	(0.141)	337
1976	0.008	0.022	0.053	(0.117)	343
1977	0.008	0.020	0.061	(0.110)	344
1978	0.010	0.025	0.074	(0.104)	344
1979	0.002	-0.002	0.092	(0.118)	344
1980	-0.013	-0.027	0.047	(0.129)	345
1981	-0.005	-0.007	0.016	(0.121)	348
1982	-0.022	-0.052	-0.052	(0.146)	346
1983	0.000	0.009	0.003	(0.154)	344
1984	0.023	0.039	0.077	(0.116)	350

Year	Non-PS (4)	New PS, preadoption (6)	New PS, postadoption (7)	If sales increase (9)	N
1985	0.003	0.007	-0.022	(0.129)	349
1986	0.002	0.001	-0.010	(0.159)	336
1987	0.009	0.007	0.033	(0.136)	340
1988	0.007	0.020	0.056	(0.126)	347
1989	0.002	0.000	0.021	(0.118)	338
1990	-0.002	-0.017	0.003	(0.107)	325
1991	-0.013	-0.038	-0.043	(-0.115)	321

Breakdowns of changes in company sales:[a]

Year	Non-PS (4)	Old PS (5)	New PS, preadoption (6)	New PS, postadoption (7)	Percent w/sales increase (8)	If sales increase (9)	If sales decrease (10)
Across all years	0.030 (0.13)	0.042 (0.13)	0.034 (0.15)	0.020 (0.15)	65	0.103 (0.087)	-0.099 (0.098)
Negative shocks	-0.096 (0.10)	-0.097 (0.10)	-0.117 (0.11)	-0.100 (0.10)			
Positive shocks	0.099 (0.09)	0.108 (0.09)	0.115 (0.09)	0.114 (0.10)			
1971	0.014 (0.11)	0.040 (0.09)	0.046 (0.11)		68	0.076 (0.07)	-0.087 (0.09)
1972	0.069 (0.10)	0.102 (0.10)	0.084 (0.11)		85	0.103 (0.08)	-0.070 (0.08)
1973	0.082 (0.11)	0.127 (0.11)	0.112 (0.13)		87	0.122 (0.09)	-0.077 (0.07)
1974	0.096 (0.14)	0.098 (0.13)	0.096 (0.14)		83	0.137 (0.11)	-0.098 (0.09)
1975	-0.017 (0.13)	-0.030 (0.15)	-0.043 (0.17)		47	0.089 (0.07)	-0.125 (0.11)
1976	0.051 (0.12)	0.071 (0.09)	0.045 (0.15)	-0.009 (0.15)	73	0.105 (0.07)	-0.088 (0.10)
1977	0.056 (0.11)	0.078 (0.10)	0.063 (0.10)	0.040 (0.21)	80	0.099 (0.07)	-0.087 (0.10)
1978	0.067 (0.10)	0.101 (0.10)	0.056 (0.10)	0.102 (0.15)	84	0.103 (0.08)	-0.078 (0.08)
1979	0.088 (0.11)	0.110 (0.13)	0.071 (0.11)	0.121 (0.15)	83	0.123 (0.10)	-0.058 (0.07)
1980	0.054 (0.13)	0.041 (0.12)	0.016 (0.14)	0.057 (0.13)	69	0.110 (0.09)	-0.096 (0.09)

Breakdowns of changes in company sales:[a]

Year	Non-PS (4)		Old PS (5)		New PS, preadoption (6)		New PS, postadoption (7)		Percent w/sales increase (8)	If sales increase (9)		If sales decrease (10)	
1981	0.023	(0.12)	-0.006	(0.12)	0.004	(0.13)	0.054	(0.15)	56	0.093	(0.09)	-0.080	(0.08)
1982	-0.044	(0.14)	-0.077	(0.14)	-0.063	(0.17)	-0.022	(0.15)	38	0.091	(0.08)	-0.138	(0.11)
1983	0.011	(0.14)	0.003	(0.16)	-0.057	(0.22)	0.028	(0.15)	55	0.102	(0.10)	-0.117	(0.12)
1984	0.071	(0.11)	0.077	(0.12)	0.079	(0.11)	0.112	(0.13)	77	0.118	(0.10)	-0.063	(0.05)
1985	-0.026	(0.13)	-0.010	(0.14)	-0.002	(0.13)	-0.034	(0.13)	44	0.082	(0.08)	-0.103	(0.10)
1986	-0.025	(0.17)	0.017	(0.15)	0.007	(0.15)	0.007	(0.12)	52	0.100	(0.10)	-0.128	(0.12)
1987	0.024	(0.13)	0.047	(0.13)	0.042	(0.18)	0.050	(0.16)	63	0.110	(0.09)	-0.096	(0.10)
1988	0.056	(0.11)	0.083	(0.13)	-0.012	(0.11)	0.032	(0.18)	74	0.108	(0.09)	-0.087	(0.09)
1989	0.019	(0.12)	0.023	(0.10)	-0.043	(0.22)	0.037	(0.13)	59	0.088	(0.09)	-0.073	(0.09)
1990	0.000	(0.11)	0.026	(0.09)			-0.014	(0.10)	53	0.076	(0.08)	-0.078	(0.07)
1991	-0.044	(0.12)	-0.035	(0.10)			-0.050	(0.13)	37	0.063	(0.06)	-0.107	(0.09)

NOTE: All figures represent means, with standard deviations in parentheses, except for 1971-1990 values in columns (1) and (2), which represent actual values.

a. Changes in company sales have had upper 1 percent and lower 1 percent, across full sample, of values removed.

Table A4.4 Definitions and Descriptive Statistics for Employment Change Regressions

Demand shock definitions and descriptive statistics are given in appendix table A4.3. Below are descriptive statistics of variables which are interacted with demand shocks.

Means (s.d.)	NPS	Old PS	New PS, preadoption	New PS, postadoption	Sample size[a]	Brief definition
Table A4.5						
PS status	0.650	0.181	0.095	0.074	6308	Profit-sharing status in year t (dummy)
Table A4.7						
Unionized proportion	0.264 (0.250)	0.141 (0.244)	0.281 (0.293)	0.206 (0.253)	6300	Proportion of company workforce covered by union contract in 1991
Majority of union members in PS	0.000	0.271	0.454	0.347		Majority of union members participating in PS in 1991 (dummy)
Table A4.8						
Column 1	0.724				2625	
PS "substitutes" for fixed pay		0.114	0.028	0.023		See bottom of table A4.8
PS "added on" to fixed pay		0.050	0.034	0.027		See bottom of table A4.8
Column 2	0.755				2802	
PS "substitutes" for fixed pay		0.080	0.018	0.021		See bottom of table A4.8
PS "added on" to fixed pay		0.080	0.025	0.021		See bottom of table A4.8
Column 3						
Compensation not reported	0.614	0.207	0.100	0.079	2681	Co. compensation not reported

242

Means (s.d.)	NPS	Old PS	New PS, preadoption	New PS, postadoption	Sample size[a]	Brief definition
Table A4.9						
Cash or combo plan	0.000	0.055	0.028	0.061	5146	PS contribution paid as cash or to cash/deferred plan (dummy)
Deferred plan	0.000	0.095	0.055	0.037		PS contribution put in pension trust (dummy)
Table A4.11						1991 proportion of employees who are:
Clerical/technical	0.210	0.249	0.189	0.248	3728	Clerical/technical (nonexempt)
Proportion in PS	0.000	0.947	0.975	0.961		Covered by PS if clerical/technical
Production/service	0.509	0.489	0.523	0.450	4057	Production/service (nonexempt)
Proportion in PS	0.000	0.914	0.921	0.847		Covered by PS if production/service
Professional/admin.	0.280	0.261	0.289	0.302	3933	Professional/administrative (exempt)
Proportion in PS	0.000	0.949	0.970	0.946		Covered by PS if professional/admin.
Table A4.10						
Profit-sharing formulas	NPS	PS				Employer's PS contributions tied to:
Percent-of-profits	0.000	0.046			4592	Percent of profits (dummy)
Discretionary	0.000	0.022				Wholly discretionary (dummy)
Percent-of-pay	0.000	0.036				Percent of participant's pay (dummy)
Other	0.000	0.068				Other formula (dummy)

NOTES: PS = profit sharing; NPS = non-profit-sharing.

a. Descriptive statistics based on samples for regressions 1 and 3 in indicated tables (except appendix table A4.8 which uses all regressions). Old PS = PS adopted prior to 1975; New PS = PS adopted 1975 or later. PS companies are restricted to those with more than 90 percent of employees covered.

Table A4.5 Profit Sharing and Employment Changes

Dependent variable: change in ln(employment)

Demand measure	Unemployment rate		GNP		Company sales	
	(1)	Paired (2)	(3)	Paired (4)	(5)	Paired (6)
Positive demand shock	2.688***		1.265***		0.532***	0.576***
	(0.713)		(0.360)		(0.033)	(0.060)
Negative demand shock	2.396***		1.246***		0.573***	0.638***
	(0.478)		(0.251)		(0.041)	(0.075)
Profit-sharing interactions:						
Old (pre-1975) PS						
Positive demand shock	-0.514	-2.139	-0.259	-0.396	0.084	0.036
	(1.094)	(1.355)	(0.574)	(0.685)	(0.056)	(0.086)
Negative demand shock	0.747	0.945	0.268	-0.104	-0.095	-0.115
	(0.724)	(0.894)	(0.395)	(0.480)	(0.066)	(0.105)
New (post-1975) PS						
Preadoption:						
Positive demand shock	0.199	0.602	-0.486	-0.385	-0.104	-0.098
	(1.490)	(2.082)	(0.770)	(0.956)	(0.072)	(0.104)
Negative demand shock	0.434	-0.327	0.926	0.627	-0.076	-0.026
	(0.853)	(1.100)	(0.536)	(0.658)	(0.071)	(0.103)
Postadoption:						
Positive demand shock	1.691	1.196	0.112	0.140	-0.042	0.094
	(1.540)	(2.071)	(0.819)	(1.107)	(0.077)	(0.21)
Negative demand shock	-3.176**	-1.129	-1.225**	-0.051	0.001	-0.106
	(1.367)	(1.910)	(0.575)	(0.781)	(0.084)	(0.131)

Demand measure	Unemployment rate		GNP		Company sales	
	(1)	Paired (2)	(3)	Paired (4)	(5)	Paired (6)
Defined benefit plan						
Positive demand shock	0.821*	-2.712***	-0.879***	-1.199**	-0.046	-0.079
	(0.451)	(1.038)	(0.310)	(0.477)	(0.032)	(0.053)
Negative demand shock	-1.551**	2.557***	0.196	1.120***	0.110***	0.142**
	(0.646)	(0.723)	(0.229)	(0.373)	(0.042)	(0.069)
Old PS presence	0.045	0.067	0.036	0.056	-0.025	0.023
	(0.090)	(0.095)	(0.093)	(0.097)	(0.073)	(0.077)
Old PS • year	-2E - 04	-5E - 04	-1E - 04	-5E - 04	3E - 04	-2E - 04
	(0.001)	(0.001)	(0.001)	(0.001)	(0.001)	(0.001)
New PS, preadoption	0.089	0.007	0.180	0.033	-0.106	-0.074
	(0.136)	(0.152)	(0.146)	(0.154)	(0.111)	(0.125)
New PS • year, preadoption	-1E - 03	-4E - 05	-2E - 03	-2E - 04	1E - 03	1E - 03
	(0.002)	(0.002)	(0.002)	(0.002)	(0.001)	(0.002)
New PS presence, postadoption	-0.124	-0.082	-0.006	-0.031	0.061	0.008
	(0.178)	(0.241)	(0.181)	(0.245)	(0.140)	(0.192)
New PS • year, postadoption	1E - 03	7E - 04	-8E - 05	2E - 04	-7E - 04	-3E - 04
	(0.002)	(0.003)	(0.002)	(0.003)	(0.002)	(0.002)
R-squared	0.059	0.026	0.056	0.022	0.268	0.246
N	6308	2003	6308	2003	6188	1937
Dependent variable mean	0.009	0.014	0.009	0.014	0.010	0.010
(s.d.)	(0.167)	(0.218)	(0.167)	(0.218)	(0.149)	(0.197)

NOTES: Standard errors in parentheses. Regressions 1, 3, and 5 include (instrumented) wage change, dummies and time trends for 25 industries. Definitions and descriptive statistics in appendix tables A4.3 and A4.4.
*Statistically significant at p <.10   **p <.05   ***p <.01.

Table A4.6 Discontinuous Measures of Sales Demand Shocks

Dependent variable: Change in ln(employment). Demand measure: Change in ln(company sales). See appendix 4 text for discussion.

	Theoretical expectation of coefficient sign (1)		Full sample, assuming EDL = 1.8 percent of workforce				Restricted sample, with separate EDL by firm			
			Paired (2)		Paired (3)		Paired (4)		Paired (5)	
	PS	NPS	PS	NPS	PS	NPS	PS	NPS	PS	NPS
Not recovering from a prior negative shock:										
1. Positive shock	positive	positive	0.623*** (0.051)	0.480*** (0.034)	0.692*** (0.082)	0.497*** (0.065)	0.886*** (0.084)	0.438*** (0.042)	0.823*** (0.162)	0.660*** (0.139)
2. Big negative shock (continuous)	positive	positive	0.601*** (0.100)	0.643*** (0.062)	0.626*** (0.159)	0.653*** (0.118)	0.559*** (0.173)	0.670*** (0.074)	0.498 (0.315)	0.854** (0.218)
3. Big negative shock (dummy)	positive (size=EDL)	0	0.030* (0.016)	0.019* (0.009)	0.045* (0.025)	-0.001 (0.019)	0.038 (0.025)	0.021* (0.011)	0.015 (0.046)	0.023 (0.039)
4. Small negative shock	0	positive	0.176 (0.954)	0.209 (0.560)	-1.414 (1.489)	0.378 (1.128)	-1.256 (0.855)	-0.155 (0.483)	-1.898 (1.498)	-0.758 (1.892)
Recovering from a prior negative shock:										
5. Negative shock	positive	positive	0.409*** (0.069)	0.581*** (0.045)	0.404*** (0.111)	0.680*** (0.087)	0.180 (0.140)	0.552*** (0.054)	0.263 (0.240)	0.635*** (0.175)
6. Big positive shock (continuous)	positive	positive	0.540*** (0.017)	0.723*** (0.061)	0.477*** (0.168)	0.480*** (0.115)	0.730*** (0.208)	0.730*** (0.087)	0.959** (0.405)	0.430* (0.275)
7. Big positive shock (dummy)	negative (size=EDL)	0	0.021 (0.017)	-0.037*** (0.009)	0.033 (0.025)	-0.006 (0.019)	0.007 (0.029)	-0.040*** (0.012)	-0.039 (0.052)	-0.005 (0.042)

	Theoretical expectation of coefficient sign (1)		Full sample, assuming EDL = 1.8 percent of workforce				Restricted sample, with separate EDL by firm			
			(2)		Paired (3)		(4)		Paired (5)	
	PS	NPS	PS	NPS	PS	NPS	PS	NPS	PS	NPS
8. Small positive shock	0	positive	0.123 (1.177)	-0.498 (0.668)	1.996 (1.801)	-0.801 (1.303)	4.668** (1.891)	-0.089 (0.527)	4.409 (3.063)	-0.578 (2.264)
R-squared			0.270		0.241		0.255		0.267	
N			6188		1770		4120		537	

NOTES: All regressions also include dummies and time trends for 25 industries, dummies and time trends for profit sharing, and defined benefit plans interacted with demand shocks. Standard errors in parentheses.

PS = profit sharing; NPS = nonprofit sharing;EDL = theorized positive excess demand for labor by profit-sharing firm. Calculated as (labor demand elasticity * mean profit share/payroll) = (0.5* .036) for columns 2 and 3 (since .036 is median profit share/payroll), and (0.5* within-co. mean) for columns 4 and 5. See appendix 4 text.

*Statistically significant at p <.10   **p <.05   ***p <.01.

Brief definitions: (see appendix table A4.3 for demand shock descriptive statistics)	Proportion experiencing shock in column:							
	(2)		(3)		(4)		(5)	
	PS	NPS	PS	NPS	PS	NPS	PS	NPS
Not recovering from negative shock (product demand increased last period):								
1. Positive shock: increase in product demand	0.120	0.345	0.351	0.518	0.061	0.409	0.385	0.480
2. Big negative shock (continuous): decrease in demand which is predicted to exhaust EDL	0.033	0.097	0.092	0.160	0.015	0.105	0.091	0.160
3. Big negative shock (dummy): dummy for decrease in demand which is predicted to exhaust EDL	0.033	0.097	0.092	0.160	0.015	0.105	0.091	0.160

4. Small negative shock: decrease in demand, if not predicted to exhaust EDL	0.014	0.038	0.040	0.060	0.006	0.057	0.037	0.071
Recovering from negative shock (product demand decreased last period):								
5. Negative shock: decrease in product demand	0.045	0.133	0.130	0.208	0.017	0.148	0.108	0.186
6. Big positive shock (continuous): increase in demand which is predicted to reestablish EDL	0.032	0.098	0.088	0.159	0.014	0.102	0.082	0.166
7. Big positive shock (dummy): dummy for increase in demand which is predicted to reestablish EDL	0.032	0.098	0.088	0.159	0.015	0.102	0.082	0.166
8. Small positive shock: increase in demand which is not predicted to reestablish EDL	0.009	0.025	0.025	0.038	0.005	0.039	0.028	0.050
N		6188		1770		4120		537

248

Table A4.7 Profit Sharing, Unions, and Employment Changes
Dependent variable: change in ln(employment)

Demand measure	Unemployment rate		GNP		Company sales	
	(1)	Paired (2)	(3)	Paired (4)	(5)	Paired (6)
1. Positive demand shock	2.730***		1.271***		0.543***	0.570***
	(0.726)		(0.367)		(0.033)	(0.059)
2. Negative demand shock	1.739***		0.935***		0.526***	0.626***
	(0.481)		(0.256)		(0.044)	(0.080)
Unionized proportion times:						
3. Positive demand shock	-2.041	0.589	-1.408	-1.421	-0.006	0.026
	(1.699)	(3.776)	(0.864)	(1.918)	(0.091)	(0.182)
4. Negative demand shock	1.372	2.502	0.812	2.236	0.064**	-0.111
	(1.111)	(2.618)	(0.604)	(1.452)	(0.100)	(0.193)
Majority of union members in PS:						
Old (pre-1975) PS						
5. Positive demand shock	-1.805	-2.164	-1.239	-0.408	-0.008	-0.135
	(1.566)	(2.413)	(0.761)	(1.147)	(0.083)	(0.137)
6. Negative demand shock	1.440	1.894	0.842	1.013	-0.096	-0.155
	(1.101)	(1.837)	(0.557)	(0.958)	(0.094)	(0.150)
New (post-1975) PS						
Pre-adoption:						
7. Positive demand shock	-0.659	-1.123	-0.435	-0.453	-0.151	-0.213
	(1.708)	(2.743)	(0.794)	(1.164)	(0.093)	(0.139)

8. Negative demand shock	0.590	-0.454	0.612	-0.389	-0.180*	-0.296*
	(1.052)	(1.600)	(0.584)	(0.870)	(0.109)	(0.160)
Postadoption:						
9. Positive demand shock	0.667	0.402	-0.852	0.991	0.306**	-0.241
	(2.112)	(2.880)	(1.152)	(1.650)	(0.119)	(0.180)
10. Negative demand shock	-0.987	-2.060	-0.545	-0.777	-0.288*	-0.391
	(2.271)	(4.490)	(0.840)	(1.723)	(0.150)	(0.255)
11. Unionized proportion	0.000	0.000	0.000	0.000	0.000	0.000
	(0.000)	(0.000)	(0.000)	(0.000)	(0.000)	(0.000)
R-squared	0.056	0.028	0.054	0.028	0.267	0.252
N	6300	1700	6300	1626	5670	1639
Dependent variable mean	0.008	0.012	0.008	0.012	0.011	0.010
(s.d.)	(0.174)	(0.222)	(0.174)	(0.222)	(0.150)	(0.201)

NOTES: All regressions include demand shocks interacted with presence of defined benefit plan, plus dummies and year trends for old PS, preadoption new PS, and postadoption new PS. Regressions 1, 3, and 5 also include dummies and time trends for 25 industries and pay changes. Definitions and descriptive statistics in appendix tables A4.3 and A4.4. Standard errors in parentheses.
*Statistically significant at p <.10 **p <.05 ***p <.01.

Table A4.8 Compensation Levels and Employment Changes

Dependent variable: Change in ln(employment).   Demand measure: Change in ln(company sales).

	(1) Looking at levels of pay		(2) Looking at levels of pay in relation to output		(3)
	PS "substitutes" for regular pay[a]	PS "added on" to regular pay[a]	PS "substitutes" for regular pay[b]	PS "added on" to regular pay[b]	Compensation not reported
1. Positive demand shock	0.543*** (0.044)		0.509*** (0.041)		0.563*** (0.042)
2. Negative demand shock	0.749*** (0.064)		0.691*** (0.059)		0.645*** (0.048)
Profit-sharing interactions					
Old (pre-1975) PS					
3. Positive demand shock	0.317*** (0.072)	0.005 (0.127)	0.387*** (0.075)	0.184 (0.112)	-0.033 (0.091)
4. Negative demand shock	0.041 (0.095)	-0.272* (0.164)	-0.112 (0.106)	0.107 (0.142)	-0.098 (0.105)
New (post-1975) PS					
Preadoption					
5. Positive demand shock	-0.234 (0.155)	-0.207 (0.139)	-0.217 (0.182)	-0.156 (0.178)	0.183 (0.110)
6. Negative demand shock	-0.352* (0.206)	0.053 (0.176)	0.188 (0.240)	-0.264 (0.193)	-0.243 (0.107)
Postadoption					
7. Positive demand shock	-0.268 (0.211)	-0.340** (0.170)	-0.137 (0.179)	-0.466** (0.224)	-0.090 (0.118)

	(1)	(2)	(3)	(4)	(5)
8. Negative demand shock	-0.675***	0.143	-0.568**	-0.063	0.080
	(0.232)	(0.241)	(0.259)	(0.257)	(0.120)
R-squared	0.327		0.315		0.291
N	2625		2802		2681
Dependent variable mean	0.009		0.010		0.009
(s.d.)	(0.107)		(0.110)		(0.175)

NOTES: Standard errors in parentheses. All regressions also include dummies and time trends for 25 industries, dummies and time trends for old PS and pre- and postadoption new PS (instrumented) average wage change, and defined benefit plans interacted with sales changes.
a. Profit sharing assumed to "substitute" for regular pay if average compensation in old PS firms is less than 102 percent of industry average, or if average compensation in new PS firm went up by less than 2 percent. Profit sharing assumed to "add on" to regular pay if these conditions do not hold.
b. Profit sharing assumed to "substitute" for regular pay if average unit labor costs in old PS firm are less than industry average, or if average unit labor costs in new PS firm, relative to industry, declined. Profit sharing assumed to "add on" to regular pay if these conditions do not hold.
Definitions and descriptive statistics in appendix tables A4.3 and A4.4. See text and bottom of table 4.7 for further discussion.
*Statistically significant at p <.10   **p <.05   ***p <.01.

Table A4.9 Cash vs. Deferred Profit Sharing and Employment Changes

Dependent variable: Change in ln(employment)

Demand measure	Unemployment rate		GNP		Company sales	
	(1)	Paired (2)	(3)	Paired (4)	(5)	Paired (6)
1. Positive demand shock	2.723***		1.228***		0.525***	0.537***
	(0.679)		(0.343)		(0.031)	(0.055)
2. Negative demand shock	2.779***		1.473***		0.550***	0.626***
	(0.456)		(0.240)		(0.038)	(0.067)
Cash or combo plan						
Old (pre-1975)						
3. Positive demand shock	0.081	-5.713**	-0.096	-0.938	0.100	-0.280*
	(1.797)	(2.707)	(0.946)	(1.376)	(0.094)	(0.150)
4. Negative demand shock	1.043	-1.222	0.472	-2.445**	-0.041	0.339
	(1.215)	(1.833)	(0.655)	(0.989)	(0.128)	(0.254)
New (post-1974), preadoption						
5. Positive demand shock	0.875	0.269	-0.361	-1.236	0.107	0.122
	(1.741)	(2.470)	(0.910)	(1.168)	(0.086)	(0.126)
6. Negative demand shock	0.113	-1.233	0.499	0.140	-0.067	-0.010
	(1.042)	(1.418)	(0.644)	(0.819)	(0.084)	(0.116)
New (post-1974), postadoption						
7. Positive demand shock	3.826	2.263	0.476	-1.331	-0.008	-0.019
	(2.460)	(3.707)	(1.309)	(1.960)	(0.120)	(0.188)
8. Negative demand shock	-2.544	1.143	-0.722	1.610	0.091	-0.010
	(2.173)	(3.425)	(0.889)	(1.326)	(0.131)	(0.192)

	(1)	(2)	(3)	(4)	(5)	(6)
Deferred plan						
Old (pre-1975)						
9. Positive demand shock	-1.159	0.031	-0.016	0.136	0.065	0.250**
	(1.419)	(1.776)	(0.744)	(0.886)	(0.075)	(0.101)
10. Negative demand shock	0.101	0.417	-0.367	0.006	0.019	-0.136
	(0.933)	(1.158)	(0.511)	(0.619)	(0.087)	(0.123)
New (post-1974), preadoption						
11. Positive demand shock	0.692	0.373	0.373	0.569	-0.151*	-0.139
	(1.826)	(2.349)	(0.964)	(1.116)	(0.078)	(0.104)
12. Negative demand shock	-0.810	0.416	-0.046	0.708	0.022	0.058
	(1.081)	(1.327)	(0.687)	(0.789)	(0.087)	(0.117)
New (post-1974), postadoption						
13. Positive demand shock	1.016	2.639	-0.418	1.295	-0.063	0.155
	(2.117)	(3.323)	(1.115)	(1.441)	(0.100)	(0.144)
14. Negative demand shock	-4.534**	0.066	-1.789**	-1.230	0.081	-0.105
	(1.835)	(3.284)	(0.766)	(0.993)	(0.111)	(0.158)
R-squared	0.062	0.030	0.059	0.030	0.276	0.264
N	6419	2169	6419	2169	6338	2097

NOTES: Standard errors in parentheses. All regressions include demand shocks interacted with presence of defined benefit plan, and separate time trends for old and new cash and deferred plans. Regressions 1, 3, and 5 also include dummies and time trends for 25 industries, and average wage change. Definitions and descriptive statistics in appendix tables A4.3 and A4.4.
*Statistically significant at $p < .10$ **$p < .05$ ***$p < .01$.

Table A4.10 Profit-Sharing Formulas and Employment Changes

Dependent variable: Change in ln(employment)

Demand measure	Unemployment rate		GNP		Company sales	
	(1)	Paired (2)	(3)	Paired (4)	(5)	Paired (6)
1. Positive demand shock	2.846*** (0.824)		1.187*** (0.414)		0.473*** (0.037)	0.582*** (0.080)
2. Negative demand shock	2.581*** (0.551)		1.411*** (0.289)		0.607*** (0.045)	0.749*** (0.099)
Percent-of-profits plan						
3. Positive demand shock	2.050 (2.423)	1.466 (3.512)	0.399 (1.274)	0.580 (1.792)	0.058 (0.126)	0.112 (0.197)
4. Negative demand shock	-0.619 (1.675)	-0.074 (2.452)	-0.587 (0.869)	-0.360 (1.241)	-0.031 (0.126)	-0.342* (0.188)
Discretionary plan						
5. Positive demand shock	-1.357 (3.168)	-18.005*** (4.851)	-1.022 (1.718)	-8.463*** (2.497)	0.358** (0.181)	-0.556** (0.259)
6. Negative demand shock	-2.080 (2.569)	-1.852 (3.593)	-1.187 (1.214)	-2.074 (1.722)	-0.146 (0.190)	0.335 (0.277)
Percent-of-pay plan						
7. Positive demand shock	-0.131 (2.532)	-3.250 (3.525)	0.254 (1.361)	-1.052 (1.866)	0.251** (0.124)	0.299 (0.195)
8. Negative demand shock	-0.201 (1.933)	0.688 (2.745)	0.034 (0.971)	0.096 (1.353)	-0.165 (0.185)	0.005 (0.304)

Other formula

9. Positive demand shock	-1.486	-1.450	-0.694	-0.392	0.046	0.186
	(1.994)	(2.685)	(1.047)`	(1.373)	(0.102)	(0.167)
10. Negative demand shock	1.396	1.516	0.200	0.540	0.041	-0.194
	(1.382)	(1.904)	(0.704)	(0.964)	(0.128)	(0.207)
R-squared	0.057	0.054	0.053	0.053	0.262	0.284
N	4592	1084	4592	1084	4499	1046
Dependent variable mean	0.003	0.014	0.003	0.014	0.006	0.010
(s.d.)	(0.173)	(0.235)	(0.173)	(0.235)	(0.156)	(0.216)

NOTES: Standard errors in parentheses. All regressions include demand shocks interacted with presence of defined benefit plan, and separate dummies and time trends for each plan formula. Regressions 1, 3, and 5 also include dummies and time trends for 25 industries, and instrumented wage change. Definitions and descriptive statistics in appendix tables A4.3 and A4.4.
*Statistically significant at $p < .10$ **$p < .05$ ***$p < .01$.

Table A4.11 Profit Sharing, Occupation, and Employment Changes

Dependent variable: Change in ln(employment)

Demand measure	GNP			Company sales		
	Clerical/technical (1)	Production/service (2)	Professional/administrative (3)	Clerical/technical (4)	Production/service (5)	Professional/administrative (6)
Interaction of occupation proportion with:						
1. Positive demand shock	2.396** (1.020)	1.445*** (0.516)	0.669 (0.845)	1.687*** (0.122)	0.811*** (0.056)	1.160*** (0.105)
2. Negative demand shock	4.777*** (0.723)	2.258*** (0.353)	3.327*** (0.582)	1.911*** (0.122)	1.163*** (0.071)	1.772*** (0.118)
Interaction of occupation proportion, times percent of occupation in PS, with:						
Old PS						
3. Positive demand shock	-0.965 (2.094)	-1.191 (1.180)	-0.630 (2.087)	-0.827*** (0.270)	0.077 (0.128)	0.243 (0.254)
4. Negative demand shock	-1.616 (1.478)	0.525 (0.830)	1.765 (1.466)	0.561 (0.395)	-0.253 (0.147)	0.477 (0.350)
New PS, preadoption						
5. Positive demand shock	2.731 (3.665)	-0.584 (1.469)	0.965 (2.212)	-0.316 (0.463)	0.028 (0.186)	0.087 (0.231)
6. Negative demand shock	0.704 (2.394)	1.955 (1.036)	2.015 (1.592)	0.578 (0.416)	-0.056 (0.161)	-0.709*** (0.237)
New PS, postadoption						
7. Positive demand shock	-1.923 (2.941)	2.235 (1.815)	2.230 (2.742)	-0.497 (0.361)	-0.210 (0.208)	-0.380 (0.262)

8. Negative demand shock	-4.249	-1.364	-4.123**	-0.457	-0.245	-0.048
	(2.309)	(1.412)	(1.933)	(0.308)	(0.234)	(0.410)
R-squared	0.061	0.065	0.055	0.209	0.231	0.150
N	3728	4057	3933	3728	4057	3933
Dependent variable mean	0.008	0.008	0.008	0.008	0.008	0.008
(s.d.)	(0.158)	(0.158)	(0.158)	(0.158)	(0.158)	(0.158)

NOTES: Standard errors in parentheses. Regressions were run separately for each occupation group to reduce multicollinearity. Regressions also include dummies and time trends for 25 industries and (instrumented) average wage change. Definitions and descriptive statistics in appendix tables A4.3 and A4.4.
*Statistically significant at $p < .10$ **$p < .05$ ***$p < .01$.

Bibliography

Abowd, John M. 1989. "The Effect of Wage Bargains on the Stock Market Value of the Firm," *American Economic Review* 79 (September), pp. 774-800.

Addison, John T., Kornelius Kraft, and Joachim Wagner. Forthcoming. "German Works Councils and Firm Performance." In *Employee Representation: Alternatives and Future Directions,* by Bruce Kaufman and Morris Kleiner. Madison, WI: Industrial Relations Research Association.

Akerlof, George, and Janet Yellen. 1986. *Efficiency Wage Models of the Labor Market.* New York: Cambridge University Press.

Alchian, Armen A., and Harold Demsetz. 1972. "Production, Information Costs, and Economic Organization," *American Economic Review* 62, pp. 777-795.

Allen, Steven G., and Robert L. Clark. 1987. "Pensions and Firm Performance." In *Human Resources and the Performance of the Firm,* Morris M. Kleiner, Richard N. Block, Myron Roomkin, and Sidney W. Salsburg, eds. Madison, WI: Industrial Relations Research Association.

Askwith, M.E. 1926. *Profit-Sharing: An Aid to Trade Revival.* London: Duncan Scott.

Axelrod, Robert M. 1984. *The Evolution of Cooperation.* New York: Basic Books.

Baker, George, Robert Gibbons, and Kevin J. Murphy. 1993. "Subjective Performance Measures in Optimal Incentive Contracts." Draft, Harvard Business School (May).

Baker, George P., Michael C. Jensen, and Kevin J. Murphy. 1988. "Compensation and Incentives: Practice vs. Theory," *Journal of Finance* 43, 3 (July), pp. 593-616.

Balderston, C. Canby. 1937. *Profit Sharing for Wage Earners.* New York: Industrial Relations Counsellors.

Bartlett, Will, John Cable, Saul Estrin, Derek C. Jones, and Stephen C. Smith. 1992. "Labor-Managed Cooperatives and Private Firms in North Central Italy: An Empirical Comparison," *Industrial and Labor Relations Review* 46, 1 (October), pp. 103-118.

Bashir, Abdel-Hameed Mohamed. 1990. "Profit-Sharing Contracts with Moral Hazard and Adverse Selection," *American Journal of Islamic Social Sciences* 7, 3, pp. 357-383.

Bassi, Laurie J. 1984. "Estimating the Effect of Training Programs with Non-Random Selection," *Review of Economics and Statistics* 66, pp. 36-43.

Becker, Brian E., and Craig A. Olson. 1992. "Unions and Firm Profits," *Industrial Relations* 31, 3 (Fall), pp. 395-415.

Belcher, John G. 1991. *Gain Sharing: The New Path to Profits and Productivity.* Houston: Gulf Publishing.

Bell, D. Wallace, and Charles G. Hanson. 1987. *Profit Sharing and Profitability: How Profit Sharing Promotes Business Success.* London: Kogan Page.

Bell, Linda, and David Neumark. 1993. "Lump Sum Payments and Profit-Sharing Plans in the Union Sector of the United States Economy," *Economic Journal* 103, 418 (May), pp. 602-619.

Ben-Ner, Avner, and Derek C. Jones. 1992. "A New Conceptual Framework for the Analysis of the Impact of Employee Participation, Profit Sharing, and Ownership on Firm Performance." Working Paper No. 92/1, Department of Economics, Hamilton College.

Bensaid, Bernard, and Robert J. Gary-Bobo. 1991. "Negotiation of Profit-Sharing Contracts in Industry," *European Economic Review* 35, pp. 1069-1085.

Berlin, Jesse A., Colin B. Begg, and Thomas A. Louis. 1989. "An Assessment of Publication Bias Using A Sample of Published Clinical Trials," *Journal of the American Statistical Association* 84 (June), pp. 381-92.

Bhargava, Sandeep. 1991. "Profit Sharing and Profitability: Evidence from U.K. Firm Level Data." Draft, St. John's College, Oxford (April).

Blanchflower, Daniel. 1991. "The Economic Effects of Profit Sharing in Great Britain," *International Journal of Manpower* 12, 1, pp. 3-9.

Blanchflower, Daniel, and Andrew Oswald. 1987a. "Shares for Employees: A Test of Their Effects." Discussion Paper No. 273, Centre for Labour Economics, London School of Economics.

_____. 1987b. "Profit Sharing—Can It Work?" *Oxford Economic Papers* 39, pp. 1-19.

_____. 1988. "Profit-Related Pay: Prose Discovered?" *Economic Journal* 98, pp. 720-730.

Blanchflower, Daniel, and Mario D. Garrett. 1990. "Insider Power in Wage Determination," *Economica* 57, pp. 143-170.

Blanchflower, Daniel, N. Millward, and Andrew Oswald. 1991. "Unionism and Employment Behavior," *Economic Journal* 101, 407 (July), pp. 816-834.

Blanchflower, Daniel, Andrew Oswald, and Peter Sanfey. 1992. "Wages, Profits, and Rent Sharing." Working Paper No. 4222, National Bureau of Economic Research (December).

Blasi, Joseph R. 1988. *Employee Ownership: Revolution or Ripoff?* New York: Harper and Row.

Blasi, Joseph R., and Douglas L. Kruse. 1991. *The New Owners*. New York: HarperCollins.

_____. 1993. "Employee Ownership and Participation. Trends, Problems, and Policy Options," *Journal of Employee Ownership Law and Finance* 5, 2 (Spring), pp. 41-73.

Blinder, Alan. 1986a. "Comment," *NBER Macroeconomics Annual 1986*. Cambridge, MA: MIT Press.

_____. 1986b. "On the Share Economy...A Bottle Half Full," *Challenge*, November-December, pp. 51-52.

Bloom, Steven. 1985. "Employee Ownership and Firm Performance." Ph.D. Dissertation, Department of Economics, Harvard University.

Bonin, John P., and Louis Putterman. 1987. *Economics of Cooperation and the Labor-Managed Economy*. Chur, Switzerland: Harwood Academic Publishers.

Bowie, James A. 1922. *Sharing Profits with Employees*. London: Sir Isaac Pitman and Sons.

Bradley, Keith Saul Estrin, and Simon Taylor. 1990. "Employee Ownership and Economic Performance," *Industrial Relations*, 29, 3, pp. 385-402.

Bradley, Michael D., and Stephen C. Smith. 1991. "Firm Size and the Effect of Profit Sharing." Draft, Department. of Economics, George Washington University.

_____. 1992. The Comparative Institutions of Profit Sharing: The U.S. Computer Industry," *Journal of Economic Issues* 26, 2 (June), pp. 573-582.

Brickley, J.A., S. Bhagat, and R.C. Lease. 1985. "The Impact of Long-Range Managerial Compensation Plans on Shareholder Wealth," *Journal of Accounting and Economics* 7, pp. 115-129.

Brickley, J.A., and K.T. Hevert. 1991. "Direct Employee Stock Ownership: An Empirical Investigation," *Financial Management* 20, 2, pp. 70-84.

Brower, F. Beatrice. 1957. "Sharing Profits with Employees," *Studies in Personnel Policies* 162. New York: National Industrial Conference Board.

Brown, Charles. 1990. "Firms' Choice of Method of Pay," *Industrial and Labor Relations Review* 43, 3 (January), pp. 165S-182S.

Bullock, R.J., and Mark E. Tubbs. 1990. "A Case Meta-Analysis of Gainsharing Plans as Organization Development Interventions," *Journal of Applied Behavioral Science* 26, 3, pp. 383-404.

Bureau of Labor Statistics (BLS). *Employee Benefits in Medium and Large Firms* (various issues). Washington, DC: Government Printing Office.

Burton, John. 1986. "Review Symposium: The Share Economy," *Industrial and Labor Relations Review* 39, 2 (January), pp. 285-90.

Cable, John R., and Felix R. Fitzroy. 1980a. "Cooperation and Productivity: Some Evidence from West German Experience," *Economic Analysis and Workers' Management* 14, 2, pp. 163- 180.

_____. 1980b. "Productivity Efficiency, Incentives, and Employee Participation: Some Preliminary Results for West Germany," *Kyklos* 33, 1, pp. 100-121.

Cable, John R., and Nicholas Wilson. 1989. "Profit Sharing and Productivity: An Analysis of U.K. Engineering Firms," *Economic Journal* 99 (June), pp. 366-375.

_____. 1990. "Profit Sharing and Productivity: Some Further Evidence," *Economic Journal* 100, 401 (June), pp. 550-555.

Cahuc, Pierre, and Brigitte Dormont. 1992. "Profit-Sharing: Does it Increase Productivity and Employment? A Theoretical Model and Empirical Evidence on French Microdata." Working Paper 92.45, Cahiers Ecomath, University of Paris (June).

Calvo, Guillermo A.R. 1987. "The Economics of Supervision." In *Incentives, Cooperation, and Risk Sharing: Economic and Psychological Perspectives on Employment Contracts,* Haig R. Nalbantian, ed. Totowa, NJ: Rowman and Littlefield.

Card, David. 1990. "Comment." In *Paying for Productivity: A Look at the Evidence,* Alan S. Blinder, ed. Washington, DC: Brookings Institution, pp. 140-141.

Cardinal, Laura B., and I.B. Helburn. 1986. "Union Versus Nonunion Attitudes Toward Share Arrangements," Industrial Relations Research Association 39th Annual Proceedings, pp. 167-173.

Carstensen, Vivian, Knut Gerlach, and Olaf Hubler. 1992. "Profit Sharing in German Firms: Institutional Framework, Participation, and Microeconomic Effects." Paper prepared for the WZB Workshop, "Institutional Frameworks and Labor Market Performance," Hannover University, Berlin (October).

Cheadle, Allen. 1989. "Explaining Patterns of Profit Sharing Activity," *Industrial Relations* 28, 3 (Fall), pp. 387-400.

Chelius, James, and Robert Smith. 1990. "Profit Sharing and Employment Stability," *Industrial and Labor Relations Review* 43, 3 (January), pp. 256S-273S.

Christensen, Laurits, Dale Jorgenseb, and Lawrence Lau. 1975. "Transcendental Logarithmic Production Frontiers," *Review of Economics and Statistics* 55, pp. 28-45.

Coates, Edward M. 1991. "Profit Sharing Today: Plans and Provisions," *Monthly Labor Review* (April), pp. 19-25.

Colletti, Jerome. 1969. *Profit Sharing and Employee Attitudes: A Case Study of the Deferred Profit Sharing Program at Motorola, Inc.* Madison, WI: University of Wisconsin Center for the Study of Productivity Motivation.

Conte, Michael A., and Jan Svejnar. 1988. "Productivity Effects of Worker Participation in Management, Profit-Sharing, Worker Ownership of Assets and Unionization in U.S. Firms," *International Journal of Industrial Organization* 6 (March), pp. 139-151.

_____. 1990. "The Performance Effects of Employee Ownership Plans." In *Paying for Productivity: A Look at the Evidence,* Alan S. Blinder, ed. Washington, DC: Brookings Institution, pp. 143-182.

Cook, Thomas D., and Donald T. Campbell. 1979. *Quasi-Experimentation: Design and Analysis Issues for Field Settings.* Boston: Houghton Mifflin.

Cooke, Willam N. 1993. "Employee Participation, Group-Based Pay Incentives, and Firm Performance: A Union-Nonunion Comparison." Draft, Wayne State University.

Cooper, Russell. 1988. "Will Share Contracts Increase Economic Welfare?" *American Economic Review* 78, pp. 138-154.

Czarnecki, Edgar R. 1969. "Effect of Profit-Sharing Plans on Union Organizing Efforts," *Personnel Journal* (September), pp. 763-773.

D'Art, Daryl. 1992. *Economic Democracy and Financial Participation: A Comparative Study.* New York: Routledge.

Dawes, Robyn M., and Richard H. Thaler. 1988. "The Effects of Worker Participation on Enterprise Performance: Empirical Evidence from French Cooperatives," *International Journal of Industrial Organization* 3, pp. 45-59.

Defourney, Jacques, Saul Estrin, and Derek C. Jones. 1985. "The Effects of Worker Participation on Enterprise Performance: Empirical Evidence from French Cooperatives," *International Journal of Industrial Organization* 3, pp. 197-217.

Denton, D. Keith. 1991. "What's Wrong With These Employees?" *Business Horizons* (September/October), pp. 45-59.

Doherty, Elizabeth M., Walter R. Nord, amd Jerry L. McAdams. 1989. "Gainsharing and Organization Development: A Productive Synergy," *Journal of Applied Behavioral Science* 25, 3, pp. 209-229.

Dyer, Lee, Felician Foltmam, and George Milkovich. 1985. "Contemporary Employment Stabilization Practices." In *Human Resource Management and Industrial Relations,* Thomas A. Kochan and Thomas A. Barocci, eds. Boston: Littel, Brown, pp. 203-214.

Eaton, Adrienne. 1992. "New Production Techniques, Employee Involvement, and Unions." Draft, Department of Labor Studies, Rutgers University (August).

Eaton, Adrienne, and Paula Voos. 1992. "Unions and Contemporary Innovations in Work Organization, Compensation, and Employee Participation." In *Unions and Economic Competitiveness*, Paula Voos and Laurence Mishel, eds. Armonk, NY: M.E. Sharpe, pp. 173-215.

Eckalbar, John C. 1992. "Profit Sharing and Employment, Economic Modelling (April), pp. 104-110.

Economic Report of the President. 1992. Washington, DC: U.S. Government Printing Office.

Estrin, Saul, Derek C. Jones, and Jan Svejnar. 1987. "The Productivity Effects of Worker Participation: Producer Cooperatives in Western Economies," *Journal of Comparative Economics* 11 (March), pp. 40-61.

Estrin, Saul, and Nicholas Wilson. 1987. "The Microeconomic Effects of Profit Sharing: the British Experience." Discussion Paper 247, Centre for Labour Economics, London School of Economics.

_____. 1989. "Profit Sharing, the Marginal Cost of Labour and Employment Variability." Draft, Department of Economics, London School of Economics (May).

Estrin, Saul, Paul Grout, and Sushil Wadhwani. 1987. "Profit Sharing and Employee Share Ownership," *Economic Policy* (April), pp. 13-62.

Fein, Mitchell. 1981. "IMPROSHARE: An Alternative to Traditional Managing." Norcross, GA: American Institute of Industrial Engineers.

_____. 1983. "Improved Productivity Through Worker Involvement," *Industrial Management* 25, 3 (May-June), pp. 1- 12.

Finseth, Eric. 1988. "The Employment Behavior of Profit-Sharing Firms: An Empirical Test of the Weitzman Theory." Senior Thesis, Harvard University Department of Economics.

Fitzroy, Felix R., 1988. "Incomplete Contracts, Monetary Policy, and Employment in Share Economies," Draft, Wissenschaftszentrum Berlin fur Sozialforschung, Berlin, October.

Fitzroy, Felix, and Kornelius Kraft. 1986. "Profitability and Profit Sharing," *Journal of Industrial Economics* 35 (December), pp. 113-130.

_____. 1987. "Cooperation, Productivity, and Profit Sharing," *Quarterly Journal of Economics* 102 (February), pp. 23-35.

_____. 1992. "Forms of Profit Sharing and Firm Performance," *Kyklos* 45, 2, pp. 209-225.

Fitzroy, Felix, and Daniel Vaughan-Whitehead. 1989. "Employment, Efficiency Wages, and Profit Sharing in French Firms." Draft, London School of Economics (May).

Florkowski, Gary W. 1988. "The Organizational Impact of Profit Sharing." Ph.D. Dissertation, Syracuse University.

_____. 1990. "Profit Sharing and Public Policy: Insights for the United States," *Industrial Relations* 30, 1 (Winter), pp. 96-115.

_____. 1991. "Profit Sharing and Employment: Growth and Stability Effects in American Companies." Draft, School of Business, University of Pittsburgh (August).

Florkowski, Gary W., and Kuldeep Shastri. 1992. "Stock Price Response to Profit Sharing in Unionized Settings," *Journal of Labor Research* 13, 4 (Fall), pp. 407-420.

Florkowski, Gary W., and Michael H. Schuster. 1992. "Support for Profit Sharing and Organizational Commitment: A Path Analysis," *Human Relations* 45, 5, pp. 507-523.

Fosbre, Anne B. 1989. "It's Time to Change Public Opinion about Corporate Profits; One Way is to Make Use of Profit Sharing Plans to Link Pay to Profit," *Mid-Atlantic Journal of Business* 25, 6 (April), pp. 51-65.

Freeman, Richard B., and Morris M. Kleiner. 1990. "The Impact of New Unionization on Wages and Working Conditions," *Journal of Labor Economics* 8, 1, Part 2 (January), pp. S8- S25.

Freeman, Richard B., and Joel Rogers. Forthcoming. "Who Speaks for Us?: Employee Representation in a Nonunion Labor Market." In *Employee Representation: Alternatives and Future Directions,* Bruce Kaufman and Morris Kleiner, eds. Madison, WI: Industrial Relations Research Association.

Freeman, Richard B., and Martin L. Weitzman. 1987. "Bonuses and Employment in Japan," *Journal of the Japanese and International Economies* 1 (June), pp. 168-94.

Fudenberg, Drew, and Eric Maskin. 1986. "The Folk Theorem in Repeated Games with Discounting or with Incomplete Information," *Econometrica* 54 (May), pp. 533-54.

Fung, K.C. 1989. "Profit-Sharing and European Unemployment," *European Economic Review* 3, pp. 1787-1798.

Fur ubotn, E., and S. Pejovich. 1970. "Property Rights and the Behavior of the Firm in a Socialist State: The Example of Yugoslavia," *Zeitschrift fur Nationalokonomie* 30, pp. 431-454.

Gerhart, Barry. 1991. "Employment Stability under Different Managerial Compensation Systems." Working Paper No. 91-02, Center for Advanced Human Resource Studies, Cornell University.

Gerhart, Barry, and George T. Milkovich. 1992. "Employee Compensation: Research and Practice." In *Handbook of Industrial and Organizational Psychology,* Vol. 3, 2nd Ed., Marvin D. Dunnette and Leatta M. Hough, eds. Palo Alto, CA: Consulting Psychologists Press.

Gerhart, Barry, and Brian Murray. 1992. "Pay, Performance, and Participation." In *Research Frontiers in Industrial Relations and Human Resources,*

David Lewin, Olivia S. Mitchell, and Peter D. Sherer, eds. Madison, WI: Industrial Relations Research Association, pp. 193-238.

Gershenfeld, Walter J. 1987. "Employee Participation in Firm Decisions." In *Human Resources and the Performance of the Firm*, Morris M. Kleiner, Richard N. Block, Myron Roomkin, and Sidney W. Salsburg, eds. Madison, WI: Industrial Relations Research Association.

Gilman, Nicholas Paine. 1899. *A Dividend to Labor: A Study of Employers' Welfare Institutions*. Boston: Houghton, Mifflin.

Globerson, Shlomo, and Robert Parsons. 1987. "IMPROSHARE: An Analysis of User Responses," *Proceedings of the IXth International Conference on Production Research*. Cincinnati, OH: International Conference on Production Research, pp. 158-62.

Gowen, Charles R. 1990. "Gainsharing Programs: An Overview of History and Research," Journal of Organizational Behavior Management 11, 2, pp. 77-99.

Gregg, P.A., and S.J. Machin. 1988. "Unions and the Incidence of Performance Linked Pay Schemes in Britain," *International Journal of Industrial Organization* 6, pp. 91-107.

Gross, Steven E. 1989. "Customizing Compensation: The Right Diagnostic Tools," *Compensation and Benefits Review* 25, 1, pp. 24- 33.

Gross, Steven E., and Jeffrey P. Bacher. 1993. "The New Variable Pay Programs: How Some Succeed, Why Some Don't," *Compensation and Benefits Review* (January/February), pp. 51- 56.

Gross, Steven E., and Steven J. Berman. 1992. "The Role of Compensation in Planning Quality Improvement," *Journal of Compensation and Benefits* (September/October), pp. 5-8.

Gunderson, Morley, Douglas Hyatt, and James E. Pesando. 1992. "Wage-Pension Trade-Offs in Collective Agreements," *Industrial and Labor Relations Review* 46, 1 (October), pp. 146-160.

Gustman, Alan L., and Olivia S. Mitchell. 1992. "Pensions and Labor Market Activity: Behavior and Data Requirements." In *Pensions and the Economy: Sources, Uses, and Limitations of Data*, Zvi Bodie and Alicia Munnell, eds. Philadelphia: University of Pennsylvania Press, pp. 39-114.

Hamermesh, Daniel S. 1993. *Labor Demand*. Princeton, NJ: Princeton University Press.

Hamermesh, Daniel S., and Gerard Pfann. 1992. "Turnover and the Dynamics of Labor Demand. Working Paper No. 4204, National Bureau of Economic Research (October).

Hanlon, Susan C., and Robert R. Taylor. 1991. "An Examination of Changes in Work Group Communication Behaviors Following Installation of a

Gainsharing Plan," *Group and Organization Studies* 16, 3 (September), pp. 238-267.

Hanson, Charles, and Robert Watson. 1990. "Profit'sharing and Company Performance: Some Empirical Evidence for the UK." In *New Forms of Ownership*, Glenville Jenkins and Michael Poole, eds. London: Routledge, pp. 165-182.

Hart, R.A., and Olaf Hubler. 1990. "Wage, Labour Mobility, and Working Time Effects of Profit-Sharing," *Empirica* 17, pp. 115-130.

_____. 1991. "Are Profit Shares and Wages Substitute or Complementary Forms of Compensation?" *Kyklos* 44, pp. 221-231.

Hatton, T.J. 1988. "Profit Sharing in British Industry, 1865- 1913," *International Journal of Industrial Organization* 6, 1 (March), pp. 69-90.

Hausman, J.A. and D.A. Wise. 1979. "Attrition Bias in Experimental and Panel Data: The Gary Income Maintenance Experiment," *Econometrica* 47, pp. 455-473.

Heckman, James J. 1976. "The Common Structure of Statistical Models of Truncation, Sample Selection, and Limited Dependent Variables and a Simple Estimator for Such Models," *Annals of Economic and Social Measurement* 5, pp. 475-492.

_____. 1979. "Sample Selection Bias as a Specification Error," *Econometrica* 47, pp. 153-161.

_____. 1990. "Varieties of Selection Bias," *American Economic Review*, 80, 2 (May), pp. 313-318.

Heckman, James J., and V. Joseph Hotz. 1989. "Choosing Among Alternative Nonexperimental Methods for Estimating the Impact of Social Programs: The Case of Manpower Training," *Journal of the American Statistical Association* 84, 408 (December), pp. 862-874.

Heckman, James J., and Richard Robb. 1985. "Alternative Methods for Evaluating the Impact of Treatment on Outcomes." In *Longitudinal Analysis of Labor Market Data*, J. Heckman and B. Singer, eds. Cambridge: Cambridge University Press.

Hewitt Associates. 1985. *Salaried Employee Benefits Provided by Major U.S. Employers: A Comparison Study, 1979 Through 1984*. Atlanta, GA: Hewitt Associates.

_____. 1986. *Salaried Employee Benefits Provided by Major U.S. Employers in 1985*. Atlanta, GA: Hewitt Associates.

Hirsch, Barry T. 1991. *Labor Unions and the Economic Performance of Firms*. Kalamazoo, MI: W.E. Upjohn Institute for Employment Research.

Howard, Bion B. 1979. *A Study of the Financial Significance of Profit Sharing: 1958-1977*. Chicago: Profit Sharing Council of America.

268

Howard, Bion B., and Peter O. Dietz. 1969. *A Study of the Financial Signifi-cance of Profit Sharing.* Chicago: Profit Sharing Council of America.

Hsiao, Cheng. 1986. *Analysis of Panel Data.* Cambridge: Cambridge University Press.

Hubbartt, William S. 1991. "Money Talks: How to Use Financial Incentives to Motivate Employees," *Office Systems* (April), pp. 76-80.

Hublar, Olaf. 1993. "Productivity, Earnings, and Profit Sharing: An Econometric Analysis of Alternative Models," *Empirical Economics* 18, pp. 357-380.

Huselid, Mark A. 1992. "Human Resource Management Practices and Firm Performance." Draft, Institute of Management and Labor Relations, Rutgers University (October).

Ichniowski, Casey. 1990. "Human Resource Management Systems and the Performance of U.S. Manufacturing Businesses." Working Paper No. 3449, National Bureau of Economic Research (September).

_____. 1992. "Human Resource Practices and Productive Labor- Management Relations." *In Research Frontiers in Industrial Relations and Human Resources,* David Lewin, Olivia S. Mitchell, and Peter D. Sherer, eds. Madison, WI: Industrial Relations Research Association, pp. 239-272.

Industrial Participation Association. 1984. *Profit Sharing and Employee Shareholding Attitude Survey.* London: Industrial Participation Association.

Israelsen, L. Dwight. 1980. "Collectives, Communes, and Incentives," *Journal of Comparative Economics* 4, pp. 99-124.

Jehring, John J. 1956. *Succeeding with Profit Sharing: The Experiences of Profit Sharing Companies in Communicating Their Plans to Their Employees.* Evanston, IL: Profit Sharing Research Foundation.

Jehring, John J., and Bertram L. Metzger. 1960. *The Stockholder and Employee Profit Sharing.* Evanston, IL: Profit Sharing Research Foundation.

Jenkins, Glenville, and Michael Poole, eds. 1990. *New Forms of Ownership.* London: Routledge.

John, Andrew. 1991. "Employment Fluctuations in a Share Economy," *Oxford Economic Papers* 43, 1, pp. 75-84.

Jones, Derek C. 1982. "British Producer Cooperatives, 1948-68: Productivity and Organizational Structure." In *Participatory and Self-Managed Firms: Evaluating Economic Performance,* Derek C. Jones and Jan Svejnar, eds. Lexington, MA: Lexington Books.

_____. 1987. "The Productivity Effects of Worker Directors and Financial Participation in the Firm: The Case of British Retail Cooperatives," *Industrial and Labor Relations Review* 41 (October), pp. 79-92.

Jones, Derek C., and Takao Kato. 1992a. "The Incidence and Effects on Company Performance of Financial Participation Schemes: An Overview of the Japanese Experience." Working Paper No. 92/2, Department of Economics, Hamilton College.

_____. 1992b. "The Productivity Effects of Employee Stock Ownership Plans and Bonuses: Evidence from Japanese Panel Data." Working Paper No. 92/6, Department of Economics, Hamilton College.

Jones, Derek C., and Jeffrey Pliskin. 1989. "British Evidence on the Employment Effects of Profit Sharing," *Industrial Relations* 28 (Spring), pp. 276-298.

_____. 1991a. "Unionization and the Incidence of Performance-Based Compensation: Evidence from Canada," Working Paper No. 89/4, Department of Economics, Hamilton College.

_____. 1991b. "The Productivity Effects of Profit Sharing and Worker Representation on the Board." Working Paper No. 91/6, Department of Economics, Hamilton College (December).

Jones, Derek C., and Jan Svejnar. 1985. "Participation, Profit Sharing, Worker Ownership and Efficiency in Italian Producer Cooperatives," *Economica* 52 (November), pp. 449-465.

Kaden, Lewis B., and Lee Smith. 1992. *America's Agenda: Rebuilding Economic Strength.* Armonk, NY: M.E. Sharpe.

Kahneman, Daniel, and Richard Thaler. 1991. "Economic Analysis and the Psychology of Utility: Applications to Compensation Policy," *American Economic Review* 81, 2 (May), pp. 341-346.

Kandel, Eugene, and Edward P. Lazear. 1992. "Peer Pressure and Partnerships," *Journal of Political Economy* 100 (August), pp. 801-817.

Katz, Harry C., and Noah M. Meltz. 1991. "Profit Sharing and Auto Workers' Earnings: The United States vs. Canada," *Industrial Relations-Quebec* 46, 3 (Summer), pp. 515-529.

Katz, Lawrence. 1987. "Efficiency Wage Theories: A Partial Evaluation." In *NBER Macroeconomics Annual,* Stanley Fischer, ed. Cambridge, MA: MIT Press.

Kaufman, Bruce, and Morris Kleiner. Forthcoming. *Employee Representation: Alternatives and Future Directions.* Madison, WI: Industrial Relations Research Association.

Kaufman, Roger T. 1992. "The Effects of IMPROSHARE on Productivity," *Industrial and Labor Relations Review* 45, 2 (January), pp. 311-22.

Keefe, Jeffrey. 1991. "Is Incentive Pay Obsolete?" Draft, Rutgers University (November).

Kelly, John, and Caroline Kelly. 1991. "'Them and Us': Social Psychology and 'The New Industrial Relations'," *British Journal of Industrial Relations* 29, pp. 25-48.

Kertesz, Louise. 1990. "Employers Add Profit-Sharing to 401(k)s," *Business Insurance* November 19, pp. 26-7.

Keynes, John Maynard. 1964. *The General Theory of Employment, Interest, and Money.* New York: Harcourt, Brace, Jovanovich.

Kim, Joon Woo. 1988. "Bonuses and Employment in Korea." Senior thesis, Department of Economics, Harvard University.

Kim, Seongsu. 1993. "Profit Sharing and Profitability of Firms in the United States: A Simultaneous Equations Approach." Draft, Anderson Graduate School of Management, University of California, Los Angeles (March).

Kleiner, Morris M., and Marvin L. Bouillon. 1988. "Providing Business Information to Production Workers: Correlates of Compensation and Profitability," *Industrial and Labor Relations Review* 41 (July), pp. 605-617.

_____. 1991. "Information Sharing of Sensitive Business Information with Employees," *Industrial Relations* 30, 4 (Fall), pp. 480-491.

Knowlton, Philip A. 1954. *Profit Sharing Patterns.* Evanston, IL: Profit Sharing Research Foundation.

Kraft. Kornelius. 1991. "The Incentive Effects of Dismissals, Efficiency Wages, Piece-Rates, and Profit-Sharing," *Review of Economics and Statistics* 73, 3, pp. 451-459.

Kruger, Daniel H. 1986. "Profit-Sharing Arrangements and Collective Bargaining," Industrial Relations Research Association 39th Annual Proceedings, pp. 152-158.

Kruse, Douglas L. 1988. "Essays on Profit Sharing and Unemployment," Ph.D. Dissertation, Department of Economics, Harvard University.

_____. 1991a. "Profit Sharing and Employment Variability: Microeconomic Evidence on the Weitzman Theory," *Industrial and Labor Relations Review* 44, 3 (April), pp. 437-453.

_____. 1991b. "Profit Sharing in the 1980's: Disguised Wages or a Fundamentally Different Form of Compensation?" In *Structural Changes in U.S. Labor Markets: Causes and Consequences,* Randall Eberts and Erica Groshen, eds. Armonk, NY: M.E. Sharpe.

_____. 1991c. "Pension Substitution in the 1980's: Why the Shift Toward Defined Contribution Plans?" Working Paper No. 3882, National Bureau of Economic Research (November).

_____. 1992. "Profit Sharing and Productivity: Microeconomic Evidence from the United States," *Economic Journal* 102, 410 (January), pp. 24-36.

LaCivita, Charles, and Robert Pirog. 1992. "Implementing the Share Economy," *Southern Economic Journal* 58, 4, pp. 1095- 1102.

Latta, Geoffrey W. 1979. *Profit Sharing, Employee Stock Ownership, Savings, and Asset Formation Plans in the Western World.* Philadelphia: Industrial Research Unit, The Wharton School.

Lawler, Edward E. 1971. *Pay and Organizational Effectiveness.* New York: McGraw-Hill.

Lawler, Edward E. 1987. "Pay for Performance: A Motivational Analysis." In *Incentives, Cooperation, and Risk Sharing: Economic and Phychological Perspectives on Employment Contracts.* Haig Nalbantian, ed. Totowa, NJ: Rowman and Littlefield, pp. 69-86.

Lawler, Edward E., Gerald Ledford, and Susan Mohrman. 1989. *Employee Involvement in America.* American Productivity and Quality Center.

Lazear, Edward P. 1979. "Why Is There Mandatory Retirement?" *Journal of Labor Economics* 87, 6 (December), pp. 1261-84.

_____. 1986. "Salaries and Piece Rates," *Journal of Business* 59, 3, pp. 405-431.

_____. 1992. "Compensation, Productivity, and the New Economics of Personnel." In *Research Frontiers in Industrial Relations and Human Resources,* David Lewin, Olivia S. Mitchell, and Peter D. Sherer, eds. Madison, WI: Industrial Relations Research Association, pp. 341-380.

Leamer, Edward E. 1978. *Specification Searches, Ad Hoc Inference with Non-experimental Data.* New York: Wiley and Sons.

Lee, Michael B., and Yinsog Rhee. 1992. "Bonus, Union, and Labor Productivity in South Korea between 1972-89." Draft, Department of Management, Georgia State University (December).

Leonard, Jonathan. 1986. "Employment Variation and Wage Rigidity: A Comparison of Union and Non-union Plants." Draft, University of California, Berkeley.

Levine, David. 1987. "Efficiency Wages in Weitzman's Share Economy," *Economics Letters,* 23, 3, pp. 245-249.

_____. 1989. "Efficiency Wages in Weitzman's Share Economy," *Industrial Relations* 23, 3 (Fall), pp. 321-334.

_____. 1992a. "Piece Rates, Output Restriction, and Cohesiveness," *Journal of Economic Psychology* 13, 3 (September), pp. 473-490.

_____. 1992b. "Public Policy Implications of Imperfections in the Market for Worker Participation," *Economic and Industrial Democracy* 13, 2 (May), pp. 183-206.

Levine, David, and Laura D'Andrea Tyson. 1990. "Participation, Productivity, and the Firm's Environment." In *Paying for Productivity: A Look at the Evidence,* Alan S. Blinder, ed. Washington, DC: Brookings Institution, pp. 183-244.

Lewis, H. Gregg. 1986. *Union Relative Wage Effects: A Survey.* Chicago: University of Chicago Press.

Lewis, John Spedan. 1954. *Fairer Shares: A Possible Advance in Civilisation and Perhaps the Only Alternative to Communism.* London: Staples Press.

Lindop, Esmond. 1989. "The Turbulent Birth of British Profit- Sharing," *Personnel Management* (January), pp. 44-47.

Lissy, William E. 1991. "Currents i Compensation and Benefits," *Compensation and Benefits Review,* 23, 2, pp. 7-12.

Long, Richard J. 1989. "Patterns of Workplace Innovation in Canada," *Industrial Relations-Quebec* 44, 4, pp. 805-826.

_____. 1992. "The Incidence and Nature of Employee Profit Sharing and Share Ownership in Canada," *Industrial Relations-Quebec* 47, 3, pp. 463-488.

Maddala, G.S. 1983. *Limited Dependent and Qualitative Variables in Econometrics.* Cambridge, England: Cambridge University Press.

Manski, Charles F. 1989. "Anatomy of the Selection Problem," *Journal of Human Resources* 24, 3 (Summer), pp. 341-360.

Manski, Charles F., and Steven R. Lerman. 1977. "The Estimation of Choice Probabilities from Choice Based Samples," *Econometrica* 45, 8 (november), pp. 1977-1988.

Markham, Steven E., K. Dow Scott, Beverly L. Little, and Steven Berman. 1992. "Gainsharing Experiments in Health Care," *Compensation and Benefits Review* 24, 2 (March/April), pp. 57-64.

Masternak, Robert L. 1991/92. "Gainsharing Programs at Two Fortune 500 Facilities: Why One Worked Better," *National Productivity Review* 11, 1 (Winter), pp. 71-86.

Masternak, Robert L., and Timothy L. Ross. 1992. "Gainsharing: A Bonus Plan or Employee Involvement?" *Compensation and Benefits Review* 24, 1 (January/February), pp. 46-54.

May, Bess Ritter. 1991. "Earn More Profits by Sharing Them," *Supervision* (May), pp. 3-5.

McAdams, Jerry L., and Elizabeth J. Hawk. 1992. *Capitalizing on Human Assets.* Scottsdale, AZ: American Compensation Association.

Metzger, Bert. 1966. *Profit Sharing in Perspective.* Evanston, IL: Profit Sharing Research Foundation.

_____. 1975. *Profit-Sharing in 38 Large Companies,* Vol. 1. Evanston, IL: Profit Sharing Research Foundation.

_____. 1978. *Profit-Sharing in 38 Large Companies,* Vol. 2. Evanston, IL: Profit Sharing Research Foundation.

Metzger, Bert, and Jerome A. Colletti. 1971. *Does Profit Sharing Pay? A Comparative Study of the Financial Performance of Retailers With and*

Without Profit Sharing Programs. Evanston, IL: Profit Sharing Research Foundation.

Mishra, Jitendra, and Molly A. Morrissey. 1990. "Trust in Employee/ Employer Relationships: A Survey of West Michigan Managers," *Public Personnel Management* 19, 4 (Winter), pp. 443-486.

Mitchell, Daniel J.B. 1985. "Wage Flexibility: Then and Now," *Industrial Relations* 24, pp. 255-279.

_____. 1987. "The Share Economy and Industrial Relations: Implications of the Weitzman Proposal," *Industrial Relations* 26, 1 (Winter), pp. 1-17.

_____. 1993. "Profit Sharing and Employee Ownership: Policy Implications." Working Paper Series 251, Institute of Industrial Relations, University of California, Los Angeles (May).

Mitchell, Daniel J.B., and Renae F. Broderick. 1991. "Flexible Pay Systems in the American Context: History, Policy, Research, and Implications." In *Advances in Industrial and Labor Relations,* Vol. 5, David Lewin, Donna Sockell, and David Lipsky, eds. Greenwich, CT: JAI Press, pp. 95-149.

Mitchell, Daniel J.B., David Lewin, and Edward E. Lawler III. 1990. "Alternative Pay Systems, Firm Performance, and Productivity." In *Paying for Productivity: A Look at the Evidence,* Alan S. Blinder, ed. Washington, DC: Brookings Institution, pp. 15-88.

Monroe, Paul. 1896. "Profit Sharing in the United States," *American Journal of Sociology* 1 (May), pp. 685-709.

Morkes, John. 1991. "Salaries Up, Benefits Down, U.S. Researchers Say," *R&D Magazine* (June), pp. 36-38.

Nalbantian, Haig. R. (ed.) 1987. *Incentives, Cooperation, and Risk Sharing: Economic and Psychological Perspectives on Employment Contracts.* Totowa, NJ: Rowman and Littlefield.

National Civic Federation. 1920. *Profit Sharing by American Employers.* New York: National Civic Federation.

National Wages Council. 1986. "Report of the Subcommittee on Wage Reform." Singapore: Ministry of Labour.

New York Stock Exchange. 1982. *People and Productivity: A Challenge to Corporate America.* New York: New York Stock Exchange.

Nichols, Don. 1989. "Bottom-Up Strategies: Asking the Employees for Advice," *Management Review* (December), pp. 44-49.

Nickel, James E. 1990. "Can Your Organization Achieve Better Results by Sharing Gains with Employees?" *Employment Relations Today* (Autumn), pp. 173-184.

Nightingale, Donald V. 1980. *Does Profit Sharing Really Make A Difference?* Ottawa: Conference Board in Canada.

Nordhaus, William. 1986. "Introduction to the Share Economy," *Journal of Comparative Economics* 10, 4 (December), pp. 416- 420.

_____. 1988. "Can the Share Economy Conquer Stagflation?" *Quarterly Journal of Economics* 103, 1 (February), pp. 201-217.

Nuti, Domenico Mario. 1987. "Profit-Sharing and Employment: Claims and Overclaims," *Industrial Relations* 26, 1 (Winter), pp. 18-29.

O'Dell, Carla, and Jerry McAdams. 1987. *People, Performance, and Pay*. Austin, TX: American Productivity Center.

Opinion Research Corporation. 1957. *How Profit Sharing Affects Employee Attitudes*. Princeton, NJ: Opinion Research Corporation.

Ost, Edward. 1989. "Gain Sharing's Potential," *Personnel Administrator* (July), pp. 92-96.

Osterman, Paul. 1987. "Turnover, Employment Security, and the Performance of the Firm." In *Human Resources and the Performance of the Firm*, Morris M. Kleiner, Richard N. Block, Myron Roomkin, and Sidney W. Salsburg, eds. Madison, WI: Industrial Relations Research Association.

Parks, Bill. 1990. "The 'Share Economy': A Boon for Small Business?" *American Business Review* 8, 2 (June), pp. 20-24.

Parsons, Donald O. 1986. "The Employment Relationship: Job Attachment, Work Effort, and the Nature of Contracts." In *Handbook of Labor Economics*, Orley Ashenfelter and Richard Layard, eds. Amsterdam: North-Holland.

Peel, Michael, Maurice Pendlebury, and Roger Groves. 1991. "Wider Share Ownership and Employee Reporting," *Management Accounting* (May), pp. 38-39.

Peel, Michael, and Nicholas Wilson. "Labour Absenteeism: The Impact of Profit Sharing, Voice and Participation," *International Journal of Manpower* 11, 7, pp. 17-24.

Perry, Charles R., and Delwyn H. Kegley. 1990. *Employee Financial Participation: An International Survey*. Philadelphia: Industrial Research Unit, The Wharton School.

Poole, Michael. 1989. *The Origins of Economic Democracy: Profit-Sharing and Employee-Shareholding Schemes*. London: Routledge.

Poole, Michael, and Glenville Jenkins. 1990. *The Impact of Economic Democracy: Profit-Sharing and Employee-Shareholding Schemes*. London: Routledge.

Profit Sharing Council of America (PSCA). 1959. "Albert Gallatin," Profit Sharing Trends 14 (March-April), pp. 2-3.

_____. 1984. *Profit Sharing: Philosophy, Practice, Benefits to Society*. Chicago: Profit Sharing Council of America.

_____. 1989. *The 1988 Profit Sharing Survey.* Chicago: Profit Sharing Council of America.

Profit Sharing Research Foundation (PSRF). 1989. *Sources and Resources for the Study of Profit Sharing.* Chicago: Profit Sharing Research Foundation.

_____. 1992a. "Profit-Sharing Plans Garner Success in Achieving Company Objectives for Enhancing the Workplace," *PSRF Update* 1, 1 (April), pp. 2-3.

_____. 1992b. "Company Stock: A Growing Component of Larger DC- Plan Portfolios," *PSRF Update* 1, 6 (September), pp. 1-3.

_____. 1992c. "PSCA's 1992 Annual Survey Shows Change in Asset Investment Practices," *PSRF Update* 1, 8 (December), pp. 1-3.

Putterman, Louis, and Gil Skillman, Jr. 1988. "The Incentive Effects of Monitoring under Alternative Compensation Schemes," *International Journal of Industrial Organization* 6, pp. 109-119.

Quarrey, Michael, and Corey Rosen. 1986. *Employee Ownership and Corporate Performance.* Oakland, CA: National Center for Employee Ownership.

Ridder, Geert. 1990. "Attrition in Multi-Wave Panel Data." In *Panel Data and Labor Market Studies,* Joop Hartog, Geert Ridder, and Jules Theeuwes, eds. New York: Elsevier Science Publishers, pp. 45-68.

Robertson, R.N., and Chuma I. Osuorah. 1991. "Gainsharing in Action at Control Data," *Journal of Quality and Participation* 14, 6 (December), pp. 28-31.

Roomkin, Myron J., ed. 1990. *Profit Sharing and Gain Sharing.* Metuchen, NJ: Scarecrow Press.

Rooney, Patrick. 1992. "Employee Ownership and Worker Participation: Effects on Firm-Level Productivity in the United States." Draft, Department of Economics, Indiana University-Purdue University at Indianapolis, March.

Rousseeuw, P.J., and A.M. Leroy. 1987. *Robust Regression and Outlier Detection.* New York: John Wiley and Sons.

Schuster, Jay R., and Patricia K. Zingheim. 1982. *The New Pay: Linking Employee and Organizational Performance.* New York: McMillan.

Schuster, Michael. 1983. "The Impact of Union-Management Cooperation on Productivity and Employment," *Industrial and Labor Relations Review* 36 (April), pp. 425-30.

_____. 1984. "The Scanlon Plan: A Longitudinal Analysis," *Journal of Applied Behavioral Science* 20, 1, pp. 23-38.

Sen, Amartya K. 1966. "Labour Allocation in a Cooperative Enterprise," *Review of Economic Studies* 33, pp. 361-371.

Shepard, Edward M. 1986. "The Effect of Profit Sharing on Productivity," Ph.D. Dissertation, Boston College.

Shepard, Edward M. Forthcoming. "Profit Sharing and Productivity: Further Evidence from the Chemicals Industry," *Industrial Relations*.

Singleton-Green, Brian. 1992. "Lower Payrolls, Higher Pay," *Accountancy* (December), pp. 38-39.

Smith, Gillian R. 1986. "Profit Sharing and Employee Share Ownership in Britain," *Employment Gazette* 94 (September), pp. 380-384.

Smith, Stephen C. 1988. "On the Incidence of Profit and Equity Sharing," *Journal of Economic Behavior and Organization* 9, pp. 45-58.

_____. Forthcoming. "Innovation and Market Strategy in Italian Producer Cooperatives: Econometric Evidence on Organizational Comparative Advantage," *Journal of Economic Behavior and Organization*.

Stiglitz, Joseph E. 1987. "The Design of Labor Contracts: The Economics of Incentives and Risk Sharing." In *Incentives, Cooperation, and Risk Sharing: Economic and Psychological Perspectives on Employment Contracts*, Haig Nalbantian, ed. Totowa, NJ: Rowman and Littlefield.

Summers, Lawrence. 1986. "On the Share Economy," *Challenge* (November/ December), pp. 47-50.

Tehranian, H. and J.F. Waeglenin. 1985. "Market Reaction to Short-term Compensation Plan Adoption," *Journal of Accounting and Economics* 7, pp. 131-144.

Tomer, John F. 1987. *Organizational Capital: The Path to Higher Productivity and Well-Being*. New York: Praeger.

U.S. Chamber of Commerce. *Employee Benefits* (various issues). Washington, DC: Economic Policy Division, Chamber of Commerce of the United States.

U.S. General Accounting Office (GAO). 1987. *Employee Stock Ownership Plans: Little Evidence of Effects on Corporate Performance*, GAO/PEMD-88-1, October.

_____. 1988. Employee Involvement: Issues for Agencies to Consider in Designing and Implementing Plans, GGD-88-82, May.

U.S. Senate, Subcommittee of the Committee on Finance. 1939. "Survey of Experiences in Profit Sharing and Possibilities of Incentive Taxation." Washington, DC: Government Printing Office.

Usilaner, Brian, and John Leitch. 1989. "Miles to Go...or Unity at Last," *Journal for Quality and Participation* (June), pp. 60-67.

Uvalic, Milica. 1990. "The PEPPER Report: Promotion of Employee Participation in Profits and Enterprise Results in the Member States of the European Community." Prepared for the Commission of the European

Communities, Brussels. San Domenico, Italy: European University Institute, June.

Verbeek, Marno. 1990. "On the Estimation of a Fixed Effects Model with Selectivity Bias," *Economics Letters* 34, pp. 267- 270.

Verbeek, Marno, and Theo Nijman. 1992. "Testing for Selectivity Bias in Panel Data Models," *International Economic Review* 33, 3 (August), pp. 681-703.

Voos, Paula. 1987. "Managerial Perceptions of the Economic Impact of Labor Relations Programs," *Industrial and Labor Relations Review* 40 (January), pp. 195-208.

Wadhwani, Sushil, and Martin Wall. 1990. "The Effects of Profit Sharing on Employment, Wages, Stock Returns and Productivity: Evidence from UK Micro-Data," *Economic Journal*, 100, 399 (March), pp. 1-17.

Weiss, Andrew. 1987. "Incentives and Worker Behavior: Some Evidence." In *Incentives, Cooperation, and Risk Sharing: Economic and Psychological Perspectives on Employment Contracts*, Haig Nalbantian, ed. Totowa, NJ: Rowman and Littlefield, pp. 137-150.

Weitzman, Martin L. 1983. "Some Macroeconomic Implications of Alternative Compensation Systems," *Economic Journal* 93, pp. 763-83.

_____. 1984. *The Share Economy*. Cambridge, MA: Harvard University Press.

_____. 1985. "The Simple Macroeconomics of Profit-Sharing," *American Economic Review* 75, pp. 937-953.

_____. 1986. "Macroeconomic Implications of Profit-Sharing," *NBER Macroeconomics Annual 1986*. Cambridge, MA: MIT Press, pp. 291-335.

_____. 1988. "Comment on `Can the Share Economy Conquer Stagflation?'" *Quarterly Journal of Economics* 103, 1 (February), pp. 219-223.

Weitzman, Martin L., and Douglas Kruse. 1990. "Profit Sharing and Productivity." In *Paying for Productivity: A Look at the Evidence*, Alan S. Blinder, ed. Washington, DC: Brookings Institution, pp. 95-140.

Wider Share Ownership Council. 1985. *Employee Share Schemes*. London: Copeman Patterson.

Wilson, Nicholas, and Michael J. Peel. 1991. "The Impact on Absenteeism and Quits of Profit-Sharing and Other Forms of Employee Participation," *Industrial and Labor Relations Review* 44, 3 (April), pp. 454-468.

Wray, David L. 1993. "Cash Profit-Sharing Plans: An Overview," *Profit Sharing* 41, 1 (January), pp. 12-15.

Zalusky, John L. 1986. "Labor's Collective Bargaining Experience with Gainsharing and Profit-Sharing." Industrial Relations Research Association 39th Annual Proceedings, pp. 174-182.

_____. 1990. "Labor-Management Relations: Unions View Profit-Sharing." In *Profit Sharing and Gain Sharing*, Myron J. Roomkin, ed. Metuchen, NJ: Scarecrow Press, pp. 65-78.

Index

Abowd, John, 60
Akerlof, George, 24
Alchian, Armen A., 48
Askwith, M. E., 1, 2
Axelrod, Robert M., 47

Babbage, Charles, 1
Bacher, Jeffrey P., 48, 88
Baker, George, 77
Bashir, Abdel-Hameed M., 47
Bassi, Laurie J., 201
Begg, Colin B., 55
Bell, D. Wallace, 51, 52
Bell, Linda, 8–10t, 11, 36, 108, 109t,
   113, 149
Berlin, Jesse A., 55
Bhargava, Sandeep, 56t
Bias
  minimizing simultaneity, 82
  self-selection statistical, 65–68, 126,
   199–202
Blanchflower, Daniel, 12, 51, 52, 147
Blasi, Jospeh R., 5, 7, 36
Bonin, John P., 49
Bonuses
  as form of profit sharing, 13
  in gainsharing plans, 42n1
Bouillon, Marvin L., 86
Bradley, Keith, 8–10t, 56t, 108, 109t,
   112
Bradley, Michael D., 18, 55
Broderick, Renae F., 51
Brower, F. Beatrice, 51
Brown, Charles, 23

Cable, John R., 55,, 56t
Cahuc, Pierre, 26t, 29, 56t
Canada, 12, 30
Capital
  availability in deferred profit-sharing
   plans, 149
  investment when workers share in
   profits, 49–50

Card, David, 55
Cardinal, Laura B., 165
Carstensen, Vivian, 26t, 30, 56t, 114
Cash/deferred profit-sharing plans, 5–6
Cash profit-sharing plans
  conditions for adoption of, 149
  defined, 5–6
  effect of, 51, 73–74
  impact on productivity growth, 208–9
  as motivators, 152
  prediction of adoption, 192–93
  relation to employment stability, 138–
   40, 159
  tax incentives in Great Britain for, 168,
   169
Cheadle, Allen, 26t, 28
Chelius, James, 8–10t, 108, 109t
Christensen, Laurits, 197
Colletti, Jerome, 51, 52
Compensation
  conditions for deferral of, 23
  effect on labor force of decreased,
   105–6
  efficiency wage as form of, 24
  flexibility in profit-sharing plan, 24–25
  levels and growth of, 115–20, 234–36
  in old and new profit-sharing
   companies, 112–20
  profit-sharing distributions as, 120–22
  size of profit share in relation to, 81–
   83, 153
  See also Profit-sharing payments;
   Wages
Compensation systems
  deferred as worker compensation
   system, 23
  with deferred compensation, 45
  employee self-selection of, 50
  incentives in deferred, 45
  to induce worker effort, 23
  with reduced company profitability,
   24–25
Conte, Michael A., 5, 7

About the Institute

The W.E. Upjohn Institute for Employment Research is a nonprofit research organization devoted to finding and promoting solutions to employment-related problems at the national, state, and local level. It is an activity of the W.E. Upjohn Unemployment Trustee Corporation, which was established in 1932 to administer a fund set aside by the late Dr. W.E. Upjohn, founder of The Upjohn Company, to seek ways to counteract the loss of employment income during economic downturns.

The Institute is funded largely by income from the W.E. Upjohn Unemployment Trust, supplemented by outside grants, contracts, and sales of publications. Activities of the Institute are comprised of the following elements: (1) a research program conducted by a resident staff of professional social scientists; (2) a competitive grant program, which expands and complements the internal research program by providing financial support to researchers outside the Institute; (3) a publications program, which provides the major vehicle for the dissemination of research by staff and grantees, as well as other selected work in the field; and (4) an Employment Management Services division, which manages most of the publicly funded employment and training programs in the local area.

The broad objectives of the Institute's research, grant, and publication programs are to: (1) promote scholarship and experimentation on issues of public and private employment and unemployment policy; and (2) make knowledge and scholarship relevant and useful to policymakers in their pursuit of solutions to employment and unemployment problems.

Current areas of concentration for these programs include: causes, consequences, and measures to alleviate unemployment; social insurance and income maintenance programs; compensation; workforce quality; work arrangements; family labor issues; labor-management relations; and regional economic development and local labor markets.